AGRICULTURE AND INDUSTRY IN BRAZIL

AGRICULTURE AND INDUSTRY IN BRAZIL

INNOVATION AND COMPETITIVENESS

Albert Fishlow and
José Eustáquio Ribeiro Vieira Filho

FOREWORD BY

José A. Scheinkman

COLUMBIA UNIVERSITY PRESS

NEW YORK

Columbia University Press
Publishers Since 1893
New York   Chichester, West Sussex
cup.columbia.edu

Library of Congress Cataloging-in-Publication Data
Names: Fishlow, Albert, author. | Vieira Filho,
José Eustáquio, author.
Title: Agriculture and industry in Brazil : innovation
and competitiveness / Albert Fishlow and José Eustáquio
Ribeiro Vieira Filho.
Description: New York : Columbia University Press, [2020] |
Includes bibliographical references and index.
Identifiers: LCCN 2019057517 (print) | LCCN 2019057518
(ebook) | ISBN 9780231191708 (hardback) |
ISBN 9780231549523 (ebook)
Subjects: LCSH: Agricultural industries—Technological
innovations—Brazil. | Agricultural innovations—Brazil. |
Agriculture and state—Brazil. | Agriculture—Economic
aspects—Brazil. | Competition—Brazil.
Classification: LCC HD9014.B82 F545 2020 (print) | LCC
HD9014.B82 (ebook) | DDC 338.1—dc23
LC record available at https://lccn.loc.gov/2019057517
LC ebook record available at https://lccn.loc.gov/2019057518

Columbia University Press books are printed on permanent and
durable acid-free paper.

Printed in the United States of America
Cover design: Noah Arlow
Cover image: Getty Images

In gratitude to our professors, students, colleagues, and friends

———————————

CONTENTS

In this book, Albert Fishlow and José Eustaquio Vieira-Filho describe the trajectory of Brazilian agribusiness, perhaps the biggest success story in Brazil's recent economic history. In the early 1960s, Brazilians imported 30 percent of the food they consumed, and the trade balance in many products, including cereals and chicken meat, was negative.

Agriculture in Brazil was highly regulated. A government license was needed to import a bushel of wheat or to export a pound of sugar. The opening of trade and lifting of many governments controls on production and export of agricultural goods in the beginning of the 1990s was crucial for the success of Brazilian agriculture because it led to expansion and gains in economies of scale for the most efficient producers. However, the gains to the sector would have been much smaller if Embrapa, the Brazilian Agricultural Research Corporation, had not been created earlier, in 1973.

Embrapa aimed at generating knowledge and technology for Brazilian agriculture and meat production. Embrapa was not the first institution to produce R&D for this sector in Brazil—Esalq, later a founding unit of the University of São Paulo, dates from the beginning of the last century and has made many important contributions to the development of Brazilian agriculture. However, the creation of the national research corporation represented an important commitment from the federal government to technological development. In addition, after creating Embrapa, the government reorganized its program of technical and rural assistance to facilitate the adoption of new techniques by Brazilian producers.

In a Ford Foundation report written in the late 1960s on the state of Brazilian agriculture, Purdue University economist Edward Schuh wrote that "very little is known about tropical soils and how best to manage them. Very little is known about the response of these soils to fertilizer. The capability for generating and developing new, higher yield varieties is limited. . . . The point is that the research on agricultural problems in Brazil is quite limited, and the capability for a rapid expansion is not there."[1]

This book describes in detail the organization and impact of Embrapa and how it changed the bleak scenario described by Schuh, generating remarkable improvement in production processes in agriculture and meat production in Brazil, in just over four decades. Embrapa is an excellent example of how a well-managed R&D infrastructure allows a country to absorb, adapt and improve foreign technologies. As Fishlow and Vieira-Filho stress, technological absorption in agriculture has complications that are less present in other industries—climate, soil and topography differences cause uneven diffusion of knowledge among countries and even regions within a country. In the beginning, Embrapa absorbed advances from the "green revolution" but soon Embrapa started what the authors rightly call its own revolution. One of its great successes was the occupation of the Cerrado, a region that currently produces almost half of Brazil's grain output. Making the Cerrado one of the world's most productive agricultural regions involved a series of technological advances: the use of lime to correct soil acidity, the development of tropical varieties of soybeans tolerant to the Cerrado climate, improvements in pest control, and the development of nitrogen fixation that eliminated the need for chemical nitrogen fertilizers and lowered costs.

To analyze the evolution of the agricultural sector in Brazil, Fishlow and Vieira-Filho apply a unified theoretical framework that brings much clarity to the discussion. Professional economists will appreciate chapter 3 that exposits the theory, but other readers may skip this portion, while learning much from the rest of the material in this book.

In chapter 7, Fishlow and Vieira-Filho examine the effect of the expansion of Brazilian agriculture on greenhouse gas (GHG) emission. The emphasis is on livestock production, a sector that is an important contributor to GHG emissions. The authors document that in the period 1990–2015 Brazil's agriculture succeeded in using technological advances to intensify the use of resources and gain productivity. For example, while cattle herd size increased 20 percent, the area of pasture decreased 30 percent from 1990 to 2015. A decrease in slaughter age further increased total production of meat per occupied hectare, albeit to levels that are still inferior to that of other major meat exporters.

This positive overall picture of the impact of the expansion of livestock production should not distract us from the much uglier current state of affairs in the Amazon region. The Amazon Environmental Research Institute (IPAM) calculates that a resident of the state of Pará produces four times the annual emissions of a U.S. citizen, much of it from deforestation. A sizeable portion of deforested land in the Amazon ends up being used for beef cattle farming with very low productivity. The goal in this case is not to run a profitable cattle farm, which would require substantial investment, but to pillage valuable timber and establish property rights in public land, by proving possession for a certain amount of time. Speculation and land-grabbing allow for the survival of inefficient cattle farms. From 2004 to 2014, Amazon deforestation markedly diminished, a result of the intensive use of satellites to monitor deforestation in almost real time, and punishment of offenders with fines and apprehension of equipment. Since then, a weakening of the apparatus to detect and punish violators has led to a renewed increase in deforestation. This situation will only get worse as a result of the 2018 election that brought to power a candidate that had pledged to slash environmental regulations. As of April 2020, the Brazilian legislature is considering a proposal from the Bolsonaro administration that shortens the minimum time of possession and weakens other requirements for acquiring property rights over previously public land. If passed, this legislation will be an enormous gift to public land grabbers.

The authors describe two other success stories of government interventions that helped create R&D infrastructure in Brazil. The first is Petrobras, the national oil company that became a world leader in deepwater oil exploration. As with Embrapa, Petrobras developed a thriving network of research partners, including universities and the private sector. However, unlike Embrapa, which relied on the private sector to implement the fruits of its R&D activities, the Brazilian government often required Petrobras to monopolize the use of the results of its R&D. For instance, legislation from 2010 required a minimum share for Petrobras in oil production from each block in the pre-salt layer off the Brazilian coast. This requirement slowed down the production of oil in the pre-salt layer. While Brazil's agriculture greatly benefited from the commodity boom in the early twenty-first century, the country gained relatively little from the high oil prices during that episode. In contrast, during the same period, the exploration of shale oil and gas helped turn the United States into a leading oil and gas producer.

The second story told here is that of the aeronautics complex around São José dos Campos in the state of São Paulo. This complex is the closest analogue in Brazil to Silicon Valley, with the Air Force Institute of Technology (ITA) playing Stanford's and UC Berkeley's role. In this environment, Embraer was founded in 1969 with the goal of producing aircraft with Brazilian technology. After privatization in 1994, as the authors describe, Embraer embarked on a major program of cost reduction and successfully built a worldwide network of suppliers. This restructuring allowed it to become the third largest producer of civil aircraft, after Airbus and Boeing.

Since the late 1970s the performance of Brazil's economy has been disappointing. Standard growth decompositions show that the principal reason for this poor outcome was the stagnation of total factor productivity (TFP), a measure of how much output an economy can produce with a fixed quantity of factors of production, such as labor and capital. In contrast to several countries in east Asia, China, or India, TFP in Brazil grew less than TFP in the United States, distancing the country further from the frontier. Agriculture was an exception to this general mediocrity. From 1990 to 2009, TFP of Brazilian agriculture grew 160 percent of the U.S. agricultural productivity growth. The history that Fishlow and Vieira-Filho recount in this excellent book would help in the design of economic policies that could deliver the long-term growth prospects that Brazil sorely needs.

José Alexandre Scheinkman

Charles and Lynn Zhang Professor of Economics at Columbia University and Theodore Wells '29 Professor of Economics Emeritus at Princeton University.

ACKNOWLEDGMENTS

First off, we would like to thank Columbia University Press for the efforts they have made—even in the midst of the ongoing battle to temper the coronavirus crisis—to ensure the timely appearance of this volume.

We also acknowledge the generous grants from former Provost John Coatsworth and from the Institute of Latin American Studies. Recent financial support to Columbia by Jorge Paulo Lemann has contributed to a revival of interest in Brazil, measured by the number of students and faculty focused on the country. This is a return to the time of social anthropologist Charles Wagley, founder of the first Center of Latin American Studies in 1961. Others, such as economists Albert Hirschman and Stefan Robock, and the historian Herbert Klein were involved.

An earlier edition of this book, with the same title, appeared in Portuguese under the aegis of IPEA in 2018. This version is not the same. Part of the change appears in the form of more extensive macroeconomic content as well as inclusion of more recent research. We are indebted to the personal commitment of Christine Puleo Reis, who enabled this more focused book to appear in English. She has been a central component of the volume's evolution.

One of us is a citizen of the United States; the other is Brazilian. One of us is beginning to think of slowing down a bit in the future; the other continues to advance at an impressive pace by adding governmental experience to his qualifications. Bringing together our different specializations and nationalities, we have written a book examining the central role of innovation in advancing Brazilian growth. We present it, fully optimistic that a positive future will recur. Aggregate expansion, an improving distribution of income, and a deepening commitment to democratic values are not beyond attainment.

We have dedicated this book to our professors, students, colleagues, and friends who have contributed to our better understanding of Brazilian reality.

Albert Fishlow

José Eustâquio Ribeiro Vieira Filho

AGRICULTURE AND INDUSTRY IN BRAZIL

CHAPTER 1

Introduction

Research, technology, and productivity all play important roles in economic growth. Firm behavior and technology changes in industry have been widely studied, but few cases focus on agriculture. It is critical to study agriculture through this lens. Given the increasing scarcity of land and labor, the essential resources of agricultural production, technology is more indispensable than ever in the agricultural sector. Overall, our goal in *Agriculture and Industry in Brazil: Innovation and Competitiveness* is to outline technological change in the Brazilian agricultural sector. Exploration of the innovation pathways in its production chain is central to this analysis.

The early chapters lay the groundwork to fully understand the evolution of agricultural innovation in Brazil. Chapter 2 outlines the macroeconomic evolution of the Brazilian economy, which is the backdrop for demand and supply in agricultural production. Chapter 3 considers the theory of technical institutional change and contextualizes the debate in subsequent chapters. Chapter 4 presents a historical perspective and shows how induced institutional innovation is intimately tied to transformation in the agricultural sector. Chapter 5 provides detail on Embrapa, the Brazilian Agricultural Research Corporation founded by the Ministry of Agriculture in 1973, and traces its contribution to institutional and technological change. Chapter 6 assesses Brazil's surprising agricultural export growth over the last twenty-five years, which is inherently related to prior modernization efforts that set off the process of dynamic growth. In chapter 7, we study the advance of Brazil's agricultural frontiers, mainly due to intensive use of knowledge and technology, and examine the consequences for the environment. Chapter 8 analyzes small-scale agriculture, highlighting the regional inequalities in Brazil that leave some regions less able to innovate due to educational and technological roadblocks. Chapters 9 and 10 compare the case of Brazilian agriculture to two other industries—oil and aviation—which also expanded rapidly. Finally, chapter 11 looks to the future of Brazilian agriculture.

Many economists mistakenly consider agriculture as a sector with only minimal influence on technological generation and productivity growth. However, this is not the case. In fact, agriculture serves as a paradigmatic case for studying innovation. The Green Revolution, which used modern products such as fertilizers, pesticides, and improved seeds in developing countries, does not fully apply to the Brazilian context. Unlike Mexico and Asian countries, Brazil did not import ready-made technological packages in the 1950s and 1960s. In addition, Brazil had an unusually ambitious and centralized program of support through the Embrapa initiative.

Embrapa was founded partly to ensure food security, which had become a concern due to population growth and the rapid urbanization of the country in the late 1960s and early 1970s. With Embrapa, Brazil had the capacity to produce new knowledge and apply it to a tropical climate rather than use production techniques developed for other environments. This development process provided a novel link between sectors and research institutions that did not follow a sequential pattern. Institutional research created an ability to adapt production to local conditions and generate new technologies. The success of Embrapa shows that the revolutionary dynamics observed in Brazil depended on an institutional focus utilizing science and technology. Modern agriculture, therefore, is a knowledge-intensive sector.

In later chapters, we compare the Brazilian agricultural sector with aviation and oil production. Like agriculture, oil and aviation were also supported by public policy, which directed efforts to build institutions and provided a basis for their robustness. We highlight their shared characteristics of success, in theory as well as in practice.

At the Brazilian Petroleum Corporation, more commonly known as Petrobrás, the main initial objective was reduced dependence on oil imports. This concern was reinforced by Getúlio Vargas's nationalism, in the 1940s and 1950s, and by military governments from 1964 to 1985. Meanwhile, the national strategy for Brazilian aircraft manufacturer Embraer was driven by the integration of national territory (via aviation networks), concern over national defense/security (military aviation), and a desire to strengthen a domestic industry capable of cutting-edge technology.

The performance of Petrobrás and Embraer in a recently industrialized country like Brazil is an example of emergent global competitiveness based on technological change and the design of knowledge networks. These companies were able to adopt, assimilate, and gain external knowledge from abroad before starting an internal and virtuous cycle of innovation. These companies depended on strategic knowledge networks and external collaboration, just as the agricultural sector did.

There are challenges as well. Public intervention in Petrobrás over the past decade has placed the company in financial jeopardy, as shown by the *Lava Jato* (Car Wash) corruption probe and its consequences. Development of new technologies now depends on the company's future ability to allocate financial resources to research activities. With scarce capital, technological innovations are inevitably compromised, especially the firm's ability to continue to manage strategic knowledge networks. We focus on the technological progress of Petrobrás prior to this problem. The deteriorating financial structure brought about by corruption is not analyzed, but the uncertainties that followed are recognized.

Embraer focused on the regional aviation market and specialized in the production of aircraft in response to domestic demands. When the company was privatized, it conquered the international market, but it faced challenges in productive restructuring following trade liberalization. Favorable prospects are emerging with creation of Embraer's military transport aircraft (KC 390). With a ratified agreement involving Boeing, this will reposition the company in the global market, competing with other nations in a new capacity.

Together, analysis of these three cases provides a valuable contribution to the study of technological change. Furthermore, they highlight the challenges now faced by emerging economies. Our aim is to show how innovative policies in the agricultural sector, and the leadership role of Embrapa, are similar to policies observed in the oil and aviation sectors.

Effective public policy can help expansion of the country's economy. Indeed, agriculture has truly transformed the country. For example, nearly half of a Brazilian worker's income had been used to put food on the table, but the current cost is no higher than 20 percent of a worker's income. As a result, Brazil has established itself as a leading exporter of grains, fruits, and animal products. This has led to an agricultural sector increasingly integrated with others and able to create higher value-added products. Overall, the agro-industrial sector now accounts for about one-third of the gross domestic product (GDP) and a significant portion of the domestic workforce.

Nonetheless, the agricultural sector has continuing challenges. Regional income inequality and poverty remain. Poorly conceived programs do not create the benefits they are intended to provide. Intervention is not always for the good.

All three efforts began when Brazil had highly centralized development priorities. Due to the Brazilian debt and fiscal crisis in more recent times, federal investment is now limited. In analyzing the successes and challenges of each case, we focus on a central question: What should future policy be?

We hope the discussion contained in the following pages illustrates the influence of earlier public policies as a basis for productivity growth. That pattern should be a central focus in the years ahead.

CHAPTER 2

Development Strategies in Brazil

A CONTEMPORARY VIEW

NATIONAL PERFORMANCE: BRIEF SUMMARY OF THE BEGINNINGS

Brazil was one of the world's most vibrant economies throughout the twentieth century. From a very low initial level of income per capita in 1889, when the republic was first established after years of Portuguese and domestic monarchy, much was required to accelerate progress. At that time, economic advances shifted to the states of the south. Earlier reliance on sugar exports based on slavery in the northeast had given way to coffee exports, subsidized immigration from Italy, and the beginnings of import substitution. With political change, Brazil established a policy committed to developing domestic manufacturing to supplement the declining growth of coffee exports.

The *Encilhamento* took place in the earliest years of the new republic, and by 1893, it was over. Domestic credit had rapidly expanded, as had financial speculation. Inflation was important as well. With exchange rates relatively stable, there was a shift toward larger international debt to finance larger imports of capital goods required by a burgeoning textile industry. Much remained to be done, despite lower immediate growth, as Brazil sought to stabilize.

Under new presidents Campos Salles and Rodrigues Alves, government restrictions on expenditures were instituted in response to demands of foreign bankers, and the declining exchange rate was eventually reversed. In this recession, unemployment increased and textile output barely grew. Recovery accelerated after 1906, owing more to a policy to store coffee, normalizing supply as more trees were planted, than to tariff protection, although that was quite strong as well. The Treaty of Taubaté in 1906 established government regulation of coffee production, and foreign bankers were happy to help finance that initiative. Unlike temporary Brazilian adherence to the gold standard, tariff protection remained a central government commitment.

On the eve of World War I, Brazil still had a primitive industrial structure. Textile imports represented about a third of estimated consumption. Although domestic production of processed foodstuffs increased, agricultural imports still rivaled those of iron and steel. There was virtually no domestic capital goods sector, even though an import substitution policy with some consequences was in place at that time.

The war interrupted this progress. Trade, especially imports, was curtailed; immigration was greatly reduced; and industrial growth was irregular. Inflation accelerated as fiscal deficits returned. But this experience was not as negative nor as positive as some might imagine. Generally, entrepreneurial gains during this interval were available for later investment. Also, textile imports were impeded, enabling domestic supply to grow to about 85 percent of consumption. Processed food products, more protected by distance, were slightly higher. In the 1919 census, capital goods and consumer durables were almost entirely imported.

Industrial manufacturing slowed in the 1920s, although a small gain was seen in imports of capital and intermediate goods. At the same time, foreign investment brought modern technology to the domestic production of cement and steel. Larger investment by foreign firms, increasingly from the United States, underwrote low inflation and a steady industrial and infrastructure expansion. In comparison, agricultural production showed less expansion.

The real determinant of Brazilian growth remained centered in the coffee sector, and this is where public policy really mattered. The Great Depression of 1928–29 led to a new era of active intervention, with coffee no longer financed externally but directly by the government. The exchange rate was devalued, and direct control of imports was implemented. Tariffs lost force with the rapid fall in international prices, and imports of manufactured products had already diminished as a result of earlier import substitution.

Above all, the federal government enacted a complementary fiscal and monetary intervention committed to stockpiling (and even destroying) coffee and making domestic credit available. This created a large federal deficit along with an increase in the domestic money supply. This demand-oriented policy worked. Excess supply disappeared, and the public sector began setting priorities for the first time. Servicing the international debt was put aside in the early years of the Depression, making larger sums available for essential imports.

The manufacturing sector expanded rapidly throughout the 1930s due to an increased labor supply rather than to a rising capital-output ratio. Double shifts became common. In the aggregate, about half the increase in manufacturing value added can be attributed to import substitution. Intermediate and capital goods began to lead the way for the first time. By 1939, this sector accounted for almost 10 percent of the labor force, compared to 4 percent in 1919. Labor productivity was modest during this expansion, and industrialization suffered severe shocks.

As World War II approached, the United States altered its foreign policy. Until then, direct barter trade with Germany was extensive and had been growing. After the Getúlio Vargas coup in November 1937, federal political and economic powers were centralized, and Brazil returned to freezing service on the external debt and intervening in the foreign exchange market. Brazil also experienced a large decline in exports due to the decline in GDP in the United States.

Brazilian growth began to falter at the beginning of World War II. From the double-digit rise in 1936, expansion fell to less than 1 percent between 1939 and 1942. In 1942, the United States not only helped finance a new steel plant at Volta Redonda but also provided technological assistance. The same was true for the expanded iron ore facility at Vale do Rio Doce. These policies, as well as others, reflected deeper engagement by the federal government in managing the economy.

By 1943, these efforts had produced tangible results. Growth was sharply higher, at 8 percent per year in 1943–44, with industry moving ahead by 12 percent. Two views about future policy emerged when the war ended. One was the position of Roberto Simonsen, reflective of São Paulo industrialists, which was in favor of continued intervention; a contrasting position by Eugenio Gudin argued for less federal oversight and defended agriculture and a return to a free market.

PLANNED IMPORT SUBSTITUTION INDUSTRIALIZATION IN BRAZIL

Post-World War II government policy, even after Vargas was deposed in 1945, remained committed to import substitution industrialization (ISI) and state engagement.[1] That differentiates it from earlier advances in manufacturing that were dependent on passive adjustment to changing external circumstances. The policies in favor of industrialization were based on two principles. The first focused on protectionist limits on imports, and the second focused on credit support to private investment combined with direct state-controlled enterprises.

At the beginning, in 1945, there was reason for doubt about the right choice. Coffee prices began a sharp climb upward, gaining almost 300 percent by 1950 and climbing another 50 percent by 1954. Total exports seemed sufficient to finance freely determined imports. Controlling high rates of inflation (15–20 percent), inherited from the war years and much above earlier levels, was the first priority. But from the beginning, these restrictions limited bank credit and created problems for domestic firms.

In 1947, instead of devaluation to retain the wartime expansion of exports of manufactured products to Africa and elsewhere and limit imports of consumer goods, the key decision was a return to overvalued exchanged rates. The current account deficit reduced inflation, but this implied an early need for other measures of control. Tariffs were irrelevant. They had remained at 1900 rates and were not adjusted to an ad valorem basis. Management of the exchange rate to limit imports, as well as to encourage a shift to capital goods, was necessary. That meant controlling importation of specific products and excluding products for which domestic alternatives were sufficient.

Even during the more conservative phase of Brazilian leadership, efforts toward increased federal engagement were made. The Plano SALTE in 1948 emphasized health, food production, transportation, and energy, and it was hoped that cooperation with the United States could achieve these objectives. But the Marshall Plan—and flows to Europe— dominated U.S. strategy. A mixed commission began to identify projects for which financial and technical assistance would be beneficial, but the commission didn't manage to get very far. In addition, the Brazilian Congress only approved the plan a year before the election.

With Getúlio Vargas president again—this time by popular vote— Brazilian priorities shifted somewhat. Immediate efforts were made to increase federal authority and to complete projects. New institutions were created under direct control of the state, among them the Brazilian Development Bank (BNDES) and Petrobrás. To help matters along, import management again devolved into a federal responsibility following increases in inflows during 1951 and 1952.

During those two years, Brazil altered its imports with a greater emphasis on capital goods and raw materials. Imports were increased for machinery for textiles, metal and woodworking, and road building, among others. But exports weakened, and stress began to be felt in the coffee sector, whose fixed rate meant a lower return. That led to alteration of the rules in 1953 in two stages. At the beginning of the year, slightly higher rates, along with some sector variation, were approved. By the end of the year, the Aranha Plan produced clear economic profitability for the industrial sector, and agriculture largely paid the price. Agricultural rates were kept low as were inputs required by domestic industry. Profits were high in sectors to which the government was committed, such as iron and steel, cement, heavy chemicals, and oil refineries. Many of these were later selected for continuing governmental support in Kubitschek's *Plano de Metas*.

Vargas then turned to another of his priorities, updating the minimum wage. On May 1, 1954, the nominal wage went up 100 percent. That meant a real increase of 7 percent relative to 1952. Not surprisingly, domestic reaction was divided. Vargas's electoral base in the labor movement was on one side, and leaders of industrial expansion and the military were on the other. The industry leaders wanted assurances that the economy would not move leftward. It is worth noting that Minister of Labor João Goulart left government after the large wage increase, but he was elected vice president in both 1955 and 1960.

After Vargas's suicide in 1954, a regime headed by conservative Vice President Café Filho came to power. He selected Eugenio Gudin as the minister of finance. Gudin wanted to end inflation by tightening monetary policy, controlling fiscal expenditure, and ending large transfers in resources from agriculture to industry, which was characteristic of the Vargas period. After grappling with an initial banking crisis and securing assistance from private U.S. banks, Gudin installed credit restraint, but he could not alter fiscal policy. Industrial activity slowed, and coffee producers complained about their declining profits. Gudin resigned after a mere seven months, having been in full opposition to the better exchange rate conceded to coffee.

Before Gudin resigned, however, he saw to the issuance of SUMOC Instruction 113. This was central to the great surge in industrial development in the late 1950s and early 1960s. Foreign firms were allowed to invest at favorable exchange rates that were not available to Brazilian entrepreneurs. This investment policy became the source for expansion of consumer durables, particularly automobiles, and new capital goods in the late 1950s. With elections coming up, Congress did not approve a proposal to end the multiple exchange rate system, despite preliminary discussions with the International Monetary Fund (IMF).

Regularly scheduled elections brought a new president in October. Juscelino Kubitschek, often known as JK, won by a leading minority vote of 36 percent, with Goulart as vice president. Conservatives and the military were horrified, and there was talk of a potential coup, which was narrowly averted by War Minister Henrique Texeira Lott.

JK was committed to high rates of economic growth, and subsequent inflation and deteriorating exchange rates were simply a bother. Innovative structuralism dominated conventional monetarism. Price increases and compensating rises in wages were soon to become the rule rather than the exception. Initially, Finance Minister José Maria Alkmin was able to manage quite well. Price increases went down in 1957 to around 7 percent, benefiting from good agricultural harvests. During the same year, a tariff structure was put in place, replacing the specific levels—for some time outmoded—with an ad valorem structure. This ended the need to regularly modify categories of exchange rates that had been adopted earlier.

But direct control continued in two respects. First, when coffee prices fell substantially the following year, the sector received a large transfer of resources—a multiple of expenditures for Brasilia. Second, imports of industrial products became subject to complete restriction once domestic firms began to satisfy local demands. Local inflation increased as a result, and a large increase in minimum wages in July 1956 gave inflation a further boost. Early on, with lower inflation in 1957 and a booming economy, real wages rose. But as prices adjusted in 1958, much of that gain was eroded, creating dissatisfaction within the growing urban labor force.

Alkmin left in June 1958, and Lucas Lopes replaced him. He had been a close associate of Kubitschek in Minas Gerais for many years. He served the new administration as president of the development bank BNDES, which was established in the early 1950s by Vargas. Assisted by Roberto Campos, his successor as head of BNDES, they immediately began work on a monetary stabilization program, the PEM. This undertaking was a vain attempt to impose controls on credit expansion and gradually lessen increments in the money supply. It was expected to take at least two years to achieve price stability. And, as explicitly stated, government expenditures to construct Brasilia were exempt from cutbacks.

Those objectives, however, could not compete with the Plano de Metas and its intent to achieve an advance of fifty years within the next five.

Thirty specific targets were grouped into five categories. Energy received priority, with more than 40 percent of expected outlays; transportation came next, with more than 25 percent; basic industries, cement, steel, aluminum, paper and cellulose, and rubber were the other priorities; agriculture and education were included, each with minimal changes.

Resources for these undertakings were designed to emanate from a different style of interaction with the private sector. For the first time, large foreign investment was welcomed into Brazil in what was intended to be a tripartite process of cooperation, with the other two components being the federal government and domestic investment. But that structure occurred infrequently. The automobile sector was totally foreign owned. On the other side, government outlays for roadways and increased generation of electricity represented the largest component of its expenditure during the period.

Foreign investment was certainly present, under the favorable terms of Instruction 113. A growing number of state-owned enterprises also managed to achieve their targets, some with participation from the United States, Germany, and Japan. Economic advance proceeded rapidly as credit from the Bank of Brazil continued to be available, and state banks encountered no federal limit. In addition, construction of a new capital, Brasilia, was rushed to functional operation by the end of the presidential term. That alone involved a federal outlay estimated to be 2 to 3 percent of national income over five years, but assistance to coffee producers and state enterprises was much larger.

For Kubitschek, high growth and the official dedication of the new capital overshadowed the IMF stabilization program. The IMF made limited resources available as the PEM was being prepared, but criticisms began to escalate once it was approved by Congress. Greater limitations were desired. Soon they were joined, but on the other side, by both coffee producers and industrialists who wanted subsidies.

As the debate increased in 1959, there was little doubt about how JK would decide. He was willing to accept a higher rate of inflation as the price of rapid industrial advance. Lucas Lopes suffered a heart attack in June, and soon after that Brazil made a widely publicized decision to break off all discussions with the IMF. That improved JK's domestic reputation in preparation for a possible return to the presidency in 1965. He also increased minimum wages at the end of the year by more than 50 percent.

Everything was focused on completing Brasilia on time. Costs were secondary; aircraft transported cement, and road construction was accelerated to be ready to carry the new trucks and cars that were being produced. In April 1960, on the anniversary of Tiradentes's death by hanging and brutal quartering after he led opposition to Portuguese rule, Brasilia became the new capital. Most of the government remained in Rio while development continued, and the original urban concept did not survive. Construction workers remained, encircling the capital, and the population continued to expand.

Janio Quadros, a conservative UDN candidate, easily won election in October 1960 with 48 percent of the vote. Inflation was continuing to mount, along with rapid growth. This time, the symbol of the new president was the broom he used to indicate the need for far-reaching reform. After inauguration, Quadros announced his commitment to serious domestic restriction to end inflation and, somewhat surprisingly, a much wider reaching out to communist countries, including Cuba, Russia, China, and, prospectively, Indonesia. Indeed, Quadros did not even attend the annual meeting of the Organization of American States (OAS) in Rio, and he did not plan to attend the beginning of the Alliance for Progress in Punta del Este.

A fascinating record of U.S. diplomatic efforts during the short period before Quadros's resignation in August as well as the later ascension of Vice President João Goulart is now available. These issues of U.S. foreign relations specify the abundance of help at the beginning, and the progressive dissatisfaction of the United States as Goulart assumed control. What emerges is the dire economic condition of Brazil in 1961. Facing massive external debt along with fiscal and balance of payments deficits, in an early meeting in Brasilia with Treasury Secretary Dillon, attending the OAS sessions in April, Quadros argued that his foreign policy was designed only to bring along the domestic left, supporters of Goulart. Public meetings with Che Guevara, Yuri Gregorian, and Fidel Castro certainly caught the public eye in Brazil—as well as in the United States.

Brazil needed immediate postponement of the scheduled amortization of public debt, both official as well as private, as well as continued entry of capital. Specific numbers were prepared. The United States pressured a very reluctant IMF to go along. Indeed, the IMF sent a mission to Brazil at the end of April; it was kept secret, and could stay only a few days rather than the typical two weeks and more.

In July, a program of assistance finally became available. Despite its magnitude and a willingness of all debtors to go along, the plan was unable to resolve the rapidly deteriorating political conditions. By that time, Quadros had failed to sustain congressional support of his dual, and incompatible, policies. His sudden decision to resign occurred at the end of August, and his speech suggested he might reconsider. When no one intervened, he was off to Europe and rapidly forgotten—at least until his surprise victory over Fernando Henrique Cardoso in the 1975 São Paulo mayoral race.

The first reaction to Goulart's right to succession was an attempt by the military as well as conservative politicians and the new industrial elite to impede that constitutional right. The United States was disposed negatively. Eventually, an agreement was reached to allow Goulart to assume the position, but with less power. Brazil committed itself to a parliamentary structure, with Tancredo Neves serving as prime minister. That resolved the immediate political threat, but it did little to help the economy. Inflation continued its acceleration, output increases began to diminish, and the flow of foreign capital began to fall.

Despite efforts to use the parliamentary form of governance, little emerged. Tancredo enunciated virtually all the changes regarded as necessary since the efforts of Lucas and Campos in 1958. As before, there was little enthusiasm either within the Congress or by the president. Attempts to gradually reduce inflation failed, and a high rate of growth continued. With prices and wages accelerating, something different was necessary. The IMF wanted immediate substantial disinflation, even if the price was limited expansion, and strong popular protests made little difference.

Congressional elections were scheduled for October 1962, and Goulart supporters were already planning a referendum restoring full powers to the president, which was approved by a large majority in early January 1963. Part of that undertaking was preparation of a formal plan to submit to the IMF to avoid impending default on the government debt.

The Plano Trienal, issued at the end of 1962, was principally the product of Celso Furtado, originally head of the Superintendency for Development of the Northeast (SUDENE), a new structure created to deal with poverty in the northeast. This attempt reiterated the possibility of gradually fighting inflation while continuing growth at past levels. Criticisms abounded regarding the consistency of the effort, and additional resources from the IMF did not appear, although a concession of $60 million was offered for declining Brazilian exports.

By the middle of 1963, the issue had transformed into when, not if, military intervention would occur. The annual rate of growth fell to the lowest level since the Great Depression, 0.1 percent. Differences about economic stabilization were forgotten as inflation rose to its highest historic levels—close to 100 percent annually. The focus now centered on politics more generally, with a deteriorating income distribution increasingly the cause as changes in prices outran cost increases. Public conflict between officers and lower ranks occurred in all three divisions of the armed services. Radical promises of agrarian reform, forcible further nationalization of foreign assets, and limits to profits abounded in presidential appearances. Military leaders were dismissed. On the other side, the middle class marched in opposition.

The end came more quickly and decisively than anyone imagined. In the evening of March 31, the military moved from Minas Gerais toward Rio, and they were joined by other forces the next day. Goulart, also known as Jango, had returned to Brasilia but then had to leave again in search of asylum in Uruguay. The coup d'etat had succeeded. On April 15, the head of the Army, Castelo Branco, was sworn in as president, beginning a period of military control that was to last for twenty years, much longer than anyone expected.

Before taking up that period, we conclude this section by returning to an evaluation of the import substitution structure Brazil had mounted in the first two decades after World War II. Four elements characterize this model.

One element was reliance on commercial policy to implement a large transfer of resources from agriculture to the industrial sector. Early on, an overvalued exchange rate taxed agriculture while subsidizing industry and permitting needed imports. This advantage to industry gave way to direct fiscal support as primary export prices fell in the mid-1950s soon after the Korean War halted. Indeed, by the end of the 1950s, coffee producers demanded, and received, considerable subsidies.

A second element was a consequence of rapid industrial growth absent earlier accelerating inflation. Rising government expenditures to support subsidies, necessary infrastructure, and urbanization were not matched by increased taxes. The fiscal deficit expanded, financed by monetary expansion and the unintended domestic savings created by inflation's progressive rise.

The third element was a growing reliance on foreign capital. Direct investment within the dynamic industrial sector underwrote domestic manufacturing production. Consumer durable goods and intermediate industrial sectors then favored by the government could not have expanded under domestic auspices alone. Foreign investment was especially needed to finance imports of capital goods as export receipts stagnated after 1953.

A fourth element was put in place with the return of Getúlio Vargas in 1950 and the election of a Republican to the U.S. White House two years later. Brazil gave up on its hopes for significant U.S. assistance to propel the country forward. There was no repeat of the Marshall Plan. Even the Alliance for Progress, put in place in 1961, accomplished little until the military takeover.

Import substitution ultimately came to an end because of its inherent inability to satisfy everyone. Conflicts erupted in a whole series of areas. Implicit taxes were imposed on agriculture as subsidies to industry increased. Needed expansion and diversification of trade yielded to reliance on the domestic market. Political conflict emerged over the role of the market versus a larger and more interventionist state. Inconsistency arose between rising consumer demands associated with urbanization and a technologically backward agriculture whose variability in harvests contributed to urban inflation. Favorable exchange rates allowed special benefits to foreigners compared to domestic producers. But that advantage was countered by another difficulty. Investment in new activities tended to be bunched rather than continuous. So cyclical variability increased as industry grew in importance.

At the end of the day, accelerating inflation became the solution rather than the problem. Inadequate domestic savings were made up by undesired transfers to the public sector. Political inaction was disguised by printing more money. Unfortunately, those with the least income were the most affected.

The import substitution strategy did have some positive effects on Brazilian performance. First, the contribution of ISI during the 1950s was not, by itself, the major source of greater domestic demand for manufacturing, but many of its inputs were critical. The ratio of imports to domestic production was already quite low by 1949, and its subsequent decline during the decade accounts for less than one-fifth of the observed manufacturing growth. This is in sharp contrast to the Great Depression experience.

Second, Brazilian industrialization was not as inefficient as its highly inflated tariff structure made it appear. Impossibly high rates of effective protection are the result of administrative measures to deal with a deteriorating balance of payments and do not measure real cost differentials. Later on, there would be more ability to diversify.

Third, exchange rate devaluation early on to encourage exports would have been inadequate. Primary product specialization in the late 1950s did not represent a feasible solution. Brazil faced international competition from other producers, even in coffee. Policies and priorities logically favored industry; they were not simply prejudiced against all external market opportunities.

ECONOMIC RECOVERY, THE BRAZILIAN MIRACLE, OIL CRISIS, AND INFLATION ONCE MORE

Right after military intervention, a new plan was prepared by Roberto Campos,[2] with considerable assistance offered by Mario Simonsen, a rising star economist at the Getúlio Vargas Foundation (FGV). By November when the plan was published, some of its elements had already been put into effect.

The *Plano de Ação Econômico do Governo*, known as the PAEG, was more sophisticated than the earlier Plano Trienal. It was characterized by greater integration with international markets; a larger and more centralized fiscal capacity; a structure of subsidies and incentives favoring profits rather than wages; enactment of monetary correction to diminish inflation-induced distortion; institutional reforms modernizing and altering the rules of the social security system, internal financial markets, tax laws, etc.; and by technocratic economic management as a counterpart to authoritarian political control.

For all its supposed commitment to capitalism, this strategy never corresponded to a free enterprise prototype. The IMF was not particularly enthusiastic about this diversion from the faith and the allowance, as in the Kubitschek years, for gradualism to work to defeat burgeoning inflation. Beyond this, there was a need to restore public confidence and increase delayed investment.

Brazil's economic strategy after 1964 remained more pragmatic and was rooted in an interventionist tradition from the past. Government participation in the economy—an object of rightist criticism in 1963—increased after military intervention. Public investment, whether direct in infrastructure or through state enterprises, rose as a percentage of capital formation. Regulation of economic activity hardly withered away. Subsidies and incentives proliferated as did price controls. They were accepted and welcomed as long as private profits also grew. Public control over resources via taxes and forced savings derived from an expanded system of changes registered in social policy.

Nor did the prior emphasis on industrialization alter. Foreign investment and modern capital-intensive technology were again welcomed. Consumer durable production resumed, led by automobiles, along with further extension to intermediate goods such as steel, paper, chemical products, and others. Rising industrial production was given additional force during this period by public resources and growing public ownership as external borrowing and direct foreign assistance from USAID accelerated.

Agricultural exports were not subsidized nearly as much as manufacturing. Indeed, agriculture was implicitly taxed by continuing protection against foreign industrial imports. Agricultural production for domestic consumption received little attention because the principal foodstuffs were primarily produced by small- and medium-sized units.

Over these years, agricultural growth varied considerably, principally as a consequence of weather changes, which had large effects on stability in the total price indices. A large part of the Brazilian population existed on an income barely above subsistence at this time, and price indexes thus gave considerable weight to agricultural products. One could bargain with oligopolistic industrial producers, as the government increasingly did in 1966, to prevent even higher general rises in price. But there was still little available for agriculture beyond minimum prices and low-interest loans.

A cyclic pattern contributed to greater popular opposition to military rule from the rising urban population (table 2.1). Agriculture was far from a passive partner in stabilization policies. Large owners, particularly coffee producers, had their own interests at heart. That meant enhanced governmental demand for products when prices were low and no interference from taxes when prices were high. It took another decade before rates began to synchronize.

An important consequence of the PAEG was the reduction of real wage levels between 1965 and 1968. A new policy was adopted to end the previous technique of constantly updating required nominal wage increases. Going forward, minimum wages—the direct measure for most of the labor force and indirectly for almost all groups—were to be determined by half of the real variability in wage levels. In theory, that would reduce the annual change in wages but not affect their real value. Figure 2.1 illustrates the logic of the technique—a direct contribution of Mario Henrique Simonsen—which was much in use in the following decades.

Table 2.1 Relative Agricultural Prices

Year	% Change	P_a % Change	P_T % Difference
1952	20.1	17.3	2.8
1953	18.6	14.3	4.3
1954	25.9	22.5	3.4
1955	24.2	23.1	0.9
1956	23.9	21.0	2.9
1957	15.3	16.0	-0.7
1958	14.4	14.8	-0.4
1959	45.1	39.2	5.9
1960	30.4	29.5	0.9
1961	34.7	33.2	0.5
1962	61.8	49.5	12.3
1963	65.6	72.8	-7.2
1964	96.1	91.7	4.4
1965	47.2	65.7	-18.5
1966	38.7	41.3	-2.6
1967	22.3	30.4	-8.1
1968	12.8	22.0	-9.2
1969	23.6	22.6	1.0
1970	25.5	22.4	3.1

Source: Institute for Applied Economic Research (Ipea). International Food & Agricultural Trade Policy Council (IPC)agriculture and total price indexes.

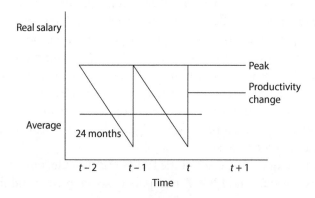

Figure 2.1 Minimum wages determined by half of the real variable in wage levels.

Source: Mario Henrique Simonsen.

Table 2.2   Real Minimum Wage

Year	Real Minimum Wage	% Change
1960	12.714	–12.2
1961	14.595	14.8
1962	12.161	–16.7
1963	11.757	–3.3
1964	13.043	11.7
1965	11.660	–11.2
1966	9.993	–13.9
1967	9.270	–7.4
1968	9.274	0.0
1969	8.784	–5.5
1970	8.645	–1.6

Source: Ipea.

However, that was not what happened. Table 2.2 provides a calculation of changes in real minimum wages from two different sources. There is little doubt about the result. As Simonsen himself wrote in 1970, "as for workers, everything confirms that they were the class prejudiced in this redistribution [monetary correction in a number of sectors], at least between 1965 and 1967, when their adjustments were less than proportional to the rise in prices."[3] Roberto Campos is less discreet: "The first sin of past laborism was the obsessive preoccupation with massively high salaries. . . . The natural result of this illusion was acceleration of the inflationary process."[4]

Prior to modest changes in the law in 1968, the rate of change of minimum wages fell far below rising prices. This meant a continuing significant reduction in real wages after earlier gains. This coincided with reduction in, and the power of, union membership. Most of the more radical leaders sought exit from the country, as did many politicians and technocrats whose political rights were canceled for a period of ten years.

Analysis of the decennial censuses leaves no doubt about the negative effects on income distribution as measured in 1960 and 1970. Between the two years, equality declined. Minimum wages were relevant for about half of the labor force. Upper-class incomes rose as a percentage of total income, and lower-class incomes—the bottom half of the distribution—fell. Nor had the stabilization program ended inflation as the PAEG had foreseen. Credit control policies and greater supervision of price increases in the industrial sector brought a continuing descent of prices in 1966, and growth prospects in the first quarter of 1967 had turned perceptibly negative.

President Castelo Branco's three-year term ended in March 1967, and a new military government headed by Arturo Costa e Silva came to power. He shifted the focus from stabilization to a resumption of economic growth, as his nomination of Antonio Delfim Netto showed. Targets became real rather than monetary, similar to that of the PAEG.

Delfim Netto's efforts were directed at first to looser monetary policy. More and cheaper credit became available in the rest of 1967. Inflation reduction was no longer the principal target. The focus explicitly shifted from demand-based inflation to cost-based pressure on prices. Unemployment represented a unique opportunity to accelerate growth without generating additional inflation. Growth began to pick up, and a short-term plan was published in 1968, the *Programa Estrategico do Desenvolvimento* (PED). The best parts of the abandoned Plano Decenal appeared as supplementary volumes.

This PED was notable in two respects. First, the document was a joint effort of Ipea and the Ministry of Finance. Delfim brought a small group of academics from the University of São Paulo (USP) to the ministry when he was appointed. At the same time, a group of foreign economists participated in Ipea under an AID contract. Their collaboration, based more on background than on governmental experience, culminated in a macroeconomic plan consistent with Delfim's desire for higher rates of growth.

Second, this approach accurately foresaw an opportunity for continuing expansion at greater speed than the IMF and the World Bank thought feasible. The PED conveyed the desire of domestic entrepreneurs for greater continuity in policy and assessed the need for exports of manufactured goods rather than the substantial reliance on coffee and other primary products. The PED understood how larger state participation, including many more enterprises under direct control, could play a leading role in stimulating private sector reaction.

As growth began to accelerate, inflation rates no longer remained a prime consideration. Nor was government investment slowed by concerns about the fiscal deficit. If exports were to grow in this environment, a variable exchange rate rather than a fixed rate was necessary. This change showed up in August 1968. So, too, did subsidies for exports of manufactured products. The result was the Brazilian Miracle—the years between 1968 and 1973 when average expansion was consistently high. Cumulatively, national product increased almost 90 percent, close to doubling.

Economic output did not falter when the military stepped up their control in December 1968 with Institutional Act No. 5, which permitted greater centralization of revenues at the federal level as well as an end to mayoral and gubernatorial elections. Despite political problems such as the kidnapping of ambassadors and torture of many of those arrested, the economy did not falter. President Emílio Garrastazu Medici—the successor to Costa e Silva—publicized "Brazil: Love it or leave it," and his own popularity was substantial as growth continued to increase.

The First National Development Plan (I PND) was instituted in 1971 after João Paulo dos Reis Velloso became planning minister. Economic growth of 9 percent, annual inflation below 20 percent, and an increase in foreign investment were among the principal objectives. A goal to smooth the flow of science and technology to the productive sector was new and included promotion of research programs. In addition, an expanded infrastructure to enhance economic development was high on the agenda. Among the goals were construction of the Itaipu hydroelectric power plant, funds to complete the Rio-Niterói bridge, and construction of the Trans-amazôn highway, linking the state of Paraíba to the state of Amazonas. Agriculture was specifically included in the plan as rising prices rewarded producers of primary goods.

High growth persisted until the end of Delfim Netto's term. But negative forces were set in motion in 1973. First, as the economy continued its rapid ascent, price inflation was calculated by excluding some increases, even as public sector prices were repressed. Second, at the end of the year, a substantial rise in oil prices affected international capital flows after the Israeli war.

The new government was led by General Ernesto Geisel. Velloso remained minister of planning, and Mario Simonsen entered as finance minister. A follow-up plan had been under way in 1973. The II NDP in 1974, already under way, had to adapt to these events if it were to be relevant. Simonsen emphasized the danger of accelerating inflation and slowed product growth. Compared to the 14 percent rise in GDP in 1973, the consumer index made only a small gain (13 percent). In 1974, Brazil grew by 9 percent while prices rose by 27 percent.

To be sure, oil prices were a factor. Brazil was heavily dependent on oil imports, which represented more than 80 percent of domestic consumption. The government decided to focus on alternative energy sources, launching the National Alcohol Program (Pró-Alcool, the National Ethanol Program) and expanding resources for the Brazilian nuclear program through the construction of nuclear plants. At the same time, more resources were committed to expand spending on offshore oil exploration by Petrobrás.

This model has been praised for the extraordinary growth it fostered between 1968 and 1973; a rate of aggregate expansion in excess of 10 percent a year is no mean achievement. But the government was rightly criticized for its failure to distribute income more equitably and to increase access to public services for the poor. Indeed, assuring both increased production and fairer income distribution soon became the issue of the day throughout the developed as well as the developing world.

Here we stress the special character and importance of Brazilian integration into world capital markets as a component of the model. Despite rapid and unprecedented export volume growth—about 10 percent since the mid-1960s—and favorable primary price trends of the same magnitude, Brazilian recovery involved even more rapid import expansion. The current account balance moved from a surplus in 1965 to a deficit of 2.3 percent of GDP in 1971–1973. By the end of 1973, before the rise in oil prices had its full consequence, the external debt registered 17 percent of GDP, compared to about 10 percent in 1967.

That acceleration of product growth represented debt-led rather than export-led growth. External resources, predominantly on commercial terms as Brazil for the first time became a factor in the euro-dollar market, guaranteed availability of foreign exchange for voracious import requirements. Those resources also permitted a surge in investment that did not have to be financed domestically at the expense of consumption. Internal capital market reforms were not necessary to achieve equivalent finance.

External indebtedness continued to expand after 1973 at even more rapid rates. Quadrupling of oil prices caught Brazil just when internal bottlenecks and cyclical excesses were creating internal economic adjustment problems, such as resurgent inflation. Especially vulnerable to the rise in oil prices, Brazil opted to postpone its adjustment to this external imbalance and relied more heavily on debt, which was equivalent to betting on a return to lower oil prices in the future. By the end of 1978, external debt was more than $40 billion, representing 25 percent of GDP. The II PND objectives had been partly achieved, with an increase in gross fixed capital formation in relation to GDP (18.8 percent in 1970, 20.2 percent in 1971–1973, and 22.3 percent in 1974–1978) to go along with mounting indebtedness.

Other countries were also affected. The East Asian countries chose a different path. They accepted the rise in petroleum prices along with devaluation and slower expansion. Soon they began to grow again, and they had less indebtedness and a stronger commitment to exports of manufactured goods. They started from much lower incomes as a result of choosing this option, but they began a continuing rise to middle-income levels.

There was now a clear shift to debt-led growth in Brazil, but this debt-financed adjustment yielded progressively fewer positive returns. Development turned into a stop-go alternation, reflecting the absence of a strategy to deal with both the external crisis and the accumulating social disparities. Debt management was weak, permitting a large acquisition of reserves and corresponding domestic monetary expansion. Limitations on imports—held virtually constant in nominal terms between 1974 and 1978 through stricter controls—began to create supply bottlenecks. Despite subsidies, exports of manufactured goods continued to lag.

Brazil and other Latin American and developing countries were accumulating debt at a rapid pace, but also at a higher cost as commercial banks adjusted interest rates to keep pace with rapidly rising market rates. The danger of this process of slower expansion and now debt-led debt began to appear in a variety of publications. When the next military president, João Figueredo, was selected in the fall of 1978, options were diminishing. A decision to restrain growth more forcefully under Simonsen and to adjust was short-lived. When oil prices went up again in June 1979 with the Iran-Iraq War, Brazil had yet to make much progress either in greater petroleum production or in expansion of the ethanol alternative. The second round of import substitution directed toward capital goods permitted some progress, but that help was minor.

The government finally began to recognize the magnitude of the crisis confronting Brazil. Delfim Netto, waiting in the wings as minister of agriculture, was now appointed minister of the presidency's secretariat of planning (*Seplan* in Portuguese). A new liberalization package and a heterodox strategy were proclaimed. Delfim's second term guiding economic policy proved much less successful than his first—there was no economic miracle this time. In the beginning, high growth returned, 7.2 percent in 1979 and 9.1 percent in 1980. But Brazil paid a high price for this in large fiscal and trade deficits. Inflation went up to 100 percent, twice the initial target. State enterprises were restricted to small price increases. The heterodoxy originally advanced in 1979 gave way to orthodox austerity in November 1980 in an effort to calm the external banks that were no longer willing to finance this growing debt. Debt-led debt finally came to an inglorious end.

Soon thereafter, in 1982, the IMF provided and a series of unfulfilled and constantly adjusted targets, but high inflation did not cease. Current price increases were regularly indexed higher than inflation and were resistant to any reduction and prone to acceleration.

With continuing deterioration of the macroeconomic scenario and negative growth, the military regime rapidly lost strength. Large marches in favor of immediate elections and an end to military rule began in 1983. By 1985, the military fully retreated and ceded power to civilian rulers through the same indirect presidential elections previously employed. A fusion occurred between the Brazilian Democratic Movement Party (PMDB), still in a minority, and some members of the Social Democratic Party (PDS). With this arrangement, Tancredo Neves (PMDB) was elected president and José Sarney (PDS) vice president.

Tancredo Neves never served, becoming ill and dying before the inauguration. Instead, José Sarney assumed leadership of the New Republic. The government confronted two immediate tasks: restructuring the political system inherited from prior military rule and ending a continuing inflation of more than 200 percent annually, which had defied IMF efforts for many years.

The 1988 Constitution accomplished its first objective. After considerable debate and mounting differences, new political parties were established that complicated decisions when compared to the two-party structure previously in place. Frequently, individual ambitions dominated substantive divergence. By 2018, the Constitution included almost a hundred amendments, and more than thirty-five parties were represented in Congress. Relatively few politicians remained loyal to their initial party commitments.

The heterodox 1986 Cruzado Plan, intended to implant price stability, had less success. After a rapid decline in prices, inappropriately sustained by intervention, the PMDB won a congressional majority. Price and wage controls had to be scrapped; they were no longer working. Soon after, Finance Minister Dilson Funaro was dismissed from office. Despite a sequence of substitutes (Bresser, Verão, and Collor) and a variety of plans, relief was temporary at best. The international community saw Brazil as being unable to honor its commitments to private creditors (interest payments and debt). Inflation accelerated to 80 percent a month by March 1990, prior to the inauguration of President Fernando Collor de Mello, a novice who had won the November elections with a promise to fight inflation.

The much-awaited Collor Plan had roots in the Erhard Plan of post-World War II West Germany. It was thought that a sharp reduction in the quantity of money in circulation would achieve quick success. Despite achieving a large primary surplus on the fiscal side, this shock treatment did not work due to Brazil's erratic monetary policy, fluctuating exchange rate, and labor market disequilibrium. No single anchor was in place to guarantee future price stability. Both heterodox and orthodox approaches[5] for stemming inflation need to persuade the public of the likely success of the endeavor. Otherwise, initial confidence in the undertaking rapidly fades, and inflation returns as governments have no alternative but to increase the quantity of money to finance their increasing nominal expenditures.

After Collor's impeachment was approved by the House of Representatives in October 1992, Vice President Itamar Franco assumed the presidency. He promised to restore economic growth to earlier high levels, but inflation persisted despite attempts to reduce it. A coherent economic policy could hardly be implemented when the average ministerial stay was less than two months. That all changed when Fernando Henrique Cardoso took office as finance minister in 1993. He brought together a group of economists who formulated a revised strategy to fight inflation, correcting some of the mistakes in the Cruzado Plan. The Real Plan foresaw a period of gradual adjustment lasting about a year. After its initial successes, that time was cut just a bit shorter, in part to provide greater support for Cardoso's run for the presidency.

Stabilization was programmed much differently under this plan. The ideas set forth by Andre Lara Resende and Persio Arida in 1984 were the starting point for this discussion,[6] but implementation involved many amendments and attention to details. Edmar Bacha was central to this process, with participation from Pedro Malan, Gustavo Franco, and others, many of whom came from the high-ranking private Catholic university, PUC-Rio. A speech by Cardoso in December 1993 laid out the full strategy intended well in advance.

The Real Plan began in the summer of 1993, not long after Cardoso's shift to the ministry of finance. The starting point was fiscal adjustment. A Program for Immediate Action was passed, thereby setting in motion a large fiscal operating surplus for 1994. This built on the advance in tax collection during Collor's abbreviated term and a special dimension of Brazilian reality—government expenditures were fixed in nominal form, but tax receipts varied because they were adjusted for price increases. The difference provided additional resources to the federal government. This centralization redefined relations with states and municipalities over past debt as well as permitting the Central Bank control over federal and state banks. A second part of this strategy was approval of the Social Emergency Fund in February 1994. This allowed 20 percent of federal budget resources to be held unspent, giving greater flexibility to actual expenditures. This amendment became a centerpiece of anti-inflationary policy that has continued to this day.

The second stage occurred in March 1994 with implementation of a virtual currency, the Real Value Unit (URV). Initially established to gradually convert contracts, wages, and prices to this new accounting unit, the URV was tied to the U.S. dollar. Converting contracts, wages, and prices was no simple matter, however. Existing contracts were easiest because all internal inflation was canceled by conversion to the dollar. Wages were more difficult because they were indexed over a four-month period, varying by sector. A solution was found in a technique designed by Simonsen in 1964 using the preceding average prevailing real wage. No further indexing was allowed, and a mechanism from the Cruzado Plan—subsequent elevation if real wages declined—was accepted by the unions. Fortunately, this turned out to be rare. Prices were allowed to vary, with the public sector initially fixed.

The third and final step was conversion to a new domestic currency—the *real*—on July 1, 1994. Expansion of the monetary base was deliberately limited by setting maximal quarterly limits for the next nine months. Finally, greater autonomy was granted to the Central Bank with institutional changes at the National Monetary Council. Unlike earlier efforts, these policies worked, and with inflation defeated, Cardoso won the presidential election over Lula, who argued against them in his campaign speeches.

In late 1993, permission was given for market adjustments in prices and wages rather than holding them fixed. Administered public sector prices were able to adjust as well. No automatic inflation trigger was built in, and indexing was abolished for assets of less than one year. A primary fiscal surplus and a restrictive monetary policy checked demand, and abundant international reserves, capital inflow, favorable terms of trade, and lower tariffs allowed higher income growth by permitting needed imports to exceed product expansion.

A genuine anchor was provided by a very stable, if not fully fixed, exchange rate. A monetary anchor (through targets) and an exchange rate were adopted within an asymmetric band; that is, the exchange rate was allowed to move down but had a fixed ceiling (1 real = 1 U.S. dollar). An initially hesitant audience gradually began to believe in the currency's stability. The success of the inflationary control had immediate repercussion, and Fernando Henrique Cardoso was elected president of Brazil on January 1, 1995.

Modern agriculture contributed to stabilization of prices. This was one of the five areas emphasized by Cardoso in his campaign. Creation of the Brazilian Agricultural Research Corporation (Embrapa), with its commitment to education and to active experimental research, led to gains in agricultural productivity. For the first time, continuing agricultural advances contributed to merchandise trade surpluses. Industry was not the only area meriting attention.

A large number of countries (among which Brazil stood out) had a high human development index and an "agro-industrial base" (see chapter 4). These countries were capable of taking advantage of the rising terms of trade that had prevailed since 1980. There was no need to industrialize at the expense of agriculture, as Brazil had previously done. Larger exports and diversification of products and markets could contribute positively. A basic error in the Prebisch-Singer line of thought was understating this possibility. Some of their assumptions were valid in the 1950s, but later evidence reversed these assumptions. The current problem revolves around restricting food and other agricultural imports because of their higher productivity and greater competitiveness. Suddenly freer trade has converted a positive growth in productivity into an international tariff war.

When a financial crisis threatened Brazil in early 1999, after the Asian and Russian downturns, forcing a large devaluation and recession, the government responded by assuring regular primary fiscal surpluses and raising federal revenues. Brazil received pledges of more external assistance from the IMF and other international agencies than had any other country. A failure in Brazil would have had significant regional consequences.

Social policy, the intended objective of the second term, had to yield. The Law of Fiscal Responsibility was passed in May 2000. It transformed the budgetary process, and an altered economic structure took shape. Fiscal discipline became a requirement and has remained an obligation, with mounting flexibility during recent years. Exchange rate variability was introduced. Inflation targeting became the practice of the Central Bank, replacing the previous policy based on an exchange rate anchor.

These accomplishments were appreciated more internationally than domestically. Cardoso's presidency ended with declining popularity and a rash of additional problems. A lack of rainfall in 2001 created an energy shortage; then came the U.S. downturn and the attack on the United States on September 11. In December, Argentine President Fernando de la Rúa resigned his office amid an economic collapse. Foreign inflows virtually ceased in 2002 as a clear break with recent advances threatened, and the IMF offered another agreement for greater assistance on the eve of the Brazilian election.

CONTINUITY FIRST, BUT CHANGES LATER

Luiz Inácio Lula da Silva, a labor leader and organizer of the Partido dos Trabalhadores—the Workers' Party (PT)—became president of Brazil on January 1, 2003. His inauguration brought great joy to the left, not only in Brazil but also in the rest of Latin America. Lula promised profound forthcoming change in his inaugural address, rejecting the free market policies of his predecessor and emphasizing a campaign to eliminate hunger and fight poverty.[7] The role of agriculture was central to this discourse, but in practice few measures were implemented to increase sector competitiveness.

Immediate economic challenges took priority. The exchange rate had been devalued as his victory became likely, and the Central Bank interest rate had risen to more than 25 percent, yielding much the highest real rate in the entire world. His choices of Henrique Meirelles as head of the Central Bank, who remained in that position until the end of 2010, and Antônio Palocci as minister of finance went a long way toward easing the anxiety of the international financial community. Together the two managed to restrain internal demand by enlarging the fiscal primary surplus and only slowly reducing interest rates. Recession in this first year could, and would, be blamed on the inadequate policies of the Cardoso administration.

The hopes of many fervent PT adherents that Lula would revoke this initial conservative stance, reverse prior privatization, and end globalization and foreign direct investment were dashed. Instead, to their chagrin, an early proposal by the government was for a constitutional amendment designed to limit the deficit accruing in state pensions, for the first time imposing constraints on employees in the public sector.

The economy responded with high average rates of growth in the years after recovery began to take hold in 2004. There was no miracle, but steady gains appeared not only in domestic performance but also in the export growth of commodities, favored by improving terms of trade. That led to a large positive commercial surplus, and briefly to a surplus on the current account. Brazil was able to pay off its accumulated debt to the IMF, and as exchange rates regularly strengthened, it began to attract direct foreign investment and financial inflows. Reserves increased, and interest rates moved down—too slowly as far as the industrial sector was concerned.

Upon reelection in the fall of 2006, Lula launched the *Programa de Aceleração do Crescimento* (PAC), a set of public and associated private investments designed to accelerate the rate of growth to 5 percent per year into the distant future. The largest components of the PAC, and its successor PAC II, consisted of infrastructure and Petrobrás. But this effort was slow to get fully under way and did not achieve its goals. With the commodity boom, Brazil experienced accelerated growth in 2007 and 2008, but investment managed to attain only 17 percent of GDP, too low to guarantee sustainable continuing expansion.

Subsequent to the failure of Lehman Brothers in the United States in September 2008, Brazil was caught up in the Great Recession then spreading rapidly to all parts of the world. Developing countries obtained no reprieve as the proponents of third world decoupling had hoped. Two negative quarters of performance rapidly cooled the excess expansion of domestic demand. BNDES was given increased resources to lend and reductions in taxes on consumer durables were put in place as policy offsets to declining demand.

Brazil recovered rapidly, and despite pessimistic predictions for the final year of Lula's mandate, in 2010 the growth rate was 7.5 percent, bringing back memories of the miracle years at the end of the 1960s. Interest rates, having fallen to around 5 percent, their lowest real levels in many years, again moved upward as the Central Bank sought to curb inflationary pressures. With continuing inflows of external money, the exchange rate appreciated and new taxes on entry of foreign capital were imposed. Terms of trade again turned favorable, with a major increase in petroleum prices augmenting domestic income.

Discovery of billions of barrels of oil off the coast—the pre-salt polygon—was the reason for this optimism. This volume of oil promised to place Brazil among principal world petroleum producers over the next decade, but substantial investment would be required for development. Legislation was passed elevating the role, and profit share, of Petrobrás vis-à-vis private companies. Henceforth, the latter could bid for drilling rights only through production sharing agreements rather than by operating independently. In September 2010, Petrobrás transferred sizable capital to the government in return for the proven *Tupi* field. This was the first stage of what many, especially political leaders on the left, saw as a bonanza of future riches available for expanded social programs.

The period from 2003 to 2010 saw an expansion of income at a rate of 4 percent. If 2003 is excluded, the rate increased to 4.4 percent, a much better result than that of the previous eight-year Cardoso government. Inflation came down, the real interest rate declined, poverty fell, and income distribution improved as a family allowance program (the *Bolsa Família*) incorporating more than 20 percent of the population was unfurled. The minimum wage grew artificially well beyond the rise in income and was dissociated from increases in productivity. Added to all of this were palpable improvements in education and health and greater provision of pensions for old age.

In fact, between 2004 and 2009, labor market inclusion was a principal source of income growth. The increase in formal employment, coupled with the rise in minimum wage, was the main basis for reducing poverty. On a smaller scale, social security transfers (mainly rural retirement) and social assistance programs also contributed. A similar argument has been made by Marcelo Neri, showing how the economic expansion after 2004 was decisive in this inclusion process. A new lower-middle class, encompassing about 35 million people, benefited as income distribution continued to improve.

Especially impressive was the response of Brazilian agriculture. Favored by upward movement of commodity prices and sustained by advances in productivity, export receipts increased dramatically. The contribution of agribusiness to positive trade balances was extraordinary. China rapidly expanded as a principal market for soybeans, iron ore, and other primary products. Many companies sought to move their plants from developed countries to China, where labor costs were much lower. Chinese exports rapidly grew, consisting primarily of manufactured goods.

This reduction in the price of industrial products and an increasing demand for agricultural commodities and minerals benefited the Brazilian economy. Bilateral trade between Brazil and China was insignificant in the late 1990s, but the Chinese market soon became the main destination for Brazilian exports. In return, a flow of industrial products surged, competing with domestic sectors ranging from textiles and shoes to consumer durables and even capital goods.

As a consequence, the historic conflict between industry and agriculture resumed. Fear of Brazilian deindustrialization began to mount. The exchange rate plays a strategic role in economic growth, but excess strength threatens balanced development. Concentrating exports in natural resource sectors whose prices are rising, such as mineral extraction, the steel industry, and agribusiness, can lead to an imbalance. This discussion is not new. More than thirty years ago Corden and Neary described the causal relationship between economic development concentrated on a specific sector and the decline in other sectors as the "Dutch disease."

The solution to this problem, in Brazil as well as elsewhere, seems simple: install an active policy to select intended industrial sectors for growth and limit demand for imported products and increase subsidies to promote the needed technological capacity. The BNDES could help finance much of the investment required. New legislation was approved, first in 2004 with the Program for Industry, Technology, and Foreign Trade, and when that proved inadequate due to the rise in exports of commodities, another version was later included in the PAC. Neither had much consequence. To be effective, more time and more use of market signals were needed rather than centralized direction.

The Lula government was widely lauded for economic achievements. Lula traveled abroad even more than his predecessor, and he was honored everywhere. Foreign policy became a central theme. Brazil reached out to Africa, the Middle East, and Asia. A quest for a permanent position on the United Nation Security Council moved upward on the agenda but did not succeed. Brazil asserted leadership of the developing countries in the still unfulfilled Doha Round, but with little effect.

Regular meetings with the other BRICS (Brazil, Russia, India, China, and South Africa) were established. Brazil became an active member of the G-20, an international group of the world's leading economies. At the same time, Brazil terminated ongoing negotiations for a Free Trade Area of the Americas, preferring instead to emphasize its association with other countries through regional trade cooperation, particularly with the Southern Common Market (Mercosul) in South America. Much was sought, but little accomplished. Under the leadership of Hugo Chavez, the Union of South American Nations (UNASUR) incorporated all of the countries of South America, but that was even less successful.

Close to the end of Lula's term, Brazil reached out to play a role as a mediator with Iran, in collaboration with Turkey. That quickly came to naught due to U.S. opposition. The Security Council ultimately rejected the apparent accord, with dissent only by Brazil and Turkey. But Brazil's stature as an international player was enhanced, at least for a time.

THE PARTIDO DOS TRABALHADORES FOREVER?

Dilma Rousseff won the subsequent election despite having no prior personal electoral experience. In the second round, she rather easily defeated José Serra, who was running again. Despite the publicized *mensalão* crisis of 2005, when members of Congress allied to the PT received regular payments in return for their support, Dilma managed to emerge with larger congressional gains than Lula. As before, the cabinet was large. Numerous allies were given appointments, but the PT retained control. From the start, Dilma limited and dominated her small number of close advisors.

Lula had exited with record personal approval in public polls, and Dilma entered with great popularity as well. Economic growth was quite high, income distribution had improved, and oil prices stood at record levels. There would be not only more of the same, but even better. Nonetheless, the consequences of Lula's presidency, as well as subsequent policies, proved inadequate.

The new administration inherited a complicated economic environment that became more complex due to the continuing response to the 2008 international crisis. All developed economies were forced to grow more slowly as their fiscal deficits increased. This was favorable to South-South trade expansion and was consistent with their commitment to accelerated growth.

Yet domestic investment in Brazil remained much too low to achieve 5 percent growth, let alone the 7.5 percent that was being bruited about. Brazil needed long-lived investment in infrastructure, energy generation and distribution, expansion of Petrobrás, expansion of affordable housing, and sanitation. Even larger expenditures were necessary, but committing to this would run counter to increased consumption, both private as well as public—the real source of acceleration after 2005.

The exchange rate was overvalued due to continuing high commodity prices, but export quantities were low, particularly for manufactured products. Cheap imports kept coming despite rising dissatisfaction from the domestic industrial sector. Higher levels of protection and subsidies were not a long-term solution. Foreign investment surged, particularly in automobiles. An effort to reduce the real rate of interest was seen as a possible way out.

Educational quality remained a major issue that would not be entirely resolved by spending more money, as most in the PT wanted. Brazil started far behind in comparison with both other Latin American countries and many countries in the developing world. Average public outlay per primary and secondary student was small, especially in the poorer regions. A federal social welfare program (Bolsa Familia) helped, but much inefficiency remained.

Universities expanded, and the cost per pupil of public universities was about the median of the OECD countries, basically free. With subsidies from the government, private higher education grew rapidly, but many schools were of questionable quality. Of Brazil's total public expenditure of about 5 percent of GDP, more than half went to higher learning.

Advances occurred within the public health system (SUS), but again the temptation was to provide a greater public contribution rather than better policy and state and local participation. Private insurance allowed the rich to avoid long lines and hasty medical treatment. Sophisticated modern techniques were available free for the wealthy in large urban centers, and these expenditures amounted to about half the annual 8 percent of GDP spent. Health services were extended through Bolsa Familia as well, with positive results, but coverage remained inadequate.

The pension system was heavily skewed toward the public sector. Federal, state, and municipal employees were only about a tenth of the beneficiaries, but they received about 40 percent of the outlay, an average difference 5 times larger than that for private companies. Earlier constitutional amendments in both the Cardoso and Lula governments temporarily lowered costs that would inevitably rise as the Brazilian population rapidly became older.

Taken together, cumulative social expenditures were above the OECD average, and the Dilma government had to find a way to control their magnitude while assuring greater fairness of access. Any serious political reform continued to lag. Constitutional change altering the multitude of candidacies for the Congress seemed unlikely ever to happen. Plans continued to surface to move toward a closed system but were never passed. A proportional voting system in which parties specified a list of candidates ordered by preference, together with geographic districts within states for half the members, should strengthen political parties and reduce their number. Instead, the number of parties and the size of ministerial cabinets expanded.

The legal system saw an increasing number of cases brought before it. Efforts to reduce this excess, by granting precedence to earlier Supreme Court decisions involving large majorities, moved forward with the creation of *sumula vinculante* in 2004. At the same time, Amendment 45 created a new structure, the National Judicial Council, with oversight responsibilities for the judicial system. Finally, and perhaps most important, the scope of the Federal Supreme Court and the Public Ministry were extended considerably by their abilities to deal with the *mensalão* case in 1995. That provided a basis for the even more intensive *Lava Jato* (Car Wash) experience, a corruption probe that continued from its origins in 2014.

In short, Dilma had a lot on her plate despite the favorable economic recovery in 2010. The basic priority was to further increase the power of the state and its commitment to those with lower incomes and minimal chances for advance. Dilma supported the *Minha Casa, Minha Vida* program from its beginning at the end of Lula's presidency, promising increased assistance for construction of low-priced housing in new suburbs. Dilma likewise endorsed completion of the many lagging PAC projects that had been under her control. She retained the formula for increasing minimum wages faster than income growth that had been put in place earlier.

But Dilma went further, establishing *Brasil sem Miséria* in early June, a new program to reduce the number of poor and extremely poor, expanding the number of people able to qualify for Bolsa Familia and increasing the amount of support provided. Increases were made in financial payments for the extremely poor as well, seeking to lift them out of misery.

In August a number of measures were implemented to renovate and expand industrial policy and return manufacturing to a leading role in economic development. Lower interest rates and subsidies were provided by BNDES. It is not surprising that many sectors eventually managed exemption from social security, thereby limiting the favored effect initially intended. Estimates of revived industrial activity were highly favorable, as were the number of infrastructure projects to be undertaken by a combination of public investment, private Brazilian investment, and foreign capital. Tariffs provided protection for these activities, which encouraged greater investment from abroad.

At the same time, a broader macroeconomic strategy was organized by Guido Mantega, who continued as finance minister. The *new economic matrix* policies included an array of measures designed to offer greater opportunity for central government intervention to counterbalance the slower growth of developing countries, and to limit the inflow of monetary commitments from abroad that impeded devaluation. Brazil's growth slowed in 2011, after achieving 7.5 percent the previous year.

The economic matrix had three central elements. One was a need to reduce real interest rates. Levels of 7 percent and higher placed Brazil close to the top of the international list. Second was a commitment to devaluation from a highly appreciated currency that penalized exports. At the end of 2010, the rate stood at less than two *reais* per dollar. Third was the need for a large increase in domestic investment to underwrite continuing economic expansion. Brazil's meager rate of 17 percent was inadequate, especially given the intended infrastructure renovation after years of neglect. This strategy was devised to compensate for a lack of aggregate demand. Dilma continuously insisted upon this view, even though many differed. Lula had always been prepared to compromise, but Dilma stood firm in her assessment throughout her period as president. That complicated her limited interaction with the Congress and even with the judiciary.

Getting interest rates down was relatively easy. A new Central Bank president, Alexandre Tombini, fully concurred. After all, rates had risen in the first few months of 2011 in response to earlier expansion. As a result, the SELIC rate fell continuously, from a peak of 12.5 percent in late August 2011 to 7.25 percent in the first months of 2013. Over more than a year, real rates were coming down, reaching 2 percent by the end of 2012. Dilma did more. Throughout 2012 she managed to bring lending rates down, using the Banco do Brasil and Caixa Econômica for that purpose.

Exchange rates were much more resistant. They declined by less than 20 percent during 2011, ending the year at 1.65, and declining again during the next year at a comparable rate. That was not enough to bolster exports of manufactured products, the more so because Brazil had become dependent on imports to restrain continuing rises in prices. Despite tariffs, the industrial sector failed to grow at high enough rates to make a difference.

Nor did private investment respond as imagined to these two shifts. Instead, domestic capital formation had only an initial advance—spilling over from 2010—and soon began a downward path. Quarterly investment rates in 2012 should have accelerated as interest rates declined. Instead, they fell continuously from the third quarter of 2011 on, moving to a negative value in the third quarter of 2012. Moreover, calculations of capital productivity showed a sharp fall.

Dilma descended from very high public approval after she launched her program in August 2011 to a level half as large by the end of June 2013. This was the consequence of two circumstances, one foreign and one domestic.

On the foreign side, a money market shock sent Brazilian interest rates up and devalued the real exchange rate. The U.S. Federal Reserve Bank announced a prospective tapering of acquisition of debt beginning in 2014. That meant the end of low-interest-rate policies, which resulted in large flows of resources abroad. For Brazil, Mantega and Dilma argued against the lack of concern for developing countries shown by the United States. Because of large previous inflows, much moving into reserves, Brazil was quite sensitive.

Domestically, matters were even worse. In June, domestic opposition to a policy of trivial change in bus fares in São Paulo rapidly spread to other cities. This set off a diverse set of reactions that have been commented on by many observers. We select three events that later had important consequences.

The role of the public prosecutor was enhanced, and legislation to limit its power was defeated. That came after the 2012 Supreme Court decision convicting many PT leaders of fraud in the earlier 2005 case of the mensalão. The public was already reacting badly to the large costs associated with the forthcoming World Cup in 2014 and the Olympics in 2016. That was prior to the Lava Jato scandal, which unraveled only after the election in 2014.

Second was Dilma's inability to manage the uprising well. She initially sought to use it to call for a new constitutional reform session focusing on politics, but that did not work. Little was attained in response to public demands for better health and education. Instead, her interaction with Congress deteriorated.

Third, in face of that difficulty, Dilma began to apply direct controls to hide the real extent of the fiscal deficit, postponing federal payments until the next fiscal year. In addition, she prevented public sector price increases from being passed along to restrain exchange rate weakness. Internal and external deficits increased as she faced the burden of reelection. Demand rises and reduced unemployment were used instead of dealing with the real supply bottlenecks to productivity advance.

Despite these problems, in October 2014, Dilma managed to win in the second round by 4 percentage points, down from her 2010 margin of 12 points. Figure 2.2 shows the results by state and reflects the two Brazils. Aécio Neves's loss in Minas Gerais, his home state, assured his defeat and Dilma's victory. Had Neves won there by a million votes, the two would have been virtually tied nationally.

With this bare victory, Dilma acknowledged the need for a policy change and appointed Joaquim Levy finance minister. He had a difficult stay, lasting less than a year, in a vain effort to rapidly turn Brazil around. Levy's PhD was from Chicago, and even more relevant, he had served as secretary of finance in the first Lula term, collecting greater taxes, and he also served as secretary of finance in the state of Rio de Janeiro. His appointment brought optimism to the business community.

His initial action was to reduce Mantega's forecast of 2 percent growth to 0.8 percent. That was only the beginning of a constant downward move in projections until they reached negative territory. At the same time, inflation was higher because public sector prices had to rise. Devaluation began, heightening as revisions were required. Levy did cut federal expenditures, but there was little chance of making them more malleable. Congress tired of his constant pressure to move expenditures and receipts back into balance, and the refusal of Congress to reinstate the CPMF (tax on financial transactions) for four years was the final blow.

Dilma wanted an immediate solution to the mounting recession, but that was not to be. Matters were worse than she believed. She initially allowed Vice President Michel Temer, a congressional leader from the PMDB, to try to help pass the measures needed to initiate the process of recovery. After a few months, he gave up and eventually encouraged the PMDB to prepare an alternative schedule of required measures for such a course to begin.

Lava Jato quickly came to the fore as well, with cases rapidly multiplying. Sergio Moro, a judge from the state of Paraná, led the way. Ministers, governors, mayors, and legislators were all involved. Petrobrás, legislators, Odebrecht, and other firms and individuals were soon caught up. Many ultimately decided in favor of confession rather than a prolonged prison term. These individuals, of course, provided evidence corroborating the misdeeds of others. Attorney General Rodrigo Janot led the way, with many subordinates at the state and municipal level offering assistance.

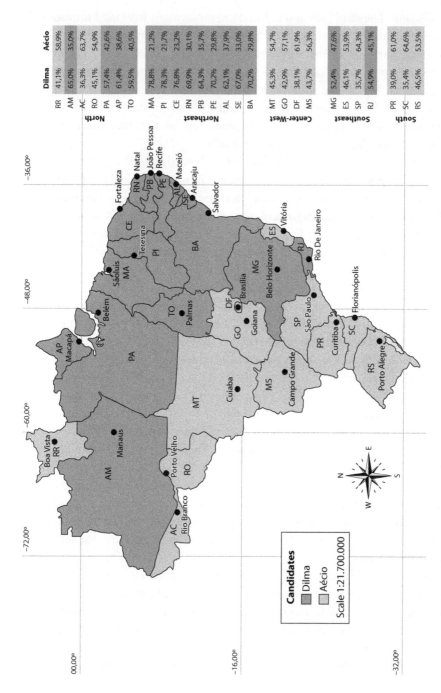

		Dilma	Aécio
North	RR	41,1%	58,9%
	AM	65,0%	35,0%
	AC	36,3%	63,7%
	RO	45,1%	54,9%
	PA	57,4%	42,6%
	AP	61,4%	38,6%
	TO	59,5%	40,5%
Northeast	MA	78,8%	21,2%
	PI	78,3%	21,7%
	CE	76,8%	23,2%
	RN	69,9%	30,1%
	PB	64,3%	35,7%
	PE	70,2%	29,8%
	AL	62,1%	37,9%
	SE	67,0%	33,0%
	BA	70,2%	29,8%
Center-West	MT	45,3%	54,7%
	GO	42,9%	57,1%
	DF	38,1%	61,9%
	MS	43,7%	56,3%
Southeast	MG	52,4%	47,6%
	ES	46,1%	53,9%
	SP	35,7%	64,3%
	RJ	54,9%	45,1%
South	PR	39,0%	61,0%
	SC	35,4%	64,6%
	RS	46,5%	53,5%

Figure 2.2   Distribution of votes between Dilma and Aécio in the second round of the 2014 elections.

Source: TSE (2014).

By March 2015, about a million people were marching on the streets asking for Dilma's impeachment, but this time, unlike two years earlier, there was no violence.

Eduardo Cunha, Speaker of the House, had sought the support of Dilma, in part to assure his continuity as a legislator immune from conviction. He finally decided to take up the question of her impeachment in December. A two-thirds vote in the House sent the matter to the Senate in April 2016, with Temer now serving in an acting role. A final vote occurred there in August 2016, with much more than the needed two-thirds of senators concurring. There was dissent, led by the PT, but it was insufficient to count. Ironically, Cunha was similarly impeached by his colleagues for substantial illegal bribery receipts, and he remains in prison as a result of Lava Jato.

As with Collor in 1993, no economic growth translated into no continuity of office. That was not only the case for Dilma. In the municipal elections held in 2016, the PT lost a number of seats, both by voter negative reaction and the rapidity with which mayors simply changed political affiliation.

THE TEMER INTERLUDE

Michael Temer's acquisition of the presidency was made permanent after the final Senate vote. But even before that, during the interim months, he had begun restructuring the cabinet. From the beginning, there was a dichotomy between the economic and political branches of government taking office. On the economic side, Henrique de Campos Meirelles and Central Bank president Ilan Goldfyn were given substantial authority to appoint professional aides. On the political side, Temer surrounded himself with old colleagues from his long service in Congress. They were all male, elderly, with many suspected of participation in the Lava Jato or associated fraudulent activity.

Some reforms occurred subsequently, but this pattern of separate centers of control persisted. Temer acquired limited support even from those who were against Dilma. Indeed, Temer himself was suspected of illegal activities. While awaiting a congressional decision on claimed illegal activity as vice president, in May 2017 an unexpected taped conversation between him and the leader of the large meat producer JBS came to light. That discussion made his agenda of a rapid congressional move to the right untenable. Pension, political, and tax reform, as well as state and local finance, were discussed but did not come to a vote. Nevertheless, some important changes were accomplished by provisional measures sent to Congress to be approved: decrees, legislation, and even constitutional amendments.

Changes in the laws governing labor unions had one principal objective—reduce their power. Unions could no longer collect dues from all workers, even those who were not members. Individuals with higher incomes could claim exemption from social security taxes by working as contractors rather than employees. Government, avoiding the extensive labor courts, wound up with a reduced role as direct negotiation between employees and entrepreneurs was encouraged. Other measures sought to encourage expansion of joint private-foreign-government infrastructure projects. With the sale of Eletrobas facilities, a division of Embraer, with Boeing taking over production of larger jets, federal coverage of state and local debt were no longer manageable.

Central to government concern, and coming first, was the large continuing fiscal deficit assured by the recession in 2015–16 and the slight recovery in 2017. Failure to generate a primary surplus meant an increase in public debt. Moreover, increased foreign capital was needed for domestic investment. A return to a positive primary surplus would require at least five more years of low interest rates and moderate growth.

Limiting future increases in central government expenditures to no more than that spent in the past year plus inflation was seen as a way to deal with this problem. This constitutional amendment occurred in December 2016. Intended to prevent real growth of outlays and thereby reduce them as a percentage of GDP, this was a novel measure. Given the frequent failure of past attempts to recover quickly, a twenty-year program was passed and was to take effect in 2018.

This effort presumes an ability to curb congressional desires by legal means. But there is no way to legislate prudent and cooperative behavior for so long. Much, inevitably, will depend on what the future holds. There is no way to assure intelligent fiscal policy by imposing narrowly defined limits in either developed or developing countries. What we must count on is negative public reaction to poor policy. Even the IMF has recognized that; its recommended policies now markedly differ from earlier fixed rules.

Democratic principles function better than centralized control in achieving results. Quasi-dictatorial realms prevent disclosure of full information. Deception can work for a time, but rarely forever. Latin America proved that proposition during the period of militarization in the 1960s through the 1980s. Leaders thought that higher growth could reconstruct political life. Ultimately, the military was cast out permanently, except in Venezuela. Decisions that would end inflation and increase growth were needed.

There are consequences, moreover, for a range of social activities when regular criticism of inadequate public provision of education, health, sanitation, housing, and so forth becomes extreme. These areas require constant real expenditure. Given the existing structure of budgetary outlays, where the poorest do not benefit as much as the rich and the young suffer from growing pensions paid to the elderly, income inequality cannot be addressed. Temer exempted education outlays from the new restrictions, and the judiciary went beyond their initial prescribed levels. Imagining that a constitutional amendment can adequately confront this situation is magical realism transferred to the realm of economic policy. What is necessary is coherent application of the Fiscal Responsibility Law (LRF) and little reliance on debts from previous budgets (*restos a pagar*).

That leaves the problem of a continually deteriorating balance of social security receipts and expenditures. As the population ages, the ratio of workers to retirees declines. This is the reason for close association of new fiscal rules with reform of the existing social security system. Without changing the age of retirement and varying privileges for a select few—including public officials and others—that negative forecast, too, will widen. This conclusion is also a needed addendum to stop further expansion of taxes and demand pressures.

We end here with two tables. The first conveys expectations of Brazilian growth through 2021 and appears just prior to the first round of the presidential election. The second focuses on longer-term fiscal sustainability under alternative interest rate and growth assumptions. Together these tables provide the basis for concern about the future.

Growth in Brazil is far from assured. Table 2.3 shows the revision downward from the 3 percent many had expected at the beginning of the year. This translated into a 2018 expectation in the neighborhood of 1.4 percent. This restrains the ability to find resources for needed public investment because required expenditures will absorb more than 90 percent of expenditures in 2019. Restricting the fiscal deficit becomes more onerous, just at a time when a new government takes over.

Table 2.3   Brazil Long-Term Scenario

	2015	2016	2017	2018	2019	2020	2021
Real GDP growth %	–3.5	–3.5	1	1.4	2.5	2.5	2.5
Private consumption %	–3.2	–4.3	1	2.2	3.2	2.8	2.7
Government consumption %	–1.4	–0.1	–0.6	–0.2	–0.5	1.5	2
Gross capital formation %	–13.9	–10.3	–1.8	3.4	6.1	5.8	5.5
Exports %	6.8	1.9	5.2	3.2	0.8	3	2.8
Imports %	–14.2	–10.2	5	6.5	4.2	6	5.5
Unemployment rate %	8.5	11.5	12.7	12	10.8	10.3	10
Inflation—IPCA % (eop)	10.7	6.3	2.9	4	4.2	4	3.8
Selic % (eop)	14.3	13.8	7	6.5	8.5	8.5	8.3
Real interest rate % (eop)							
Exchange rate (eop) R$/$	3.91	3.26	3.31	3.77	3.61	3.5	3.52
Public sector—primary (% GDP)	–1.9	–2.5	1.7	–2.2	–1.7	–1.1	–0.6
Public sector—total (% GDP)	–10.2	–9	–7.8	–7.4	–7	–6.6	–6.2
Gross public sector debt (% GDP)	65.5	70	74	76.1	78.4	80	81.4
Current account (% GDP)	–3.4	–1.3	–0.5	–1.2	–2.2	–2.3	–2.5
Foreign direct investment ($ bn)	74.7	78.9	70.7	67.1	80	80	80
International reserves ($ bn)	368.7	372.2	375.3	381.4	381.4	381.4	381.4

Source: Citibank research estimates, September 26, 2018.

Into the future, matters improved very little. Almost all estimates, whether from Brazilian sources or foreign, settle at 2.5 percent. That is inadequate for both macroeconomic policy and microeconomic reforms. Unemployment is calculated to remain high, and real interest rates rise. But that presumes a slight rise in U.S. rates. Given the expanding deficit, U.S. rates may go up more and international rates also may rise, then income inequality will return to the fore.

The public sector primary result continues to be negative, causing external debt to rise at the same time as domestic consumption growth rises faster than product. Government consumption outlays also go up. This is realistic and may be understated for a new administration. Where is the needed domestic savings for continuing gains in investment to come from?

Foreign direct investment increases a bit, and the current account deficit rises only slightly. Although domestic investment rises a little faster than GDP, the gain is certainly not enough to propel the economy forward.

Table 2.4 focuses on the primary surplus required to stabilize the public debt to GDP ratio at its 2016 level of .70. It ignores the effects of exchange rate changes and simplifies the mathematics. Orders of magnitude are what count.

Table 2.4   **Predicting the Personal Surplus to Stabilize Debt**

		Real Growth Rate		
		1%	2%	4%
Real Interest Rate	3%	1.40%	0.70%	−0.70%
	5%	2.80%	2.10%	0.70%
	7%	4.20%	3.50%	2.10%
Debt/GDP=70%				

The formula used is the following:

$$PS = D_{t=1}/Y_{t-1} (r - g)$$

where PS is the primary surplus, *D/Y* the past specific public debt/GDP ratio, *r* the real interest rate, and *g* the real growth rate.

The table is easy to understand. As the differential between the real rate of growth and the real interest rate goes up, so does the required surplus. Once one is at the point of stability in the debt ratios, a positive primary surplus permits a subsequent decline in the ratio.

Standard and Poor's, and the other rating agencies, want to see tangible progress before upping the punitive rating Brazil now possesses. Brazil is well above the 0.5 ratio that is generally a maximum for a rating allowing many foreign facilities to purchase securities to hold as part of their assets.

There is thus less hope for a low-cost external way out. Instead, the problem is now a domestic one.

FINAL WORDS

Two sharply different perceptions of Brazil's economic future remain. The election of 2018 indicates how Brazil intends to manage the range of current problems just described—and whether affairs will be better or even worse. Two extremes, one on the left and one on right, are dominant.

The PT will not return as it was. Fernando Haddad, emanating from the left, where he served as education minister and mayor of São Paulo, ran because Lula could not. He advocated traditional party positions: partial, if not complete, return to protectionism, ISI, and greater public sector expenditure. Expansion of manufacturing is a central objective. Modernization involves explicit choice of the principal sectors to lead the way. A large and even expanding state remains fundamental. After the Lula incarceration, many in the PT wanted to go further: reduction of the powers of the judiciary and the legislature, expansion of the executive, and, of course, Lula's immediate pardon.

The PT succeeded in electing many congressional deputies as well as governors and senators. But its regional concentration is altered to the northeast. The party will take a major role in opposition. A principal question remains: will Ciro Gomes or Haddad become the future leader on the left?

Jair Bolsonaro had only a small party, the PSL, supporting him. This is his ninth party during his very long congressional career. Jumping from one to another has been his style, just as in the military he spent time in the parachute corps. But he was always a back bencher until his recent magical ascent. His base is rooted in conservative groups: the military, the wealthy, those who are racist, homophobic, as well as those opposed to urban violence and corruption. On the positive side, he favors lower taxes and less government intervention, privatization, and a free market.

Faced with the challenge from the left, Brazil chose the rightward path, by a 10 percent margin. But the party also elected a large, diverse political base. Also, many politicians have decided to shift allegiance and join the PSL.

The political center and Geraldo Alckmin, in particular, despite his dominant margin in television time, failed to arouse much popular support. He and his PSDB party were seen to be associated with the corrupt and violent past instead of committed to needed future changes. Election results reduced the position of virtually all the previous political parties.

Brazil has little time to revamp the economy positively. Future opportunities to achieve the needed changes will be progressively more difficult. One must assure direct investment from abroad to undertake these efforts, a task complicated by Brazil's loss of investment grade status in ratings by the international agencies. Brazil must commit to large-scale investment in infrastructure to participate in continuing globalization. That means more and freer trade.

Brazil must also go beyond the automobile as the dominant sector and utilize investment in science and technology to assure productivity advances. Returns to investment, social and private, can be gauged and should be used. A very good place to start is the education sector. Gaps between private and public schools remain large. They are likewise geographic. Without reducing educational disparities by region and sector, income distribution will remain a serious problem.

Everywhere services have emerged as a source of productive gain. Brazil has been able to do very well in finance, but in few other areas. As a large economy, other activities where application of local intelligence can make a difference are needed, particularly in urban areas. This policy is neither free enterprise nor governmentally driven, but is a search for efficient intervention. The great strength of Brazil is its diversity: agriculture, off-shore petroleum and rich ore deposits, and vibrant examples within the service and industrial sectors.

A report produced at the end of the Lula administration conveys an optimistic PT vision of the future. That document specifies a continuing 7 percent rate of growth of GDP, along with impressive social gains and greater income equality. Those hundreds of objectives—although some are mutually inconsistent—were accumulated from ministers, ex-ministers, entrepreneurs, and society as a whole. In April 2013 at an event announcing expanded public works, Dilma Rousseff indicated that doubling income per capita by 2022 was the goal, pushing up the growth a bit. Such growth would be a miracle of Chinese proportions. That is impossible. Current Brazilian circumstances are far different: the investment rate, even if it returns to higher values, is less than half as large; the labor force already is urbanized; government outlays are badly directed; and engagement in international trade is minimal.

A different view is expressed in table 2.3 as well as in a BNDES report looking at perspectives from 2018 to 2023. That is too positive: 2018 appears with growth of 2.5 percent, however, actual expansion is likely to be only half of that. Major results in table 2.3 therefore begin with 2019. Cumulative advance in actual GDP from 2019 comes to only 13 percent. This is far more realistic. Brazil will be lucky to arrive in 2022 with a national income equal to its 2013 level.

For higher growth to occur, productivity gains will have to be generalized rather than limited to particular sectors. Industrial policy soon becomes generalized throughout the economy, meaning increased subsidies for everyone but no relative advantage for anyone. Integration of the agricultural, mineral, petroleum, manufacturing, and service sectors into a globalized economy is of the essence. Their competitiveness stems from efficiency, which is the central point of our discussion. Few countries benefit from such a diversified base. Perhaps God after all is Brazilian, but even then, he/she must be depressed by the failure to attain an economy capable of adequate expansion despite such possibilities.

Above all, this process of development depends on political persuasion. That problem is severe given the outcome of recent elections. Instead of cooperation, there is open dissent. Instead of regional diversity, there is concentration. The only solution is compromise and inclusion.

Brazilian citizens, including those who recently moved into the lower-middle class, must learn the virtue of postponing immediate gratification for the greater good. This is a different message than has been emphasized in the past. The ability to move forward to a higher and sustainable level of annual growth depends on lowering the ratio of consumption to income. But, as we have just seen, few ever take up that issue. Distributing that cost intelligently is the only path toward economic and political success.

Populism, whether of the right or the left, is perilous. Its promises are not viable, and sooner or later populism produces economic instability and political conflict.

CHAPTER 3

The Role of Agricultural Innovation

FROM THE TRADITIONAL APPROACH TOWARD A THEORY OF
TECHNICAL AND INSTITUTIONAL CHANGE

In recent years, academics and policymakers have increasingly focused on the relationship among science, technological improvements, and productivity changes based on learning processes. This interaction has been especially important in studies on industry. However, few studies exist that engage both theoretically and quantitatively with agriculture.

Over the past few decades, land has become an increasingly scarce resource, limiting agricultural output. Climate change has demanded more efficient water usage, and labor has decreased in rural areas due to an increase in urbanization and growth in the service sector. Incorporating technology into modern agriculture has become essential to achieve productivity gains and sustainable progress.

This chapter discusses technical change in agriculture, comparing the mainstream view—the idea of an agricultural treadmill—with an alternative approach to agricultural growth.[1] We discuss the diffusion of agricultural technology, productive dualism, and an induced innovation model. Then we discuss the importance of innovation and the application of external knowledge to improve agricultural growth.

Agriculture, in particular, faces limitations due to a lack of emphasis on the adoption and diffusion of technology as an endogenous component of institutional change, and on learning effects by agents in the innovation process. We attempt to dissect the case of post-1970s Brazilian agriculture and then compare it with successful examples in Brazilian industry.

THE AGRICULTURAL TREADMILL

Many economists have described the agricultural sector as an example of pure, and perfect, competition. Some hypotheses are implicit in this

description. First, there are a large number of consumers and producers in a market with a downward sloping demand curve and an upward
sloping supply curve. Second, there are no barriers to free entry and exit,
allowing for perfect mobility of labor and capital. Third, each producer
is a price taker; that is, the market determines prices. Finally, the product
is homogeneous and is not differentiated; agricultural output is a simple
commodity.

For the case of pure competition, all these suppositions are true.
Therefore, the price becomes equal to minimum average cost, with zero
profit: or marginal revenue equals marginal cost. Relaxing the second
hypothesis yields a model of perfect competition. When capital is not
instantaneously mobile, price is equal to marginal cost but different from
average cost. In this situation, profit will be positive.

Pure, or perfect, competition embodies very restrictive assumptions.
On this basis, Cochrane[2] developed a model of technological change in
agriculture that functions like a *treadmill*—farmers adopt new technology while staying in the same economic situation. Innovation results in a
reduction of cost and a shift in the production frontier. Likewise, with the
same number of inputs it is possible to produce a larger output, moving
the supply function to the right. This process is illustrated in figure 3.1,
which shows the production function on the left side and market supply
and demand curves on the right side.

New and more efficient technology shifts the production function
from f_1 to f_2 (that is, for a fixed quantity of inputs x, production increases

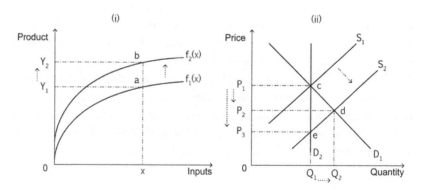

**Figure 3.1   Product market effects of new technology and a comparison with a
different range of sloping of the demand curve.** K = capital; L = labor.

from a to b). This movement affects the supply and demand equilibrium (equilibrium point c moves to d; in the extreme case of inelastic demand, equilibrium moves from c to e). Total economic welfare increases as a consequence of technological progress. Its allocation between producers and consumers depends on supply and demand price elasticities. Supply is represented by an upward sloping curve (S curve), whereas the demand can be considered with two different elasticities: a negative-sloping curve (D_1), and a vertical one (D_2). If producers can increase profit by larger sales (from Q_1 to Q_2) and thereby compensate for the decline of revenue by a fall in price from P_1 to P_2, their welfare will increase. Consumers will likewise benefit from lower prices.

When demand elasticity is zero (D_2), a large decline of price from P_1 to P_3 cannot be compensated by any increase in sales. Therefore, a sharp fall in total revenue results in a net loss to producers. In this extreme case, the entire welfare increase is transferred to consumers, who pay a lower price for the same quantity. Technological change does not benefit the adopters; the only beneficiaries are consumers.

Agricultural commodity production that absorbs less technological content is usually not tradable (that is, it is absorbed in the internal market). Modern production is directed to a global market paying a higher price. Both outcomes are characterized by low elasticity of demand, primarily in high-income economies. Agro-exporting countries, like Brazil and the United States, also face trade restrictions when commercializing their products of greater technological content. These are countries where agricultural and manufacturing sectors coexist, with agriculture playing an important role. The demand for agricultural commodities is inelastic, and the new technology in agriculture leads to a progressive transfer of the labor force to the nonagricultural sector.

Capacity to innovate is greater in the principal agro-exporting countries because technological progress is dependent on adaptive and local research. When the introduction of new technologies increases the quantity supplied and lowers product prices, producers seek innovation to reduce production costs. Those who move first and adopt early gain profits. As innovation diffuses more widely, the supply curve shifts to the right, price falls and surplus profit disappears. Laggards either incorporate the new technology or decide to leave the market.

To summarize this analysis, farmers unable to keep up with the technology treadmill tend to leave the market, moving into urban areas and into the nonagricultural sector. In turn, urban industry and services benefit from subsequent lower wage costs. In a subsistence economy, the treadmill effect transfers welfare to producers by augmenting the quantity consumed on each family farm. To develop agriculture as a business, investments in new knowledge are crucial to increase production. Mainstream economic analysis assumes that technical change is largely an exogenous process.

DIFFUSION OF TECHNICAL CHANGE IN AGRICULTURE

Zvi Griliches first presented a study of empirical regularities related to the diffusion process in agriculture, which is typically represented by a logistic function (or S-shaped curve).[3] His study, based on a simple epidemiological model of dissemination, focused on the systemic problems affecting the differential adoption of new technology in two U.S. states: Iowa, the most prosperous and innovative region in corn production, and Alabama, which was the slowest to adopt hybrid corn.

This model is as follows:[4] suppose that there are potentially N users of new technology. At time t, each of the existing adopters, $y(t)$, who have experience in using it, affects the decision of nonadopters $[N - y(t)]$. The hypothesis underlying the logistic model is that the growth in the number of adopters of a specific technology happens through the random transfer of information between nonadopters and adopters—for example, by word of mouth. Therefore, the growth $\Delta y(t)$ of users over time Δt is specified by:

$$\Delta y(t) = P\left[N - y(t)\right].\qquad(3.1)$$

P is a diffusion probability, varying with time t, for transfer between adopters and nonadopters. The average rate of transfer remains constant over time, and when it is divided by the size of the population of potential adopters, it assumes a value stated as θ. Besides being proportional to Δt and θ—which fixes the maximum percentage of diffusion in the logistic model—the diffusion probability also depends on the relative size of the adopters' population changing over time. This probability can be defined as follows:

$$P = \theta\left[\frac{y(t)}{N}\right]\Delta t.\qquad(3.2)$$

Adaptation is related to the share of adopters in the population, which varies over time, $[y(t)/N]$. For the discrete case, the diffusion of new technology is variable because it depends on the percentage of acceptance in each period. At time t in a discrete interval Δt, substituting (3.2) into (3.1), the growth among the adopters is given by equation (3.3):

$$\Delta y(t) = \theta \left[\frac{y(t)}{N} \right] [N - y(t)] \Delta t. \tag{3.3}$$

At the limit $\Delta t \to 0$, dissemination of information about the new technique is given by the probability of spread, $\beta[y(t)/N]$, relative to the size of nonadopters $[N - y(t)]$. That approximates the shape of the logistic curve.[5] It describes a first order differential equation, permitting solution for the function $y(t)$. Thus, assuming $y(0)$ equals a positive value in the open interval $(0, N)$, we have the following differential equation:

$$y'(t) = \beta \left[\frac{y(t)}{N} \right] [N - y(t)]. \tag{3.4}$$

From the equation above, it follows that:

$$y'(t) \frac{1}{y(t)[N - y(t)]} = \frac{\beta}{N},$$

by integrating both sides, the primitive integral of equation (3.4) is:

$$y(t) = N \left[1 + e^{-(\beta t + k_5)} \right]^{-1}. \tag{3.5}$$

Equation (3.5) yields a logistic function defined in the open interval $(0, N)$ and $y'(t) > 0$, where $y(t)$ does not start from zero and does not reach N. This function depends on three parameters: (i) the date of first commercial use of the technology described by the constant of integration k_5, which plots the "S curve" over time; (ii) the potential ceiling of the innovative market, specified by the size of population N; and (iii) the speed of diffusion expressed by β. When $(\beta t + k_5) \to \infty$, $y(t) \to N$. When $(\beta t + k_5) = 0$, $y(t) = \frac{N}{2}$. When $(\beta t + k_5) \to -\infty$, $y(t) \to 0$.

The relationship between the logistic function and the symmetrical bell-shaped curve is described in figure 3.2.

This logistic model presents the dynamics of embedded and not embedded knowledge. The model describes the diffusion of new information over time. The efficient use of technology by an agent influences the nonadopter's decision, leading to an ascending pattern in the beginning and a descending trajectory at the end. When knowledge is new, there is

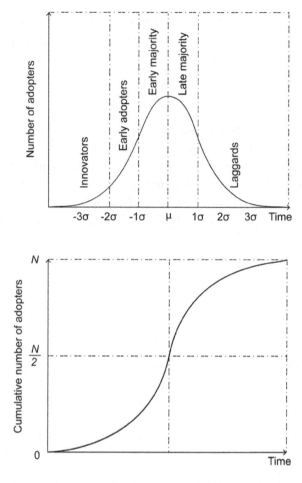

Figure 3.2 The epidemic model—the process of diffusion of technical change viewed as analogous to the spread of infectious disease.

rapid diffusion. Later on, the laggards are less likely to innovate than early adopters. Therefore, the diffusion process follows an S-shaped curve.

Logistic growth is defined by equation (3.5) where $y(t)$ is the percentage of adopters, N is the potential ceiling of adoption, or equilibrium state, and k_5 is a constant of integration that plots the curve on the time scale. This curve has some interesting properties. It is asymptotic to 0 and N and is symmetrical about the inflection point. The first derivative with respect to time is given by equation (3.4), where the growth rate is proportional to adoption attained and to the distance to reach the potential ceiling. Diffusion of technology can occur more quickly and ultimately depends on the rate of diffusion of the new knowledge.

This model provides a major contribution to the diffusion of new technology. Additional studies clarified some points. The potential ceiling of adopters can change over time because this parameter is not constant and can be endogenous to the logistic function. The diffusion process emphasizes the role of time and the transition from one productive technology to another. Time serves as a proxy for at least three distinct sets of variables: (i) cost reduction over time, as a result of the learning process and cumulative knowledge; (ii) the depreciation rate of capital; and (iii) the dissemination of knowledge.

But the diffusion process is more complex and is not always subject to a stable equilibrium. As a result, the evolutionary approach can offer a better explanation of how the potential ceiling changes over time. The diffusion of new technology can be better understood in conditions of uncertainty, limited rationality, and disequilibrium, which was extensively studied by Nelson and Winter.[6]

MODERNIZATION AND ECONOMIC DUALISM

In most treatments of economic development, agriculture is seen as a lagging sector, dependent on technological inputs produced by other sectors. Compared to industrial sectors, agricultural production is passive in terms of generation and diffusion of new knowledge. One model of economic development with institutional response is W. A. Lewis's "unlimited supply of labor." In essence, its functioning depends on the capitalist's ability to regulate wages in the "subsistence" sector of the economy. The surplus in the capitalist sector goes to company profits, but most workers (in unlimited supply) remain outside industry in low-dynamism activities.

Lewis presented a two-sector model with modern and traditional sectors coexisting in the same economic space.[7] He understood development as stages of growth with the economy moving from primary production to manufacturing. A final stage would be a service-based economy. Therefore, duality was presented between sectors. The work of Ruy Miller Paiva provided an innovative contrast, evaluating the internal diversity of the agricultural sector as intrasector duality.[8]

Paiva discussed agricultural modernization in the context of two types of agriculture: modern and traditional. In developing countries, some farmers employ modern techniques recommended by international research centers, but others have little knowledge of or use for new technology.

A single region can feature three product classes. The first requires modern techniques, without traditional farmers. The second class consists of products involving traditional techniques. The third and largest category is one in which modern and traditional farmers coexist. The process of agricultural modernization focuses on two factors: the adoption of technology and its process of diffusion. Adoption is dependent on the decision-making of producers at a microeconomic level. Diffusion is a broader process that considers the aggregate results of adoption; therefore, it presumes a macroeconomic point of view.

To investigate the *adoption process*, the modern technique is assumed to be more effective than the traditional one. Modern inputs (machinery, fertilizers, pesticides, and improvements, etc.) are represented by a single variable (X^m), and traditional inputs (land and labor) are expressed by (X^t). Furthermore, Q^m is the quantity produced with modern technology, Q^t is the quantity obtained with traditional techniques, P_q is the price of the product, P_x^m is the price of modern inputs, and P_x^t is the price of traditional inputs. The farmer chooses the modern technology when the net income between modern and traditional production satisfies equation (3.6):

$$\left(P_q.Q^m\right) - \left(\sum_{i=1}^{n} P_{xi}^m.X_i^m + \sum_{j=1}^{l} P_{xj}^t.X_j^t\right) > \left(P_q.Q^t\right) - \left(\sum_{i=1}^{n'} P_{xi}^m.X_i^m + \sum_{j=1}^{l'} P_{xj}^t.X_j^t\right), \quad (3.6)$$

with $n > n'$ and $l > l'$, in a proportion to be determined.

In this sense, the economic advantage of modern technology over traditional techniques depends on three relationships. First is the productivity of inputs, $\left(\dfrac{Q^m}{X^m}\right) \bigg/ \left(\dfrac{Q^t}{X^t}\right)$. When this relation increases (or decreases), the productivity of a modern technology is favorable (or unfavorable). Second, relative prices of modern and traditional inputs, (P_x^m/P_x^t), are relevant. An increase in land and labor prices favors the use of modern technology. Finally, the product price is related to input prices in modern and traditional production (P_q/P_x^m and P_q/P_x^t). An increase of product price compared to input price favors more intensive resource use.

The advantage of modern compared to traditional technology will then depend on productivity; the relative prices of modern and traditional inputs; and the price of the product with respect to input prices. Changes in these values may create a favorable environment for agricultural modernization. There are also transaction costs in adopting new technology. If these can be reduced, modernization will proceed faster. Taking these transaction costs into account, the economics of utilizing a modern technique is given by:

$$RT^m - CV^m > RT^t - CV^t + CT, \qquad (3.7)$$

where RT is total revenue; CV is variable costs; and CT is transaction (or opportunity) cost.

The transaction cost varies from one farmer to another, depending on background, education, local features, and the innovative environment. Figure 3.3 shows the cost of transfer. The slope of the curve is a function of access to investment, level of education, and entrepreneurship, among other characteristics. The greater the economic advantage of modern technology over traditional techniques, the greater the percentage of farmers opting to modernize. A shifting curve to the right reflects a rise in the likelihood of innovation.

The speed of the *diffusion process* depends on the gains from using new technologies as well as other factors determining development in the nonagricultural sector. Technological diffusion alters the prices of both product and traditional inputs, which affect the spread of modernization. This phenomenon can be summarized in three main steps. First,

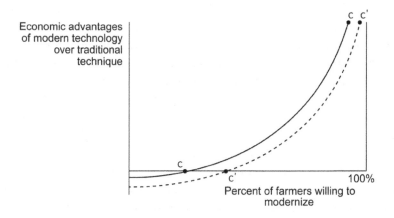

Figure 3.3   Transaction cost to switch from traditional to modern techniques.

Source: Ruy Miller Paiva, "Modernização e Dualismo Tecnológico na Agricultura," *Pesquisa e Planejamento Econômico* 1, no. 2 (1971), 190.

the diffusion of modern technology increases productivity and, *ceteris paribus*, reduces product prices. Intensification of technology reduces the price of traditional inputs (land and labor). Second, lower product price reduces the relative price of inputs (P_q/P_x^m). This reduces the gains from modern technology. Finally, after a drop in traditional input prices, the relative gain from modern technology becomes less advantageous.

This discourages agricultural modernization. More modern techniques that reduce the cost per unit of input may compensate for reductions in the price of product. If this occurs, the use of technology continues in an ascending trajectory. This process of modernization has a *self-control mechanism* because some negative elements are present, as noted previously. The result limits the potential for technological diffusion. Finally, upon reaching this limit, the growth of further modernization within agriculture becomes dependent on growth of the nonagricultural sector.

Three types of modern technologies can be differentiated. The first provides gains in productivity without a reduction in marginal cost. Some examples are inputs involving large expenditures of fixed capital, such as tractors, combines, machinery, and agricultural equipment. A second category involves productivity increases and marginal cost decreases. This technology, using fertilizers, pesticides ,and animal feed, for instance, involves low expenditures on fixed capital and high variable cost spending. The third type yields a higher return, either by increasing productivity or by reducing marginal cost. This group is characterized by harvesting techniques, proper spacing of planting, pasture units, crop-livestock-forestry units, and use of high-yield varieties. Compared to traditional techniques, this third category is preferable because net income is always higher. This is not true for the second type, nor even for the first, in which large-scale production is needed for profitability. Only the third category does not confront the self-control mechanism.

After reaching an appropriate level of modernization, further gains depend on a larger global market. Self-control mechanisms do not permit modernization to proceed faster than expansion of the nonagricultural sector. Therefore, international trade is a decisive factor. By exporting surplus production, the self-control mechanism loses its function because a fall in domestic price does not occur. Conversely, with the entry of more export producers, a decrease in international prices may discourage adoption of technology changes in the future.

The main variables responsible for agricultural modernization are productivity, the relative price of traditional and modern inputs, the level of

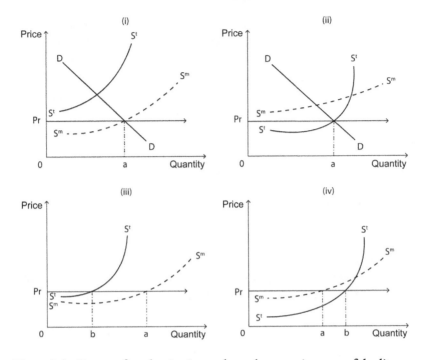

Figure 3.4   Degree of modernization and supply curves in terms of duality.

Source: Ruy Miller Paiva, "Modernização e Dualismo Tecnológico na Agricultura," *Pesquisa e Planejamento Econômico* 1, no. 2 (1971), 214–217.

farmers' education, transaction costs, development of the nonagricultural sector (which can absorb the output and the surplus labor from mechanization), and exports.

As shown in figure 3.4, agricultural advances are summarized through the relationship of supply and demand curves. Three different situations are analyzed: modern, traditional, and dual production. At the top (charts i and ii), the first two cases are presented; at the bottom (charts iii and iv), the case of dual use is depicted.

In the upper-left corner (chart i), specialization in modern techniques, exemplified by the production of fruit (such as figs, grapes, and peaches), is presented. The use of modern inputs (such as high-yield varieties, fertilizers, and pesticides) increases agricultural productivity. Traditional techniques involve a low level of productivity because these crops are highly sensitive to diseases and pests and are dependent on adequate soil management. The supply curve affected by traditional technology (S^t) stands well above the price line, allowing only production with modern technology. Another example is the mechanized production of sugarcane in the state of São Paulo. Labor costs and societal pressures against manual harvesting fires have led to nearly complete mechanization there.

The upper-right corner (chart ii) presents the opposite situation, exemplified by cassava production. The supply curve related to traditional techniques (S^t) is quite elastic in the beginning, due to favorable weather conditions and abundant land. The supply curve based on modern technology (S^m) remains above the price line in the graphic analysis. This crop is resistant to weather, pests, and disease. The supply curve using traditional technique becomes inelastic only for high-volume production in which modern techniques are preferable. Nevertheless, given the low consumption of the product, the traditional technique prevails.

At the bottom-left corner (chart iii), technological duality is represented by poultry and egg production. Cost differences are small at a low-volume output, and both modern and traditional farmers can participate. Homegrown production is inexpensive for the small producer. As production increases, the risk of disease and pests does as well, thus favoring modernization (breeding selection, feed, veterinary medicines, etc.).

Despite the number of large-scale producers using modern techniques, a small market for individual farmers remains. In the state of Minas Gerais, this duality can be seen in coffee production and is largely due to labor costs and land grade. With rising wages, there is an incentive to mechanize, but this is only possible on flatter lands. In municipalities with sloping topography, properties may adopt the manual system.

At the bottom-right corner (chart iv), there is duality, but of an opposite variety. Corn production is a good example because it largely utilizes traditional techniques that are adapted to different regional conditions. Hybrid seeds, fertilizers, machinery, tractors, and harvesters increase corn yield, but the increase in total cost eliminates widespread adoption of the most modern technology. The case of sugarcane production in the northeast is similar. Mechanized and manual-labor farms may operate side by side.

INDUCED INNOVATION MODEL

John Hicks was the first to address technological change and factor endowments.[9] He suggested that most labor-saving inventions are associated with changes in the relative prices of factors of production.

At the same time, innovation seeks to economize relatively expensive inputs in the production process. Based on these Hicksian presuppositions, Syed Ahmad developed a model utilizing the innovation possibility curve. This formalization of the induced innovation model should be seen more as an extension of the neoclassical approach than as an alternative approach.

Hayami and Ruttan, who studied agricultural development in the U.S. and Japanese economies, designed the first empirical test related to the microeconomic fundamentals of technological change. This was based on changes in prices of factors of production. Both countries are examples of the influence of factor endowments. Within the United States, advances in mechanical technology increased agricultural production, even when the market was constrained by an inelastic supply of labor. In Japan, advances in biological technology offset the constraints imposed by an inelastic supply of land.

Figure 3.5 presents induced technical change in agriculture. The graphical analysis illustrates both factor substitution and complementarity of mechanical and biological technologies. The mechanical innovation process is indicated in the left-hand panel (i), and the right-hand panel (ii) describes the advance of biotechnology. The innovation possibility curve (*IPC*) is an envelope of isoquant units corresponding to a given technological state (for example, different types of tractors, harvesters,

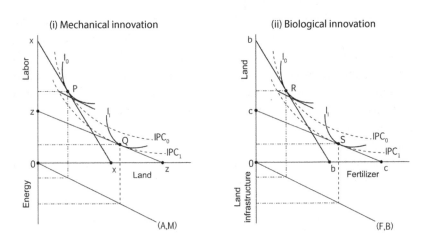

Figure 3.5   Induced technical change in agriculture.

Source: Hayami and Ruttan (1985), 91.

and planters). The transformations are shown in two periods of time (from the initial 0 to the final 1). The tangent line of relative factor prices to isoquant curve (I) determines an optimal combination of inputs. Isoquants have the same quantity of production for different combinations of factors.

For mechanical innovation, the vertical axis represents labor at the top and mechanical power at the bottom, and the horizontal axis is land. In the initial period, the minimum-cost equilibrium point is at P, an optimal combination of land and labor with relative price xx. In the second period, with an increase in the relative cost of labor (given by the line zz), there is a mechanical innovation that saves the scarce factor, using less labor and more land. There is a transition from IPC_0 to IPC_1, changing the marginal rate of technical substitution from I_0 to I_1. The new equilibrium point is at Q, implying a complementary relationship between power and land, drawn by the line (A,M). In this representation, land and mechanical power are regarded as complements and land and labor as substitutes.

In similar fashion, to understand biological innovations, the microeconomic reasoning and graphical analysis are analogous. The vertical axis represents land on top and land infrastructure on the bottom; the horizontal axis contains the biological factors (for example, fertilizers). In the initial period, the minimum-cost equilibrium point is at R, expressed by an optimal combination of fertilizer use and land with relative price bb. In the subsequent period, with an increase in the relative cost of land (given by the line cc), new varieties more responsive to fertilization are developed. That saves the scarce factor, combining less land and more fertilizer. There is a transition from IPC_0 to IPC_1, changing the marginal rate of substitution from I_0 to I_1. A new equilibrium point is at S, implying a complementary relationship between land infrastructure and fertilizer, drawn by the line (F,B). Therefore, fertilizer and land infrastructure are complements, but fertilizer and land are substitutes.

These explanations of induced innovation are based on an equilibrium assumption, but Hayami and Ruttan later suggested that technological changes are more complex. Innovation was not a smooth adjustment along the IPC curve in response to change in relative prices of factors. These authors introduced induced technical and institutional innovation, although the sequence was not formulated mathematically.

EVOLUTIONARY THEORY, COMPETITION, AND LEARNING PROCESS

All three of the models presented—diffusion, dualism, and induced innovation—fail to treat technical change endogenously. Therefore, these models are unable to incorporate important processes such as learning, searches for innovation, imitation behavior, investment decisions, and formal research and development (R&D).

In the fields of economic theory and history, efforts have been made to understand how technological change relates to organizational complexity over time. In this approach, technological change begins to be studied as a dynamic and evolutionary process. The idea that market competition is analogous to biological competition and that firms must pass a market-imposed survival test is quite reasonable.

Later, in a more systematic fashion, the evolutionary theory of technological change proposed by Nelson and Winter incorporated Schumpeterian elements. It introduced innovation searches based on business strategies, and the selection of these innovations was based on the market environment. This evolutionary approach replaced the profit-maximizing behavior of firms with decision rules and routines at the microeconomic level. Subsequent aggregation then explained the stylized facts of the macroeconomy. The production function and equilibrium optimization are abandoned. In its place, characteristics such as technique, resource allocation, investments and business strategies, policies regarding R&D, and product diversification became relevant. Two fundamental components composed this evolutionary model: a search for innovation and the market behavior of firms.

New technology can be generated internally or acquired from suppliers or competitors. Figure 3.6 is an adaptation by Ruttan of Nelson and Winter's explanation of technological search. This illustration is quite intuitive. If A is the present combination of productive factors, then the potential input-output technical coefficients are distributed around this point such that there is greater probability of finding a combination close to A than of finding one far away. In this case, the search is local. By finding a point B, the firm makes a profitability check of the new input ratio. If costs are lower at B than at A, the firm adopts point B and stops the search. Otherwise, the process continues. Thus the technology at point B describes an input-output combination and a ratio between productive factors. This will be accepted if the labor is relatively inexpensive, similar

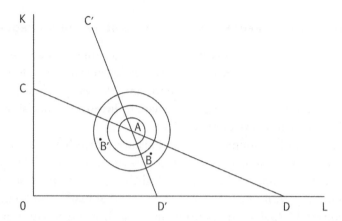

Figure 3.6   Evolutionary model: sampling and selection of new input-output coefficients.

Source: Ruttan (2001), 110.

to the relative prices described by line *CD*. If labor is relatively expensive, as described by *C'D'*, the firm rejects the technology at *B* and pursues the search for another technology, represented by point *B'*. The technology at point *B'* will be labor saving relative to point *B*.

The stochastic process of the technological search is a model with several competitors. Three groups of equations determine: (1) total output, market share, and profits; (2) productivity growth and its interaction with R&D; and (3) the dynamic of investment and capital accumulation. Search for innovation is a random process by innovative and imitative firms, and entrepreneurial strategies can succeed or fail, depending on their probability of innovating. Above-normal profit is reinvested, and successful firms grow faster than those that fail in their technological pursuits. The learning process that leads to technical change is then characterized by the search for innovation, the imitation of best practices, and the economic behavior of agents.

Winter incorporated the conditions of entry and exit of firms as well as differentiation of two industrial regimes into the original model.[10] One is related to the basic science case and the other to cumulative technology. Schemes vary in terms of technological opportunities, degree of innovation, and nature and transmission of knowledge. The first regime links innovation to new firm entry. With a higher level of external research and greater difficulty in innovating, the market is more competitive, leading to a higher rate of entry and exit. The results of this scheme's innovation process, equivalent to the basic science case of the Nelson and Winter model, are independent of the firms' current level of productivity.

The second regime is routinized and links innovation to internal R&D by established firms, which dominate the market because investment in R&D is higher. This converts the market to an oligopoly. The innovation process is cumulative over time. Therefore, the productive gains from technological innovation are dependent on the firm's current level of productivity. There is a lower level of external research, a greater probability of incremental innovation, and productivity is higher.

In the first regime, the innovation process is driven primarily by incoming firms because technological knowledge is not cumulative. In the second regime, the innovation comes from established firms as a result of first movers' advantages.

EVOLUTIONARY APPROACH TO AGRICULTURAL DYNAMICS

Capital can be defined as a combination of fixed and variable factors in a dynamic setting. Agricultural growth depends on capital growth. Fixed capital is constrained by the growth of variable capital, and vice versa. To quantify the land-saving technologies (related to variable capital), a proxy variable was obtained from the sum of expenditures on seeds and seedlings and products to adjust soil chemistry: fertilizers, agrochemicals, animal feed, and veterinary medicines. Labor-saving technologies (related to fixed capital) were represented by an estimate of the value of vehicles, tractors, machinery, and agricultural implements (given depreciation and average life span), plus rental machinery.

The Leontief production function with fixed proportions of factors is a static example of an isoquant map with inputs that are perfect complements. There is no substitutability between factors. To incorporate the dynamic nature of economic changes, as seen in figure 3.7, the expansion path of production is limited by the combination of productive factors between the two rays, $0R_1$ and $0R_2$. According to David and Arthur, technical change becomes path dependent because new technology evolves from earlier technological development.[11] At points A, B, and C, the percentage of inputs used in production varies over time. Although the substitution of productive factors is constrained by upper and lower limits (R_1 and R_2, respectively), it is possible to substitute factors within these limits.

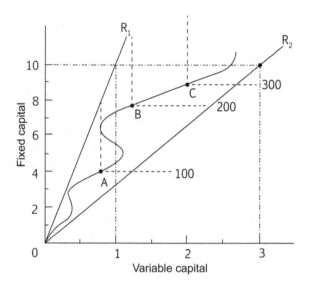

Figure 3.7   Map of isoquants in agriculture using a Leontief production function in a limited dynamic situation.

Source: Vieira Filho, Campos, and Ferreira (2005), 472.

This schematic representation of the production function can be compared to the induced innovation model by Hayami and Ruttan. Induced innovation is explained by the difference in the relative prices of inputs, as producers search for a way to limit scarce factors. Nonetheless, the shape of the innovation possibility curve (*IPC*) is independent rather than dependent, as in the evolutionary approach.

The output of agricultural activity i in period t is equal to the minimum ratio between capital employed (fixed capital, Kf_{it}; or variable capital, Kv_{it}) and their technical coefficients α and β. Then: $Kf_{it} = \alpha.Q_{it}$ and $Kv_{it} = \beta.Q_{it}$. So production Q_{it} is limited to the maximum given by the minimum combination of those two factors. If $Kf_{it}/\alpha < Kv_{it}/\beta$, there will be a surplus of the second factor. If the opposite occurs, $Kf_{it}/\alpha > Kv_{it}/\beta$, there will be surplus of fixed capital. Thus, the production function is defined as:

$$Q_{it} = min\left\{\frac{Kf_{it}}{\alpha} ; \frac{Kv_{it}}{\beta}\right\}. \tag{3.8}$$

The relation between fixed capital and variable capital is given by a constant, with $Kv_{it}/Kf_{it} = z_{it}$. Moreover, $(Kv_{it}/\beta)/(Kf_{it}/\alpha) = n$; so $(Kv_{it}/\beta).(\alpha/Kf_{it}) = n$. Thus making the substitution, the result is

$n.(\beta/\alpha) = z_{it}$. The parameters ($\alpha$ and β) are determined at the outset, with n as a constant defining proportion between the different types of capital. In the initial state of the system, z_{it} is given. Then $\alpha = 1/Af_{it}$ e $\beta = 1/Av_{it}$, where Af_{it} is the productivity of fixed capital (represented by labor-saving technologies) and Av_{it} is the productivity of variable capital (represented by land-saving technologies).

One can move forward by focusing on the internal learning mechanism. Technology adoption affects the diffusion of new knowledge. To stimulate agricultural growth, one needs technological competition and investment in management skills to increase absorption capacity.

An example of the importance of learning is the adoption of new seeds (or even increases in technological content) within production. Modern seeds are more expensive than traditional ones. These new seeds affect other productive factors, such as reduction of fuel and decrease of herbicides. If this information is correctly applied, lower expenditures will be the result. Different farmers have different learning abilities.

Vieira Filho and Silveira presented a model where the differential increase in the stock of knowledge, (Z_i), depends on investment, (I_i), absorptive capacity, (γ_i), the spillover effect in the market, (θ), the total investment undertaken by other agricultural producers, ($\sum_{j \neq i} I_j$), and external knowledge, E.[12] Thus it follows that:

$$Z_i = I_i + \gamma_i \left[\theta. \left(\sum_{i \neq j} I_j \right) + E \right]. \tag{3.9}$$

Absorptive capacity and spillovers assume values between zero and one. The greater the absorptive capacity, the greater the farmer's ability to assimilate knowledge from the investments of other producers and from external information. The greater the spillover effect, the better the agents interact, and knowledge is more easily diffused.

Producer cost (C_{it}) is the sum of operational cost (CO_i) plus the volume of investment in the period. The operating cost is constant and determined by administrative costs, such as labor, inputs, and financial expenditures. The absorption capacity of each agent reduces operational cost. The parameter (ψ_i) varies between zero and one and represents the percentage reduction in operational costs. The larger the absorptive capacity, the higher the reduction of operational and final costs. This relation can be expressed by:

$$C_{it} = CO_i \left[1 - \left(\psi_i . \gamma_{it} \right) \right] + I_{it}. \tag{3.10}$$

Consequently, absorptive capacity of agents not only influences the assimilation of external knowledge but also reduces final production costs. The learning model explains productivity, costs, and absorptive capacity of each farmer. Investment in learning increases the absorptive capacity and the accumulation of external knowledge. Therefore, investment in agriculture has two functions: (i) generating technological innovation, which increases productivity; and (ii) increasing capacity to absorb knowledge, which reduces production costs.

AGRICULTURE'S EXPANDED TECHNOLOGICAL FRONTIER

Agricultural production is not technologically dependent. Instead, there is a complementary coevolution of agricultural production and development of new technologies. The institutional framework for the development of innovation is very complex within an economic sector, let alone when multiple sectors are introduced.

Technology that solves productivity problems will be implemented rapidly in the market. The more efficient a given technology is, the stronger the response of the productive sector. This will, in turn, influence the technological trajectories of the input supplier sector, thereby creating and diffusing other innovations.

Technologies can be path dependent. Trajectories are shaped by specific technical properties. Historical context defines path dependence, whereby the past influences future trajectories. The cumulative nature of productive learning reinforces the tacit and specific nature of knowledge, which allows some producers to obtain competitive advantages. Technological innovation increases the productive capacity of land and labor, creating continuous gains.

The producer's managerial capacity is key for leveraging competitive advantages and productive gains from technological knowledge. Experience and knowledge in the use of new technology not only reduce risk from exogenous factors (climatic adversities, geographic variability, and the emergence of new plagues and diseases) but also redirect the trajectories of suppliers. This occurs through a feedback effect that adapts and enhances technology for diverse environments and producers' needs. The process of learning (via experimentation) is associated with the absorption of new knowledge.

The technological transformation of agriculture began two centuries ago, but these changes did not significantly increase agricultural

productivity until the mid-twentieth century. Until 1900, agricultural production employed manual cultivation and used rudimentary techniques.
In the 1920s, better techniques were introduced. By the 1940s, chemical
production plus the mechanical and automotive sectors benefited from a
cluster of innovations related to the internal combustion engine and petro-
chemicals, in which oil and natural gas substituted for coal. Biotechnology
later appeared, improving new seed varieties. This began in the 1970s with
the development of molecular biology and was consolidated by the 1990s
with the genetic engineering of plants and living organisms.

Figure 3.8 illustrates this trajectory and its consequences for agricultural development. The left vertical axis indicates increases in productivity, which may be low, medium, or high. The horizontal axis represents
technological content as a measure of agricultural modernization. This
ranges from restricted technology (traditional agriculture) to intense use
of technology (modern producer). The black line (AC) is the absorptive
capacity. The dotted line (S) is the upper limit of absorptive capacity, and
the dotted line (I) is the inferior limit. Finally, the main clusters of technological innovations in agriculture, such as chemical, mechanical, and
biotechnological revolutions, are located on the right vertical axis.

For a given technological content (x) different levels of productivity are
available, ranging from y_1 to y_3. For identical technology, the accumulated
knowledge stock of each producer is central to improved performance.

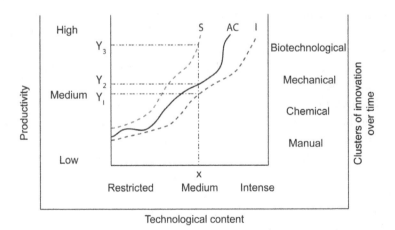

Figure 3.8   Agriculture's expanded technological trajectory.

Source: Vieira Filho (2012), 6.

The closer productivity is to y_3, the closer it is to the maximal stock of knowledge. If the productivity is low (or close to y_1), the farmer has limited absorptive capacity and little knowledge.

Productive investment has two functions. The first raises the level of technological content, increasing levels of productivity. The second is the development of absorptive capacity. By expanding technological content and absorptive capacity through increasing investment, a farmer has a higher probability of reaching higher productivity. That process shifts the absorptive capacity curve (AC) upward.

Technological revolution without learning cannot occur. Modern agriculture has incorporated chemical innovations and thereby created a need for mechanical innovation. Biotechnological innovations, in turn, influence chemical and mechanical trends. All have become essential to modern agricultural advancement.

TECHNICAL AND INSTITUTIONALLY INDUCED INNOVATION: A STANDARD MODEL

This treatment of agricultural production growth is related to earlier economic analysis in which the firm is analyzed as a nexus of contracts, specifically, a relationship of acquisition of modern inputs and services through contracts. The contractual relationship between the parties is renewed based on actual productive return within a stipulated period. Economic activity is not limited to the technological transformation of inputs into outputs because there are necessary transaction costs. These are incurred by the firm in order to utilize the market most effectively.[13] Institutions are constraints (norms) that structure social, economic, and political interaction and define the mechanisms for enforcing formal and informal rules.

Research in the agricultural sector can be considered a public good, having the attributes of nonrivalry and nonexclusivity. The first implies that the good, once offered, is distributed to all interested parties. The second refers to the inability of private producers to appropriate the gains arising from this new knowledge; it is difficult to exclude this good even from a nonpayee. Institutional arrangements therefore ensure that the result of basic research is available to the market.

When analyzing dynamic questions in the innovation process, neoclassical hypotheses with a predefined production function for all countries have been rejected. Differences in levels of productivity and growth rates cannot simply be explained by the transfer of capital and technology. Asymmetries in factor endowments between firms and countries alter production decisions and may create path dependence in certain technologies.

Here it is important to emphasize the microfoundations. The limitation of the induced innovation model is that the format of the IPC is independent of bias in technical change. In addition, the technological change is treated as an exogenous variation. The major constraint is treating internal mechanisms, such as learning, searching, and formalizing R&D processes, as if they were inserted into a black box. Important transformations are primarily directed by external forces.

The strength of the evolutionary approach lies precisely in the construction of a behavioral basis to explain firms' decisions. This evolutionary approach has not become a source of empirical studies. Simulation results define a large proliferation of stylized facts, which makes it difficult to carry out empirical tests.

Technological change is increasingly generated by institutional transformations. Changes in resource endowment, cultural endowment, and technology are important sources of institutional change. It is important to emphasize that special attention should be given to the process of institutional innovation. Ruttan seeks to examine the elements of a more general model of technical and institutional change that was presented by Hayami and Ruttan.

Figure 3.9 presents the elements that map the interrelationships among resource endowment, cultural endowment, technology, and institutions. This representation goes beyond the conventional general equilibrium model in which these elements are givens. Modeling the interactions among cultural endowment, technology, and institutional change is much more difficult.

To contextualize this model for the Brazilian case, we utilize post-1970s agricultural modernization, which is discussed in the following chapters. At the beginning, a limitation of resources stimulated institutional transformations (line C). The creation of Embrapa in 1973 was an induced institutional innovation, leading to the creation of strategies to increase the generation of knowledge and technology (line *b*).

Development of soil correction was a technological change that expanded the arable area (it can be represented by line *a*, notably by the incorporation of the Cerrado in production). With the high land prices in Brazil's southern region, several producers moved to the new agricultural

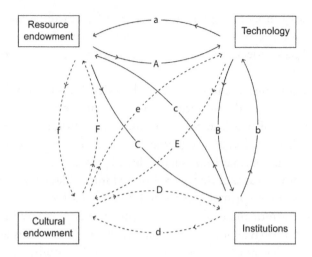

Figure 3.9   Interrelationships between changes in resource endowments, cultural endowments, technology, and institutions.

Source: Hayami and Ruttan (1985), 111.

frontier—the Midwest—incorporating their business culture into the new agricultural enterprises and local institutions (a movement that can be represented by the impact of lines f and D).

Clearly, this model of induced institutional innovation is more complex than a simple analysis of competitive equilibrium. The theoretical debate in this chapter has sought to interpret technological change in agriculture. A general approach that incorporates elements of induced innovation, evolutionary theory, path dependence, and technological trajectories is the appropriate path.

THEORETICAL AND RESEARCH CHALLENGES

This theoretical approach explains why a particular technology is not always profitable. Mathematical models are best when there is simplicity in variables and maximization of profitability. Implicitly or explicitly, technology is homogeneous and standardized, with characteristics observable by all market participants.

As discussed in later chapters, less than 1 percent of agricultural establishments (the richest) accounted for half of all production. At the other extreme, 90 percent of the (poorer) establishments accounted for approximately 15 percent of total production. In an environment favorable to technological adoption, conventional theory does not explain how this great majority survived and remained producers using traditional technologies.

Technological information is assimilated asymmetrically among private farmers. The greater the degree of access to markets and the more organized the producer, the better the ability to negotiate costs or to determine final prices based on return on invested capital. Information asymmetry arising from market imperfections that exist in credit, rural extension, education, and agrarian reform programs is ignored.

Positive social programs utilize well-designed interventions. If selection is influenced by nonobserved variables, the treatment and control groups will be systematically distinct. Then there is bias with the treatment group potentially associated with unobservable variables. Public policy should be evaluated for its real impact. Random participation in the program is ideal. Frequent mismatch between the potential and the real outcome may even provoke market failures.

To illustrate, consider the following agricultural policies in Brazil: (*i*) National Program for Strengthening Family Agriculture (Pronaf); (*ii*) agrarian reform; (*iii*) education; and (*iv*) the Food Acquisition Program (PAA). Pronaf's goal is to stimulate the generation of income of family farmers by financing capital and providing rural activities and services. According to the legislation (Law No. 11,326, dated 7/24/2006), a treatment group is defined by the area or size of the property and the income obtained from agricultural activity, as well as limits to hired labor.

To access credit, the legislation imposes a selection bias. If the agent does not expand his production area, raise his income through business diversification, and hire staff, the goal of reducing poverty and generating income will not be achieved. There is only perpetuation of extreme poverty in the countryside.

Agrarian reform (Law No. 4,504, dated 11/30/1964) is a set of measures aimed at improving land distribution through changes in ownership or use. Its goals are to satisfy the principles of social justice and to increase productivity. The legislation misinterprets what generates productivity gains. Land distribution will not increase productivity; better technology is required, and this is dependent on the ability of individuals to absorb new knowledge. Normally, settlements are deprived of basic education and rural extension infrastructure. In addition, there is limited access to electricity, sanitation, and other needed inputs. Then chances of upward mobility diminish. Although land is important, access to knowledge is the key determinant of productivity growth.

The best schools are in the more developed regions of Brazil. Rural areas lack basic resources such as good teachers and facilities. Rural producers must send their children to study in urban centers. The main policies aimed at benefiting small agricultural producers presume that the labor force employed is family-based. How, then, is it possible to participate in the treatment group and also to prioritize education? Public policies fail to consider this logic and increasingly stimulate polarization between rural and urban spaces.

The PAA (created by Article 19 of Law 10,696, dated 2/7/2003) is part of the Zero Hunger Program whose goal is to promote access to food for people living with nutritional insecurity. It encourages family farming and allows purchase of food produced by family farmers without bidding requirements. Municipalities can coordinate the distribution of the products through public welfare and education networks. The government pays a low price for products in the program. Therefore, the most efficient producers prefer to access the market directly. Only the least-efficient producers remain, offering inferior products. As a result, the policy selects suboptimal products and does not break the poverty cycle imposed on the beneficiaries because the price received does not adequately compensate for costs of production.

In summary, public policies aimed at boosting agricultural production in Brazil require new approaches to deal with the country's profound inequality. Many market imperfections are introduced by the government itself. Any intervention must be very well planned to avoid the potential reduction to social welfare.

CHAPTER 4

Brazilian Agriculture

A HISTORICAL PERSPECTIVE

Despite its massive size and an economic history based on primary goods, Brazil was a net food importer until the 1980s. Application of science and technology has resulted in a sharp rise in agricultural productivity over the past fifty years. Induced innovation based on local institutional change was essential in transforming Brazil into one of the world's largest food exporters. This success did not extend to all regions nor reduce all productive inequality.

Challenges still persist, despite large production increases. We presents the key factors that transformed Brazilian agriculture, divided into three time periods. The first period is pre-1970s, the second considers the transitional moment, and the third incorporates the 1990s to the present. The impact of technology on economizing scarce resources and reducing food prices is analyzed next. Finally, we discuss regional and productive inequalities and the inability to absorb new technologies in the Northeast and North regions. Fully recognizing and studying these regional differences is essential for the design of better public policies for the Brazilian agricultural sector.[1]

Brazilian agriculture is an excellent case for studying how the Green Revolution relied on local institutions. Brazil was one of the few developing countries to incorporate external knowledge from international research centers and adapt it to local conditions. Institutional changes were essential for promotion of R&D processes focused on evolving from a net importer of food to self-sufficiency, and ultimately, export.

Technologies from developed countries could not easily be adapted to the Brazilian environment. During the 1960s, there was less productive diversity (agricultural and livestock)and a high risk of domestic shortages.

Since the 1990s, world production has been more stable, and Brazilian agriculture has experienced a significant expansion in all its economic dimensions. This trajectory resulted from a combination of technological inputs and innovation clusters in different sectors. Absorptive capacity of farmers to recognize, assimilate, and use new knowledge was necessary. As observed by Esposti,[2] public research in agriculture can influence the ability to adopt a new technology, or, put differently, it can increase the absorption capacity of farm units. An R&D process not only generates new information but also increases a firm's ability to leverage existing information.

In a similar context, the international transfer of agricultural technology depends in part on the recipient's own research efforts (or knowledge). When the gap between theoretical and applied knowledge is narrowed, increased productivity is associated more with local selection, technical adaptation, and marginal improvements in technology than with advances in the development of international research. Economic estimates indicate that research contributes substantially to productivity gains. In countries with institutional environments that participated in collaborative research, dissemination of knowledge was more rapid.

Outlining some important historical facts creates a clearer picture. In terms of technology, modern agriculture can use chemical innovations to increase land productivity while at the same time intensifying the use of mechanical innovations to improve labor productivity. Biotechnology, such as genetically modified seeds, further advances chemical and mechanical innovations. In addition, genetic engineering and multidisciplinary exchanges induce even wider technological change.

Technical change in agriculture is typically introduced by buyers. Adoption and diffusion varies depending on the learning processes of producers. The greater the gain in productivity in the receiving sector, the greater the chance of improving technological opportunities emanating from buyers. Chiaromonte and Dosi[3] presented an analogous two-sector model describing the agricultural production chain as a relation between primary and industrial manufacturing sectors.

Upstream industry has well-defined technological trajectories that can lead to innovation in the agricultural sector. On one hand, the purchaser offers a package that brings new knowledge and a hope for better returns. On the other, the ability of farm units to combine different technological inputs leads to increased agricultural productivity. Learning by doing provides feedback. Chain analysis is useful for describing this innovation.

Figure 4.1 illustrates the historical events transforming Brazilian agriculture over the last half-century. The first period includes the 1960s, the

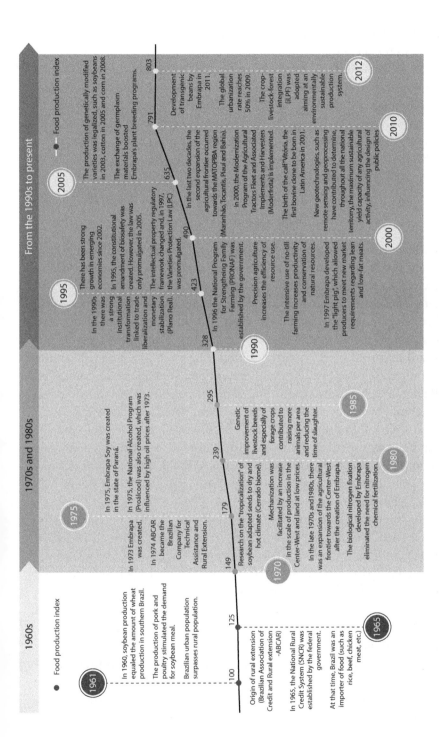

Figure 4.1 Time line of the Brazilian agricultural transformation over the last half-century.

Source: World Bank, "World Bank Indicators," 2016, https://data.worldbank.org/indicator.

second represents the following two decades, and the third period is from 1990 to the present.

From 1961 to 2012, the food production index increased more than eightfold, and during the same period the Brazilian population grew approximately 2.5 times. In 1961, the Brazilian population was about seventy-five million people. The latest demographic census estimated the population at just over two hundred million. Per capita production grew. This performance has improved domestic food security and boosted foreign trade in the most recent decades.

THE 1960s—A PROBLEM TO SOLVE

During the 1960s, soybean production had the same relative importance as wheat production in southern Brazil. Larger pork and poultry production increased demand for soybean bran, an important source of vegetable protein for animal feed. The Brazilian urban population surpassed the number living in rural areas in the mid-1960s. This demographic shift increased demand for food and stimulated greater grain consumption. Despite this, Brazil remained a net importer of food. There was low productivity and a limited food supply, but rapid growth occurred on the demand side. Public authorities had mounting concerns, and for the following two decades, Brazil experienced a fragile socioeconomic environment.

Foreign trade of agricultural products is a good indicator when comparing these three periods. Early on, production was positive (by thousands of tons) and the trade surplus was very low. In 2011, the agricultural surplus, particularly for cereals, grains, and meat production (see figure 4.2), was higher than in previous years.

At the outset, the Brazilian Association of Credit and Rural Assistance (ABCAR) served as a starting point for rural extension services in Brazil, and the Rural Credit and Assistance Associations (ACAR) of the states were part of a decentralized system. They provided credit through very restricted and specific technical assistance, as shown by Peixoto.[4] In 1965, the federal government created the National Rural Credit System (SNCR) and began to establish policies to address the dramatic instability in the national food supply.

The first initiative was credit expansion, which continued until the second oil crisis in the late 1970s. After a long decline during the 1980s, financing once again increased, reaching a peak in the mid-1990s. This second era of credit expansion was much more market-oriented,

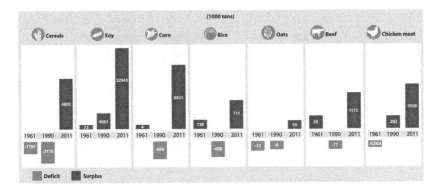

Figure 4.2   Brazilian trade balance for selected products over time (in thousands of tons).

Source: Food and Agriculture Organization, "Food and Agriculture Data," 2015, http://www.fao.org/faostat/.

including public policies targeting capital formation and rural extension services. This advance was influenced by U.S. universities engaging in Latin American research.

FROM 1970 TO THE LATE 1980s: AGRICULTURE AS A KNOWLEDGE AND SCIENCE-BASED SECTOR

In the 1970s, policymakers, clearly aware of the production problem, decided to invest in rural research and extension services. Embrapa was created in 1973. Its mission was to provide leadership for research, development, and innovation in agriculture to prevent an imminent crisis due to an inadequate food supply.

One year later, ABCAR became the Brazilian Company for Technical Assistance and Rural Extension (Embrater), under the management of the Ministry of Agriculture, and the State Enterprise for Technical Assistance and Rural Extension (Emater) was also established. Embrater was responsible for creation of national (top-down as well as universal) strategies and for the funding state-level policy designs. The objective was to provide essential rural extension services to the most vulnerable farmers.

Embrapa was a center for innovation and technical change, and Embrater enabled diffusion of applied knowledge. Embrapa was not the only institution promoting knowledge and technological development in Brazil at the time, but its creation enabled a national strategy for agricultural research to develop. Applied research needed decentralization, and in 1975, a branch of Embrapa specializing in soybean cultivation was created in the state of Paraná. Embrapa was successful because farms across the country were capable of absorbing new knowledge to increase productivity and reduce production costs.

During this period, the country faced the first oil crisis, which raised prices and production costs significantly. The relative price of oil to ethanol changed, making investment in biofuel production more attractive. Despite these oil price increases, the Brazilian economy continued its growth, relying on international credit available at low cost. Although not as intense as in previous years, economic growth was still positive.

The National Alcohol Program (*Proálcool*) was created in 1975. It sought to replace gasoline (fossil fuel) with ethanol alcohol, reducing oil dependence and the trade deficit. This was a case of induced innovation driven by institutional change.

In the 1970s, Brazilian agriculture was based on four fundamental pillars: (i) abundant rural credit, (ii) large investments in agricultural research, (iii) widespread rural extension services, and (iv) availability of cheap land. These fundamentals changed with a second wave of rising oil prices in 1979. Brazilian oil imports then accounted for more than half of domestic consumption. Globally, U.S. interest rates rose, ending international credit at low rates. These changes altered the Brazilian economy over the next decade.

From 1979 to 1993, the Brazilian automobile industry produced more than five million ethanol-powered vehicles. Production reached its peak in 1986, when ethanol-fueled cars accounted for nearly 70 percent of total sales. With economic liberalization and reduction of the federal presence in the economy in the 1990s, production subsidies were cut. Sales then fell to below 50,000 units by 1995, representing less than 1 percent of total vehicle sales.

By the 1980s, the development of agricultural knowledge and its effective use by local farmers contributed to productivity gains across the economy. This agriculture research was built on three principal objectives: (i) improvement of degraded tropical soil, (ii) plant breeding and genetic engineering, and (iii) integrated management systems.

First, research aimed to correct the acidic soils of Brazil's Center-West region, a biome known as the Cerrado.[5] These techniques allowed the arable area to be extended. Second, genetic improvements in soybean cultivation adapted seeds to the local climate and shortened the life cycle of traditional plants. This made a second harvest possible.

Production increased due to biological nitrogen fixation, a technique that reduces the use of fertilizers but permits an increase in productivity per hectare. Genetic improvement of pastures[6] favored high livestock production. Finally, in the third area, the development of high yielding seed varieties resistant to diseases helped to reduce productive losses and insecticide costs.

As the price of land decreased, there was greater access to mechanization. The agricultural frontier expanded toward the Cerrado's Center-West and raised efficiency of Brazilian agriculture and livestock production to international standards. Figure 4.3 depicts these transformations across time and location. Frontier expansion is observed, with a concentration in the Cerrado. This is an area of 204 million hectares, or approximately 24 percent of Brazil's total surface (which is 34 percent larger than the Corn Belt in the United States, equivalent to about 73 percent of the Argentine territory, and even 3.7 times larger than France). Agricultural production also spread from the South to the Center-West and more recently to the Northeast. Prior to 1980, the soil was unsuitable for most crops and incompatible with large-scale production.

In the 1970s, the pioneer states were Rio Grande do Sul, Paraná, Santa Catarina, and São Paulo. In the following decade, production increased in the states of Mato Grosso do Sul, Goiás, Minas Gerais, and Mato Grosso. During the 1990s and 2000s, the agricultural frontier expanded toward underdeveloped areas in the North and Northeast.

There has been a significant increase in mechanization, as shown by the increase of tractors per unit area (figure 4.4). This mechanical intensification was due not only to increased numbers of tractors but also to their increase in power. Mechanization does not necessarily result in a reduction in the number of rural workers. The average number of workers per holding remained stable during the period under review, with a slight decline only recently.

FROM THE 1990s TO THE PRESENT—EVOLUTION AND RESILIENCE

We consider the development of Brazilian agriculture to be a revolution rather than a process of simply importing technology from external markets. A comparison between Brazil and the world shows the trajectories of long-term crop yields (figure 4.5). When observing three distinct years (1961, 1990, and 2012), yields of cereals, fruits, oilseeds, vegetables, and meat production (bovine, swine, and poultry) all increased over time.

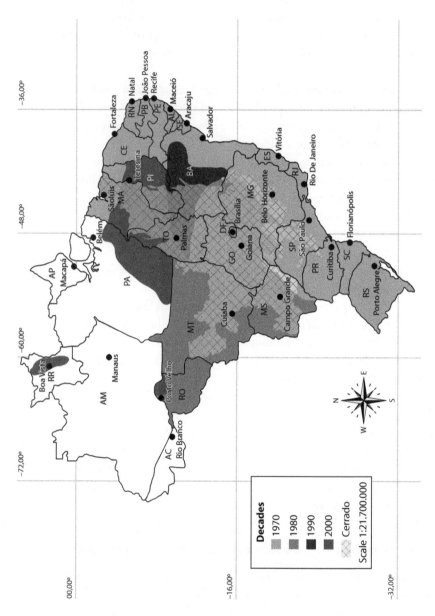

Figure 4.3   Expansion of the Brazilian agricultural frontier over time.

Source: Ibama, Instituto Brasileiro Do Meio Ambiente E Recursos Naturais Renováveis, 2015, http://siscom.ibama-gov.br/monitora_biomas/ and José Eustáquio RibeiVieira Filho (2016).

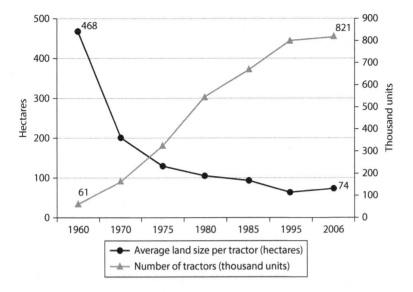

Figure 4.4   Mechanization of Brazilian agriculture over time.

Source: Various agricultural censuses, IBGE (2015).

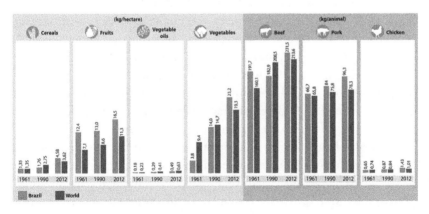

Figure 4.5   Comparison between agricultural yield of selected products from Brazil and the world, 1961, 1990, and 2012.

Source: Food and Agriculture Organization, "Food and Agriculture Data," 2015. http://www.fao.org/faostat/.

In 1961, agricultural yield was lower in Brazil than in the rest of the world, but this was about to change. It is essential to note that the Brazilian research system has managed to adapt, create, and transfer technologies to agricultural firms over a long-term period. As a result of this scientific and productive environment, Brazil has transformed into one of the world's largest food exporters.

In the 1990s, with internal reforms such as trade liberalization and an external fall in the price of agricultural inputs (chemicals, fertilizers, tractors, and machines), rapid modernization occurred. The government reduced market interventions, such as export licenses, quantitative limitations on agro-food exports, food stock control, and minimum price policy. State controls over the wheat, sugar, and ethanol sectors were also abolished.

No-till farming practices have improved seed quality, and financing programs have been created to boost investment in these techniques. In 1996, the government implemented the National Program for Strengthening Family Agriculture (Pronaf) and, later in 2000, the Modernization Program of the Agricultural Tractors Fleet and Associated Implements and Harvesters (*Moderfrota*). These programs sought to update the fleet of tractors and harvesters in Brazilian agriculture.

The government has increased agricultural credit over the last twenty years. In 1995, a constitutional amendment on biosafety was created; it was approved but not implemented until 2005. The Brazilian regulatory framework on intellectual property was changed in 1995 with signing the agreement for Trade Related Aspects of Intellectual Property Rights Including Trade in Counterfeit Goods (TRIPs). In 1997, the Varieties Protection Law (LPC) was adopted. By early 2000, the growth of the global economy—driven by emerging economies—created greater demand for food. The Brazilian trade balance reached record trade surpluses, mainly related to the growing contribution from agriculture.

In 2004, a large increase in agricultural commodity prices began, and favorable terms of trade permitted domestic consumption to expand. Soon the exchange rate began to appreciate. Manufacturing lost competitiveness, but Brazilian agriculture continued its positive performance as the price of commodities rose. This is discussed in chapter 6 in more detail.

Biofuels played an important role in both Brazilian agribusiness and the auto industry. By the end of 1990, ethanol suffered a setback. Oil prices fell in the global market. Meanwhile, sugar prices had risen worldwide, prompting domestic producers to switch from ethanol to sugar exports. At the time, there were no incentives for the Brazilian automotive industry to manufacture cars powered by ethanol engines. In contrast, flexible fuel motor technology reached Brazil in 2003. Later, in

2007, despite the entry of pre-salt offshore oil fields, the ethanol sector remained strategic. As a renewable energy, sugarcane biomass accounted for more than 15 percent of total energy supply and was the third-largest source after oil and hydroelectric energy in the country's energy matrix.

Genetic engineering techniques are essential in modern agriculture but require regulation. The use of genetically modified organisms (GMOs) has been growing since 1996 in the United States, Argentina, and Canada. In Brazil, genetically modified soybeans were illegally planted for the first time in 1997. Genetically modified planting was later legalized for soybeans in 2003, cotton in 2005, and corn in 2008. Legalization of GMO planting intensified the diffusion of biotechnology in Brazil. In 2011, Embrapa produced the first genetically modified black bean, a staple food. GMO planting simplifies management and agricultural practices, reducing the use of herbicides in pest control and increasing farmers' incomes.

Agribusiness contributed positively to Brazil's trade surplus when compared to other sectors of the economy. From 1989 to 2013, the manufacturing industry showed a trade deficit but agribusiness had a positive surplus. Brazil's total trade balance did not worsen because of the agricultural performance in those years. The second expansion of the agricultural frontier occurred in the Matopiba region (Maranhão, Tocantins, Piauí, and Bahia). Investment in R&D was critical to this process.

This success of Brazilian agriculture helped stimulate the economy. Brazilian agriculture is now a model of efficient agricultural production. A large area of degraded Cerrado land has been incorporated into productive use. Since the 1960s, the supply of beef and pork has quadrupled, and chicken production has expanded 22 times. Livestock farming grew 9 times and cereal production 6 times. Today Brazil is one of the world's largest exporters of coffee, soybeans, beef, and orange juice. These transformations[7] enabled Brazil to switch from being an importer of staple foods to being one of the largest producers and exporters in the world.

TECHNOLOGY, LAND-SAVING, AND DECLINING FOOD PRICES

Brazilian agribusiness, which includes the entire food production and distribution chain, accounted for 22 percent of GDP in 2015, with agriculture providing 70 percent and livestock 30 percent of the total. A comparative analysis of agricultural censuses (1960–2006) shows that the number of farms increased sharply until 1980. In addition, land use expanded into new agricultural areas. Since then, the number of farms has remained stable, standing at 5.1 million in 2006. The reduction of the average area per farm observed reflects the increase of land, plants, and livestock productivity, which was achieved through investment in research, science, and technology. In 2006, agriculture accounted for 321 million hectares, with 160 million hectares devoted to pasture (50 percent), 61 million hectares to crops in general (19 percent), and 100 million hectares to forests (31 percent).

The percentage of cultivated areas has been increasing, whereas areas allocated to pasture stabilized but have a downward future trend. The size of harvested area doubled from 1960 to 1980, from about 29 million hectares to 58 million hectares. After 1980, agricultural land remained stable at about 60 million hectares. Cattle pasture increased by 46 percent between 1960 and 1985. Between 1985 and 2006, pasture fell from 179 million to about 160 million hectares, a total reduction of 11 percent.

The development of Brazilian agriculture is inherently a result of productivity growth. Using an agricultural production function, an earlier study found 100 percent increase in gross income that can be explained by technology (68 percent), labor (23 percent), and land (9 percent). We used a modification of that technique, as explained in Appendix C.

Table 4.1 provides results for the changing land productivity for soybean, corn, sugarcane, cotton, coffee, wheat, and bean crops between 1960 and 2010. The accumulated production in 2010 (503 million tons) divided by productivity in 1960 (3 tons per hectare) equals the amount of land needed to apply the traditional technology (170 million hectares). Subtracting the current harvested area (41 million hectares), the land-saving effect is estimated at about 129 million hectares.

By analogy, in raising livestock, the land saved depends on productivity. Once animal productivity is calculated, the measurement of the land-saving effect is similar to that used for agricultural production. By dividing 2010 production (9,020 thousand tons) by animal productivity in 1960 (about 11 kg per hectare), the amount of land needed was approximately 806 million hectares. By subtracting the size of pasture in 2010 (160 million hectares), land-saving would be close to 646 million hectares.

There remains a mistaken perception that the growth of Brazilian beef production was based largely on pasture expansion. Although this had occurred in the past, the pattern of cattle farming has changed,

Table 4.1   Land-Saving Effect (LSE) Related to Agricultural Production—Soybean, Corn, Sugarcane, Cotton, Coffee, Wheat, and Beans—and Cattle Raising (1960–2010)

	Production	Variable	1960 Traditional	2010 Modern	Δ%	LSE	Total LSE
Agriculture	Harvested area (million hectares)	L	18.7	41.2	120	129.0	775.0 (91% of national territory)
	Productivity (tons per hectare)	A	3.0	12.2	313		
	Production (million tons)	P	55.4	503.4	809		
Livestock	Slaughtered animals (million heads)	An	7.1	41.2	477	645.9	
	Pastures (million hectares)	L	122.3	160.0	31		
	Carcass weight (kg per animal)	G	191.7	218.8	14		
	Stocking rate (animal per hectare)	S	0.06	0.26	341		
	Productivity (kg per hectare)	A	11.2	56.4	404		
	Production (thousand tons)	P	1369.1	9020.0	559		

Source: Brazilian Institute of Statistics (IBGE), *Agricultural Censuses for 1960 and 2006* and Food and Agricultural Organization of the United Nations, *Food and Agricultural Data*, 2015.

and land productivity gains now account for 79 percent of Brazil's growth in output.

The total land-saving effect, for both agricultural and livestock production, was 775 million hectares, almost the size of Brazil (851.5 million hectares). In other words, technological change was responsible for saving around 91 percent of Brazil's surface while providing much more food for national and international markets.

Meat production in Brazil comes from extensive cattle raising, with few animals per hectare. An additional 70 million hectares—currently dedicated to pastures—could be converted into agricultural areas, doubling the area for food production. In addition, 90 million hectares of arable land are still unexplored. Unlike other countries, where land is a scarce factor, Brazil has great potential to increase production.

During an economic boom, with increases in output, employment, and income, innovations reduce production costs, expand profits, and extend the production frontier outward. There are two effects: one is producers' response to productivity changes, and the other is the indirect

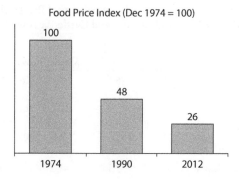

Figure 4.6   Deflation of food prices over time.

Source: Based on Barros (2013).

impact of rising consumer income. The first shifts the supply curve upward, whereas the second increases the demand for food. In the first case, prices fall; in the second, prices rise.

Productivity increase permits a better distribution of income. The fall in food prices from 1974 to 2012 (figure 4.6) was important in reducing poverty in Brazil. Since 1974, food prices fell more than half by 1990 and by almost 75 percent in 2012. This decline has generated positive effects even during the 1980s, when Brazil faced high inflation. Even after the boom in commodity prices of the mid-2000s, domestic prices rose less in Brazil than elsewhere.

Alves, Souza, and Brandão[8] studied a time series of food prices from 1970 to 2009. They used an econometric analysis covering three subperiods: (i) 1970–1978, (ii) 1978–2005; and (iii) 2005–2009. In the first and last of these, food prices rose at rates of 5.2 percent and 2.7 percent per year. In the second subperiod, the Brazilian economy experienced a sharp decline in food prices. For the whole period from 1970 to 2009, food prices declined by 23 percent.

PRODUCTIVE CONCENTRATION, LACK OF ABSORPTIVE CAPACITY, AND STRUCTURAL CHALLENGES

Most of production growth is attributed to the growth of technology, producing more with fewer resources. Producers have a limited knowledge capacity, thereby limiting potential benefits. Moreover, these agents continue to have limited access to new technologies.

Table 4.2   Stratification of Income from Brazilian Agricultural Production (2006)

Groups	Minimum Wage Equivalent (MWE)*	Number of farms (thousands)	%	Annual Gross Production Value (R$ billions)	%
Extreme poverty	0–2	3.242	69.6	6.5	3.9
Low-income	2–10	960	20.9	18.5	11.1
Middle-income	10–200	416	9.0	59.9	35.9
High-income	>200	23	0.5	81.7	49.0
Brazil		**4.641**	**100**	**166.7**	**100**

Source: IBGE, Agricultural Census of 2006.

*MWE = gross production value per month/monthly minimum wage

We highlight the concentration of production in table 4.2, subdividing productive units by income and production distribution. Agricultural units are efficient in the upper part of the distribution but are not in the lower-income group. The richest 10 percent of agricultural establishments (middle and high income) are responsible for 85 percent of gross production value. In contrast, 90 percent of the poorest establishments (which include extremely poor and low-income farmers) accounted for only 15 percent of production. In the extreme poverty group alone, 63 percent of establishments contributed less than 4 percent of production. The variations among regions and crops indicate the structural heterogeneity of Brazilian agriculture.

This heterogeneity makes technological adoption difficult. To achieve continuing agricultural development in Brazil, growth with productive inclusion of low-income farmers is necessary. In chapter 8, we assess patterns of income inequality and technology utilization in family farms.

About 3.2 million establishments are in extreme poverty. As shown in figure 4.7, extreme poverty is concentrated in the Northeast region. In other regions, poverty is not a predominant feature. The Center-West has the lowest percentage of extreme poverty. To reduce rural poverty, public policies must be regionally differentiated.

Although Brazilian agriculture has had tremendous growth in total factor productivity (TFP), many family units demonstrate a limited capacity for technology absorption. According to the 2006 agricultural census, the low educational levels of most farmers, coupled with poor management, limits their capacity to absorb external knowledge.

Figure 4.8 shows that 90 percent of farm owners did not possess a basic education (up to elementary school completion), 27 percent were illiterate, and 12 percent were uneducated. These farmers do not know how to

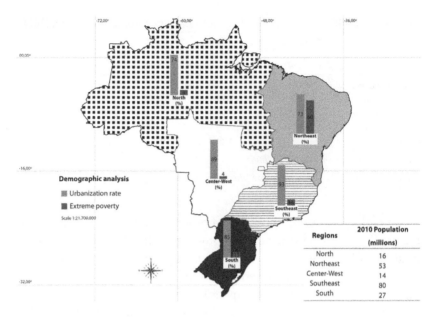

Figure 4.7   Demographic analysis of rural exodus by region, 2006.

Source: IBGE Agricultural Census (2006).

Figure 4.8   Percentage of farm owners by educational levels and regions, 2006.

Source: IBGE Agricultural Census (2006).

seek guidance for the use of new technologies, leading to underutilization or inefficient use of inputs. The Northeast has the worst educational performance, with 59 percent being illiterate and uneducated farmers, 36 percent with an elementary education, and only 6 percent with a secondary and higher education. These numbers illustrate the significant gap in comparison with other regions.

Figure 4.9 shows that only 22 percent of agricultural entrepreneurs received some type of technical assistance in 2006; the vast majority did not. In the Northeast, 92 percent of agricultural managers did not receive any technical support, and only 3 percent received regular guidance. The South has better indicators than any other region. Productive scale varies among regions. In the South and Northeast there is a predominance of small farms, whereas Center-West farming is predominantly large-scale. Small-scale production in the South utilizes better institutions and infrastructure, but the Northeast has a low incorporation of technical assistance. The Northeast and North regions are solely dependent on public funds for technical assistance. In the Northeast,

Figure 4.9   Percentage of agricultural entrepreneurs receiving technical assistance by region, 2006.

Source: IBGE Agricultural Census (2006).

there is little other investment. The participation of cooperatives in this region is only 3 percent.

Low overall labor productivity reveals the dualistic nature of agriculture in Brazil. Intensive and large-scale production coexists alongside a vast number of small and relatively unproductive agricultural units. This labor productivity gap has been falling in some segments.[9]

Public policy has an important role. There must be much greater access to rural extension and better education. Broader knowledge about Brazilian agriculture is a good place to start.

———

CHAPTER 5

Embrapa

A CASE OF INDUCED INSTITUTIONAL INNOVATION

Technology is a result of accumulated knowledge. There are many ways to absorb knowledge. In industry, a company can develop technology or interact with established firms. Collaboration can increase economic efficiency by providing access to advanced techniques. Similarly, agricultural research is needed for the development of modern agriculture. Embrapa, the Brazilian Agricultural Research Corporation, is a successful intermediary example. It has permitted Brazil to develop a domestic research network that is also capable of absorbing external knowledge from abroad.

In Brazil, passive assimilation of knowledge from international research centers was not a secret. In this chapter, we explain why this Brazilian model was successful. How did restructuring of agricultural research work? What are the limitations? Why did the innovation and learning process continue over the long term? The organization of innovation applied to local conditions has played a central role in the transformation of Brazilian agriculture over the past fifty years.

APPLIED RESEARCH AND PRODUCTIVITY GAINS IN AGRICULTURE: THE CREATION OF EMBRAPA

Both agriculture and industry are part of a broader process ranging from supply to distribution that includes research, scientific application, and technology. Vieira Filho, Campos, and Ferreira[1] and Vieira Filho and Silveira[2] state that technical change increasingly becomes embodied within productive units. Transformation is just as relevant in the agricultural sector as it is in industry, and technological innovation was an impressive part of Brazil's agricultural revolution.

But technological innovation in agriculture differs from that of industry. An illustrative example is germ plasm. Srinivas and Vieira Filho[3] explain that germ plasm is a specific technology exhibiting a complex mix of knowledge and routines. Germ plasm is genetic material that can change relative prices of agricultural inputs (land, labor, and capital) and generate induced innovation, but learning processes and knowledge transfer among regions is less automatic in agriculture than it is within industry.

Climate variation, soil differentiation, and topographic form are root causes of uneven diffusion of knowledge among and within countries. Natural factors account for some of this, but the design of public policies also has a role. When policies define objective strategies for increasing the capacity to absorb external knowledge, gains in technology adaptation and diffusion become noticeable. Brazil, India, and the Philippines all developed internal institutional environments capable of utilizing knowledge generated within international agricultural research networks.

Esposti[4] states that some regions (or countries) act opportunistically as free riders in absorbing the technological content of international research. This greatly reduces the need for investments in learning and technological adaptation. Agricultural producers vary in their degree of absorptive capacity of external knowledge, and they are also affected by climate and geographical diversity. A country's own internal research efforts increase benefits from the spillover effects of international knowledge by stimulating the diffusion of new information.

During the transition from the 1960s to the 1970s, public dispute emerged between two groups, one supporting agrarian reform and the other committed to modernization of agriculture. The former had its roots within the Alliance for Progress, and the latter was dependent on new research. Schultz[5] had shown much earlier that agriculture could be a dynamic sector if it absorbed modern production technologies. Change in traditional agriculture could occur through agrarian reform, but research was key to a new dynamic.

By 1960, Brazil was a net importer of food, including cereals and chicken. Soybean, corn, and beef production were exclusively for domestic consumption. Coffee accounted for more than 50 percent of Brazil's total exports. From the 1970s onward, rapid urbanization, high international prices of agricultural commodities, and dependence on imports were important factors that altered the government's food production strategy. By that time, society understood that what was happening in the countryside also affected cities. Low productivity had general consequences; increasing basic food prices strained urban families' budgets. The central question became how to increase output.

Brazil's response was to create Embrapa in 1973, a case of induced institutional reform à la Hayami and Ruttan. Since then Brazil has been increasing investment in building institutions responsible for absorbing external knowledge and diffusing new technologies locally. The tripod of credit, research, and rural extension was fundamental in leveraging sectoral competitiveness and transferring technology to producers.

Research was financed with national public resources, but decentralized units received the benefits. In 1974, the national system of technical assistance and rural extension was implemented to disseminate techniques and information through state research organizations (known as Ematers). Within this institutional system, Embrapa's main goal was to eliminate the food production shortage. From the outset, the future of Embrapa depended on results.

A CLUSTER OF TECHNOLOGICAL INNOVATIONS AND PRODUCTION GROWTH

Embrapa coordinated agricultural research on a national basis. Success resulted in increased soybean production in the 1980s, livestock growth and grain productivity in the 1990s, and expansion of the agricultural frontier and development of Brazilian agribusiness, including environmental sustainability. The main function of public research was to develop solutions through the generation, adaptation, and transfer of technologies.

Brazil's agricultural transformation demonstrates how local institutions can absorb external knowledge to achieve productivity growth. After the 1970s, agricultural productivity in Brazil increased through a cluster of innovations that correspond to three time periods: prior to 1985, the 1980s and 1990s transition, and post-1990. Two growth patterns can be distinguished during this time, one prior to 1985 and the other after 1985.

The first period, from the early 1970s to the mid-1980s, marks the beginning of the first growth period. Arable land was expanded toward central Brazil, leading to increased grain production (notably soybeans) and to field mechanization. The technique of liming to correct soil acidity transformed the Cerrado biome into a thriving agricultural region. Expansion of the agricultural frontier required soybean seeds that were more tolerant of climate stress and less attractive to insect pests. Biological nitrogen fixation through inoculation of bacteria in soybean seeds permitted increased production with less fertilizer usage.

Eliminating chemical nitrogen fertilization also lowered costs. The agricultural frontier expanded because the marginal price of land remained relatively low. Large-scale mechanization was introduced later in areas with flatter terrain and adequate rainfall.

The second period was characterized by a high demand for grains, influenced by the meat production chain. Growing urbanization and the eventual end of inflation enabled the poor to increase consumption. Barros and Goldenstein[6] explained that consuming more beef, pork, and chicken indirectly increased demand for nutritional inputs (i.e., animal feed), such as soybean meal, corn, and other grains.

In parallel, imported Brachiaria grass improved pasture land, reducing the average age at slaughter, and transformed the Cerrado into a region producing a high cattle yield. This increased the international competitiveness of Brazilian beef exports. Martha, Alves, and Contini[7] showed that the growth of livestock production in Brazil depended heavily on the expansion of the pasture area until 1985. Afterward, growth was based on carcass weight rather than on number of cattle per hectare. Brazil became the number two country in beef exports.

Figure 5.1 shows the increase in share of gross production value from the Center-West region's agricultural production. Large gains were made

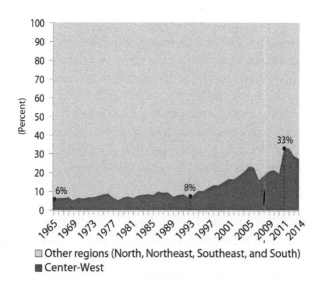

Figure 5.1   Increase in share of gross production value from the Center-West region's agricultural production.

Source: Ipeadata (2015) and IBGE (2015b)—Municipal Agricultural Research.

between 1965 and 2014, increasing gross production value from 6 percent to almost 33 percent, with increases primarily in the 1990s. The Center-West's contribution has been greater than that of the South and Southeast regions since 2011. At the other extreme, the Northeast region was the third producing region in the 1960s but has seen a fall in its contribution, from 24 percent to 13 percent, because it lags in technological development.

The third time period follows from the second wave of increased productivity due to intensification of land use, better production management practices, and the introduction of biotechnology (GMO production and genetic engineering of animals). The intensive use of land permitted two summer crops in the same field each year. Thanks to the shorter soybean cycle from seeds adapted to a tropical climate, another crop can be planted after the first. Most common is corn, but cotton, sorghum, or sunflowers also may become the second crop. Dual planting provides better use of the soil and a national comparative advantage over international competitors.

A second crop also provided feed for raising pigs and chickens. A satisfactory economic return was now possible with this increased production. Final prices for corn were higher in the offseason when fewer supplies were available, and costs were lower because the seed planted was from the previous harvest. Therefore, it was marketed at a lower price. No new investment in fertilizer was required because part of the treatment from the first crop remained in the soil. Figure 5.2 shows that the *safrinha*

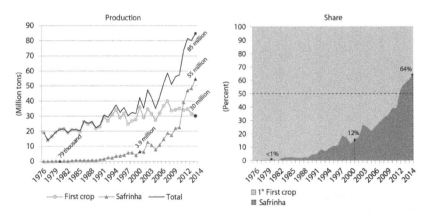

Figure 5.2   Corn production (first crop and safrinha), 1976 to 2014.

Source: Conab (2015).

(small crop) represented less than 1 percent of the total (79,000 tons) in 1980. In 2001, when the production of corn safrinha began to grow rapidly, its share was close to 12 percent (or 3.9 million tons). In 2011, the amount harvested exceeded production of the first crop, and the term *safrinha* no longer described this crop. This plentiful harvest came to be called the second crop, with approximately 54 percent of total production, equivalent to 39 million tons. In 2014, the total production of corn (first and second crops) reached 85 million tons, with the second crop now producing approximately 64 percent of the total.

Since 1990, *no-till farming* has become a fundamental soil preparation technique in Brazil. This reduces the effects of erosion, improves soil attributes, conserves water, and sequesters carbon. Unlike the plowing and grading techniques common to the European experience, no-till farming rapidly developed in Brazil as a competitive advantage. Innovation contributed to natural resource conservation. The fundamental principle is based on not breaking up soil and using a straw cover after harvesting and crop rotation. The objective is to address soil erosion, soil compaction, excessive exposure to the elements during soil preparation, and simultaneously improve the management of water resources and land fertility. Figure 5.3 shows the beginning of the no-till technique in 1973, with 180 hectares planted, but the practice did not intensify until the 1990s.

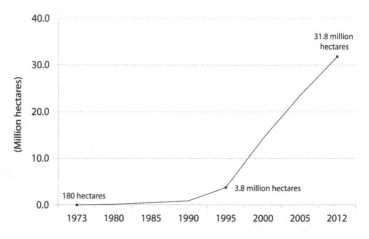

Figure 5.3   Evolution of no-till farming in Brazil, 1973 to 2012 (million hectares).

Source: FEBRAPDP (2015).

In 1995, 3.8 million hectares were planted, and 31.8 million hectares were planted in 2012. The cultivation of soybeans represents about 90 percent of the planted area.

This diffusion of *biotechnology* is the most recent technological advance. Biotechnology aims to improve economic variables (increase productivity and reduce costs) and to reduce the inputs harmful to the environment and human health. In 1997, illegal GMOs were first planted in Brazil (soybeans). At first, the adoption rate was slow. In 2003, genetically modified soybeans were legal but more than 80 percent of the planted area used conventional seeds. In 2005, planting GMO cotton was legalized.

As in Europe, there was local opposition to the use of GMO techniques. This slowed production until 2005, when the biodiversity law was enacted. Subsequently, diffusion increased. Genetically modified corn was authorized in 2008. There was greater diffusion of GMO soybean production due to its scope and scale economies. As for cotton, the absence of these possibilities imposed a longer learning period and less diffusion. Producers reaped direct benefits from GMO production: simplified management, cost reduction, and income gains. In 2014, the area planted with GMO soybean, corn, and cotton varieties was 93 percent, 83 percent, and 67 percent, respectively (figure 5.4). These are high levels compared to international standards.

Biotechnology has permitted advances in animal genetic engineering as well. In 1997, a pig bred with a lower fat content and a higher carcass

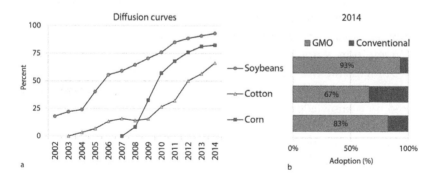

Figure 5.4   Diffusion curves (a) and percentage of adoption (b) of genetically modified soybeans, corn, and cotton planting in Brazil, 2002 to 2014.

Source: Céleres (2014).

weight was developed to respond to market demand. In 2001, the first bovine was cloned in Latin America using practically the same method that resulted in the birth of Dolly the sheep in 1996, the world's first cloned animal. Other achievements included coffee genome sequencing and the development of beans resistant to golden mosaic virus, whose commercial cultivation was approved by the National Technical Biosafety Commission (CTNBio) in 2011.

In recent years, *crop-livestock-forest integration* has been employed to recover areas of degraded pastures. Different productive systems have been introduced in the same area, including those for food, fiber, and energy. The application of appropriate planting techniques and systems improved soil fertility. That made it possible to reduce agrochemical usage, expand areas for agricultural purposes, and minimize environmental liabilities. This diversity reduces the risk of climatic and market losses. Soybeans are the main crop in integrated systems. After the harvest, the pasture provides food for animals during the dry season when forage is scarce. This, in turn, boosts livestock productivity.

Forests can be reconciled with agricultural and livestock activities in the same area. Crop-livestock-forest integration contributes to pest control and carbon storage. For example, in the cattle rearing and fattening phase, the meat yield from degraded pasture is around 30 kg/ha per year, whereas it reaches 450 kg/ha in a pasture recovered by integration systems for the same period and area.

When comparing the amount produced by harvested areas comprising different crops, only soybean and coffee yields doubled until 1985 (figure 5.5), a result that is directly related to the first wave of institutional transformations. After 1985, increase in yields became generalized, with cotton, rice, coffee, soybeans, and corn tripling the amount produced per hectare.

In addition, world urban population surpassed rural population in 2009, increasing the global demand for food. Consumption of animal and vegetable protein also rose. The cluster of innovations detailed here, based on a knowledge network centered in Embrapa, allowed expansion of agricultural areas, productive growth, and increased international competitiveness. Brazilian results were extraordinary. Food production increased more than eightfold while population only doubled.

THE ROLE OF EMBRAPA IN AGRIBUSINESS DEVELOPMENT

As discussed by Alves[8] and Correa and Schmidt,[9] the success of the Embrapa model derives from four characteristics: (i) political

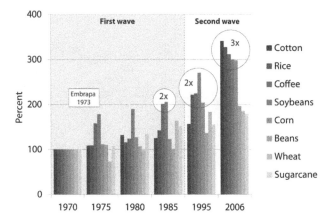

Figure 5.5 **Percentage change in yield (kilograms per hectare) of different crops in Brazil, 1970 to 2006.**

Source: Various agricultural censuses, IBGE (2015).

independence and adequate levels of public funding, (ii) investment in human capital, (iii) development of innovation networks, and (iv) engagement in intellectual property law. The agricultural sector had a specific problem, and the creation of Embrapa represented the solution.

From 1973 to 1982, Embrapa was bold and forward thinking. Staff was hired (for the company's core and complementary activities) and infrastructure investments were made at an average annual cost of R$1.1 billion at 2013 prices. The funds came from the Brazilian government with the understanding that Embrapa would modernize the sector, which was the long-term goal. However, results needed to be seen as rapidly as possible in the short term to justify a contribution of this magnitude. Efficient dissemination of Embrapa's results was fundamental to success, and special attention was given to the company's public relations activities. The direct communication with the presidency and the National Congress, as well as the sector's powerful lobby, was decisive in assuring continuing funding over the next period as well.

Annual costs reached R$1.8 billion. Figure 5.6 shows the evolution of resources invested in three phases: prospect, consolidation, and results. Spending as a share of agriculture GDP increased, especially in the first two phases, consolidation and results. The apex of the series occurred in 1996 at a 1.38 percent budget share. This matched the shares in developed

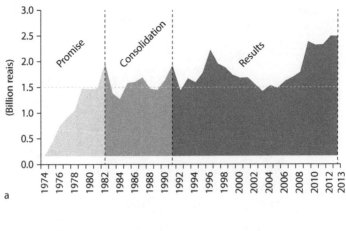

a

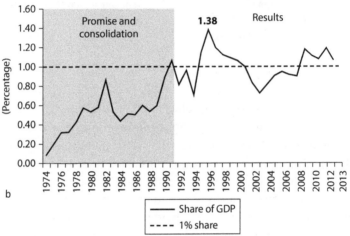

b

Figure 5.6   Government expenditures on Embrapa (a) and its budget share of Brazilian agricultural GDP, 1974 to 2012 (b).

Source: Embrapa/DAF (2015b).
Note: Prices adjusted by the IGP-DI; PLOA + PAC at current values.

countries such as Canada (1.2 percent), the United States (1.4 percent), and Australia (0.8 percent).

Human capital was needed to address specific problems in Brazilian agriculture. There was a similar need to stimulate interaction and cooperation with international research networks. Scientific training focused on researchers at all levels: bachelor's degree, master's degree, and doctorate. Embrapa maintained a graduate (doctoral-focused) program that met domestic

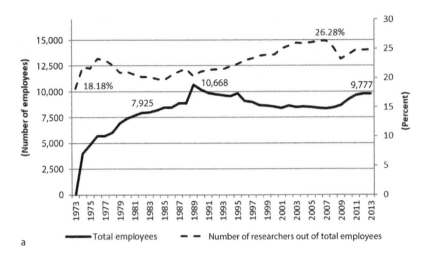

a   ━━━Total employees   ━ ━ Number of researchers out of total employees

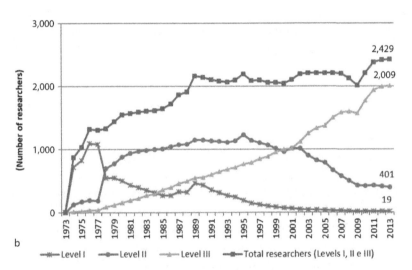

b   ━✳━Level I   ━●━Level II   ━✕━Level III   ━■━Total researchers (Levels I, II e III)

**Figure 5.7   Embrapa's employee and researcher training levels, 1973 to 2013.
(a) Total number of employees versus researchers; (b) qualification of researchers.**

Source: Embrapa/DGP (2015c).

interests but also incorporated the standards of research centers in developed countries. In the first ten years, 20 percent of the institution's total budget was allocated to training and professional improvement. The salary level, in addition to social benefits, was attractive. Merit promotion prevailed. There was notable success in encouraging academic proficiency (figure 5.7).

After 2000, the number of PhD researchers surpassed those with master's degrees. In 2013, the total number of employees was 9,777, including 2,429 researchers. Of the total number of researchers, 83 percent had a doctoral degree.

The third element was development of strategic innovation networks. Collaboration with foreign institutions was fundamental. Embrapa initiated cooperation with the Consultative Group on International Agricultural Research, which most recently contributed to Brazil's relationship with Africa, Latin America, and Asia. Cooperation with the U.S. Department of Agriculture permitted transfer of information on adapting soybean cultivation. In France, agreements were signed with three institutions: the National Institute for Agronomic Research, the Agricultural Research Centre for International Development, and the Research Institute for Development. In Japan, a partnership with the International Research Center for Agricultural Sciences was achieved. In addition, several bilateral cooperation agreements have been implemented, including Inta-Argentina, CSIRO-Australia, BBSRC-UK, Corpoica-Colombia, Inia-Uruguay, and Inia-Chile.

Within this research network, the exchange of germ plasm boosted breeding programs, increasing the yield of crops and forage. Cutting-edge agricultural research could be developed only with an intensive technical and scientific cooperation program. To strengthen relations with U.S. scientists, the first virtual laboratory abroad (Labex) was created in 1990, allowing the exchange of experience and definition of joint work. With the success of this initiative, the project expanded to Europe (2002) with Agropolis International in France, South Korea (2009), and China and Japan (2012). There was an inverse flow of researchers from partner institutions for research activities within Embrapa. The objectives of the program were (i) to generate innovative technologies for Brazilian agriculture, (ii) to promote collaborative research at the frontier of knowledge, (iii) to strengthen multidisciplinary and institutional networks, and (iv) to monitor international trends.

Finally, Embrapa's mission has always been to seek solutions for applied technological development. The organization was based on decentralized research units, but planning was on a national scale. Units were distributed across the country by ecoregional areas, products, and basic themes (figure 5.8). Embrapa's role was not to sell technologies and compete with the private sector. The public sector had a regulatory role. Embrapa's function was to produce inputs and genetic material that would stimulate

Figure 5.8   Number of Embrapa's ecoregional units, products, and basic themes.

Source: Embrapa (2015a).

Note: The figures identify the number of Embrapa units in each state.

the market to disseminate technologies. Embrapa works with the private sector when necessary to conduct high-risk and long-term strategic research on crop maturation. Embrapa also works to avoid conflicts of interest, such as the development of a crop that reduces the use of highly profitable agrochemicals or even the development of research in areas without immediate market interest.

In the 1990s, the National Agricultural Research System (SNPA) was established, comprising Embrapa (forty-six decentralized units and

Table 5.1 Number of Protected Varieties in Brazil's SNPC (1998–2016)

Protected Varieties by Products	Protected Varieties over Time									
	1998	2000	2002	2004	2006	2008	2010	2012	2014	2016
Total varieties (a)										
Soybeans	64	145	207	312	406	464	568	700	774	769
Wheat	7	27	39	67	84	90	104	134	140	131
Sugarcane	7	26	41	52	72	83	97	117	113	107
Cotton	1	13	31	48	57	61	66	67	76	70
Corn	2	19	27	31	50	42	53	52	50	36
Coffee	0	0	0	1	6	7	7	9	17	17
Others*	23	59	112	249	385	608	822	1004	1133	1082
Total	**104**	**289**	**457**	**760**	**1060**	**1355**	**1717**	**2083**	**2303**	**2212**
Embrapa Varieties (b)										
Soybeans	18	51	72	99	131	141	163	178	172	171
Wheat	3	9	13	21	33	35	37	43	45	42
Sugarcane	0	0	0	0	0	0	0	0	0	0
Cotton	0	6	12	20	21	24	26	28	31	26
Corn	2	17	24	25	27	28	42	44	42	28
Coffee	0	0	0	0	0	0	0	1	1	1
Others*	7	18	34	55	67	82	126	162	191	216
Total	**30**	**101**	**155**	**220**	**279**	**310**	**394**	**456**	**482**	**484**
Embrapa Participation (b/a)										
Soybeans	28.1	35.2	34.8	31.7	32.3	30.4	28.7	25.4	22.2	22.2
Wheat	42.9	33.3	33.3	31.3	39.3	38.9	35.6	32.1	32.1	32.1
Sugarcane	—	—	—	—	—	—	—	—	—	—
Cotton	—	46.2	38.7	41.7	36.8	39.3	39.4	41.8	40.8	37.1
Corn	100.0	89.5	88.9	80.6	54.0	66.7	79.2	84.6	84.0	77.8
Coffee	—	—	—	—	—	—	—	11.1	5.9	5.9
Others*	30.4	30.5	30.4	22.1	17.4	13.5	15.3	16.1	16.9	20.0
Total percentage	**28.8**	**34.9**	**33.9**	**28.9**	**26.3**	**22.9**	**22.9**	**21.9**	**20.9**	**21.9**

Source: Developed by the authors, with SNPC data (2016).

*Includes vegetables, flowers, fruits, and grains of lesser importance in terms of productive value.

sixteen offices), state research organizations, universities, and other public and private institutions working in agriculture. It sought to align agricultural research with development policies, eliminating overlap and inefficient resource allocation. Vieira Filho and Vieira have shown that the role of scientific research in the development of agricultural varieties changed significantly after the promulgation of the Varieties Protection Law in Brazil in 1997.[10]

Table 5.1 presents information on the number of protected varieties in the National System of Varieties Protection (SNPC) organized by product. From 1998 to 2016, the number of protected varieties in Brazil rose from 104 to 2,212. For soybeans, there were 64 protected varieties in 1998 and 769 by 2016, with 22 percent owned by Embrapa. Of the 171 soybean varieties protected by Embrapa, 76 were GMO varieties. Embrapa plays an important role for other varieties as well: corn (78 percent), cotton (37 percent), and wheat (32 percent).

Innovation in the sector has been continuous. The mechanisms protecting intellectual property are essential in the organization and management of agribusiness knowledge and innovation, strengthening both public and private research.

From 2000 onward, the seed industry underwent restructuring. By 2016, several companies had become important players in specific crop improvement programs. Figure 5.9 illustrates the five largest companies

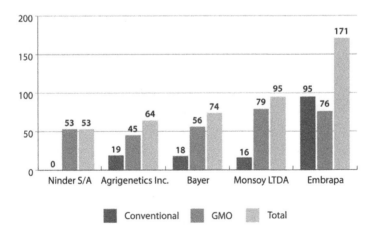

Figure 5.9   Number of protected soybean varieties, both conventional and GMO, distributed by the main holders.

Source: Authors' own work, with National System of Varieties Protection data (2016).

in the area of genetic improvement (conventional and GMO) in the soybean market, according to SNPC data.

Dissemination of technology by public research institutions—with Embrapa central to this process—has only been partially achieved in Brazil because producers have access to markets and can also access technical assistance and rural extension. Underequipped farmers remain on the sidelines of the agricultural modernization. Large producers buy inputs at a lower price and sell their products at a higher value. Small-scale producers pay a high price for inputs and sell their output at lower prices. It is to these inequalities that we now turn.

CHAPTER 6

The Competitiveness of Agribusiness in International Trade

Progressive globalization has characterized world trade since the 1960s. First effects occurred in the developed countries, which was soon followed by the Asian countries of South Korea, Taiwan, Hong Kong, and Singapore. Brazil had high tariffs and quotas on imports of manufactured products and saw a decline in trade participation and an increased focus on domestic markets.

By the late 1980s, matters had begun to change in Brazil. Trade protections began to loosen, and this liberalization continued with further elimination of barriers during the Collor presidency. Mercosul took shape with neighboring countries seeking to expand market access, principally in manufacturing. Since 1994, the Real Plan to end chronic and rising inflation has prevailed. Earlier efforts, including the Cruzado Plan and other attempts to slow the increases, all failed. With more price stability and increasing productivity in the agricultural sector, an important beneficiary of this new macroeconomic environment was the primary sector. Brazil became one of the bulwarks of commodity trade, along with the United States and the European Union.

GATT had given way to the World Trade Organization (WTO), and trade and foreign investment expanded. A growing demand for food,[1] fiber, and energy[2] emerged on a global scale. Brazil's participation in the international market was determined by a combination of the development of technology, the availability of arable land, and sustained productivity growth.

The rise in Brazilian agribusiness owing to international trade is the focus of this chapter. First, we consider how many individual crops fared, both in production and sales abroad, from the 1990s to the present.

We use a constant market share model to analyze export growth from four sources: (i) world trade growth, (ii) the commodity effect, (iii) the market effect, and (iv) the competitive effect. Brazilian success occurred during four subperiods due not only to strong global demand but also through gains in competitiveness.

GLOBAL EXPANSION IN THE FIRST DECADE OF THE TWENTY-FIRST CENTURY

Increased economic growth in China, India, and Brazil led to the inclusion of their own consumers in the global market. Other countries likewise contributed to a growing demand for food. As a consequence, food producers increasingly escaped the extreme poverty in which they had been enmeshed. Competition for scarce resources (oil and arable land) increased.

With the U.S. invasion of Iraq in 2003, the world's potential oil supply narrowed. Higher oil prices were related, on one hand, to the increase in demand and, on the other, to the contraction in the supply of oil and its derivatives. Modern agriculture is energy intensive, so the price of oil directly affects farmers' costs. In addition, mainly in regard to corn production,[3] a positive association of higher oil prices with biofuel prices was observed. Increases in food prices were thereby linked to increases in energy prices. Figure 6.1 shows the correlation between food and oil prices.

Moreover, agricultural subsidies from developed countries (United States and in Europe) limited supply from countries with more efficient production such as Brazil and Argentina. This prevented distribution of cheaper products on the international market. Tariff and nontariff barriers further reduced the global competitiveness of primary products.

Finally, global agricultural production has been directly affected by climate change. Greenhouse gas emissions coming mostly from developed regions have continued. The United States did not sign the Kyoto Protocol in 1997 seeking to curtail these emissions. Although China, India, and Brazil ratified that protocol, these developing countries were not required to issue control reports until the Rio + 20 Conference in 2012. Thereafter, in Copenhagen and Paris, a more serious response, no longer requiring ratification, took form.

Only the European Union sought to meet the earlier agreed-upon targets, but their results fell short. Throughout the 2000s, adverse climate

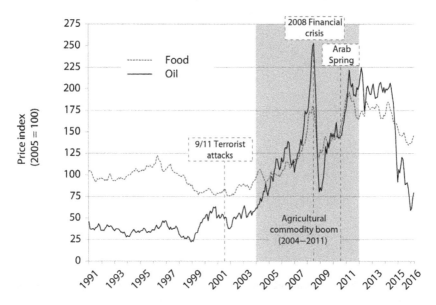

Figure 6.1   Global food and oil price indices, 1991 to 2016.

Source: IMF (2016).

conditions such as prolonged droughts and extreme cold weather in Russia, Kazakhstan, Canada, Australia, and Argentina reduced production of grain exports. In 2016, in Paris, the world went further, seeking to more fully incorporate the developing countries while setting objectives more realistically. Unfortunately, the United States has withdrawn from the Paris Accords and abdicated its leadership. However, the most recent international meeting in Poland made positive advances.

Figure 6.2 presents an analysis of global grain supply and demand from 1998 to 2011. The stocks-to-use ratio indicates the level of carryover stock as a percentage of total demand. By adding carryover stocks to total production, total supply is the sum of all end uses, including food consumption, export programs, seeds, and wastes, and provides the year-end carryover stock. The relationship between carryover stock and total demand indicates whether current and projected inventory levels are critical or abundant.

This ratio can also be used to indicate how many days of supply are available to the world marketplace under current usage. The smaller the indicator, the less the capacity of the existing stock to meet demand conditions. In the period we focus on in this chapter, grain stocks were

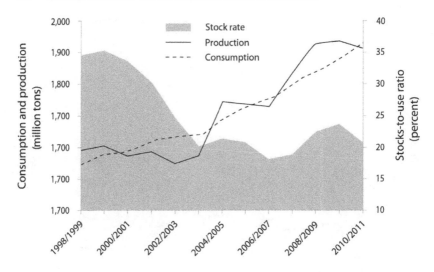

Figure 6.2   Supply, demand, and quantity of grain stocks in the world, 1998 to 2011.

Source: World Bank (2011).

reduced to historically low levels. This can be explained by several factors: (i) the growth of food demand, which surpassed the growth of production; (ii) the impact of climate change on production, leading to restrictions on export of grains; and (iii) the greater share of grain exports from nontraditional markets, such as Latin America, whose production was more variable than that of traditional OECD exporters.

Brazilian primary exports achieved a growth rate of 19 percent, a result associated with the boom in global commodity markets since 2004 with rising prices of agricultural goods. Although the macroeconomic environment was unfavorable due to exchange rate appreciation in the same period, the moment was opportune for increasing investments and, consequently, increasing productivity with only a small negative effect on the upward trajectory of agricultural exports.

OVERVIEW OF BRAZILIAN AGRIBUSINESS IN THE INTERNATIONAL CONTEXT

Table 6.1 shows value added as a proportion of GDP for the agricultural, industrial, and service sectors. The GDP share of agriculture has been declining in all analyzed countries. Although the domestic share of

Table 5.1 Value Added by Agriculture, Industry, and Services Sectors in GDP and Growth Rates for Selected Periods (1992–2013)

Value-added (% of GDP)	Regions	1992	1994	1999	2008	2013	Rate of Geometric Growth			
							1992–1994	1994–1999	1999–2008	2008–2013
Agriculture	World	..	..	4.3	3.1	3.1	..	..	-3.7	0.4
	Middle-income countries	17.8	17.0	14.3	10.2	10.0	-2.5	-3.3	-3.7	-0.4
	Low-income countries	41.4	41.2	37.8	33.5	32.4	-0.3	-1.7	-1.3	-0.7
	High-income countries	..	..	2.0	1.5	1.6	..	..	-3.4	1.3
	Brazil	7.7	9.9	5.3	5.4	5.6	13.0	-11.5	0.1	0.8
	Argentina	5.9	5.5	4.8	7.2	7.3	-4.0	-2.67	4.61	0.42
	China	21.4	19.5	16.1	10.3	9.4	-4.5	-3.8	-4.8	-1.9
	India	28.7	28.3	24.5	17.8	18.6	-0.8	-2.8	-3.5	0.9
	Russia	7.4	6.6	7.3	4.4	4.0	-5.3	2.0	-5.5	-1.8
	United States	..	..	1.2	1.1	1.5	..	..	-0.3	4.9
Industry	World	..	..	28.9	28.0	26.4	..	..	-0.4	-1.2
	Middle-income countries	36.0	37.1	35.4	37.5	35.1	1.6	-1.0	0.6	-1.3
	Low-income countries	17.9	17.0	19.6	21.0	21.3	-2.5	2.9	0.8	0.2
	High-income countries	..	..	27.6	26.0	24.5	..	..	-0.6	-1.2
	Brazil	38.7	40.0	24.8	27.4	24.4	1.7	-9.1	1.1	-2.3
	Argentina	30.6	29.0	28.2	33.1	28.7	-2.7	-0.5	1.7	-2.7
	China	43.0	46.1	45.3	46.8	43.7	3.5	-0.4	0.4	-1.4
	India	25.8	26.4	25.2	28.3	30.5	1.2	-0.9	1.3	1.5
	Russia	43.01	44.72	37.2	36.1	36.0	1.97	-3.6	-0.3	-0.1
	United States	..	..	23.3	21.6	20.5	..	..	-0.8	-1.1
Services	World	..	..	66.8	69.0	70.5	..	..	0.4	0.4
	Middle-income countries	46.2	45.91	50.3	52.3	54.8	-0.3	1.8	0.4	0.9
	Low-income countries	40.76	41.86	42.7	45.5	46.4	1.3	0.4	0.7	0.4
	High-income countries	..	..	70.4	72.5	73.9	..	..	0.3	0.4
	Brazil	53.6	50.2	69.8	67.2	70.0	-3.3	6.8	-0.4	0.8
	Argentina	63.3	65.4	66.8	59.6	63.8	1.6	0.4	-1.2	1.3
	China	35.6	34.4	38.6	42.9	46.9	-1.7	2.4	1.2	1.8
	India	45.5	45.3	50.3	53.9	50.9	-0.2	2.1	0.8	-1.2
	Russia	49.6	48.7	55.5	59.5	60.0	-1.0	2.7	0.8	0.2
	United States	..	..	75.5	77.2	78.1	..	..	0.3	0.2

Source: World Bank, "World Bank Indicators," 2016, https://data.worldbank.org/indicator.

agriculture was falling, manufacture of primary products plays an important role in the production process; this newer activity is counted as part of the industrial sector. Moreover, the service sector also now plays a relevant role, especially in high-income countries.

One must understand the dynamic interaction among sectors, especially within industry and agriculture, in addition to considering the weight of research and innovation in increased productivity. Much of the technological development applied to the agricultural sector is developed abroad. As economies become more complex and diversified, it is necessary to distinguish between contributions of different sectors within the production chain. In recent decades, the greater demand for agricultural technologies produced by industry has contributed to a boost in global food production.

Agribusiness is part of a productive chain that includes inputs, production, transformation, and final consumption. This chain involves activities from research and technical assistance to industrial processing and manufacturing, transportation, marketing, credit, export, port services, and distribution.[4]

Table 6.2 shows GDP per capita from 1992 to 2013, together with the urbanization rate and population size for several countries and regions. GDP per capita has grown substantially in middle-income countries and in emerging economies such as Brazil, China, and India. The world's urban population reached 50.5 percent in 2008. In middle- and low-income countries, the rural population is quite significant, but the growth of urbanization continues on an upward path.

Demographic data show that the global demand for food has been growing significantly due to an increasingly urban population and expanding industrial production that requires raw materials that must be imported. In relation to the dynamics of income, consumption, and production,[5] consumption is growing rapidly in China and far beyond its own production capacity. According to Figueiredo and Contini,[6] a similar growth pattern is happening with India, whose population may soon surpass that of China.

Table 6.3 presents economic indicators for the agricultural sector. Brazil and Argentina had the greatest increase in arable land, and emerging countries showed the highest growth in agricultural crops and livestock. In Brazil, the agricultural production index in 2013 was around 140, the second highest, just behind India. Brazil stands out among all analyzed countries in terms of land and labor productivity. For example, from

GDP per Capita, Urbanization Rate, and Total Population (1992–2013)

Indicators	Regions and countries	1992	1994	1999	2008	2013	Rate of Geometric Growth (RGG) 1992–1994	1994–1999	1999–2008	2008–2013
GDP per capita (constant 2005–US$)	World	5861.2	5959.5	6494.8	7649.6	7907.8	0.8	1.7	1.8	0.7
	Middle-income countries	1156.8	1227.1	1408.0	2151.9	2655.2	3.0	2.8	4.8	4.3
	Low-income countries	284.1	271.6	288.5	345.8	407.4	-2.2	1.2	2.0	3.3
	High-income countries	22428.0	23012.8	25818.2	30379.4	30759.1	1.3	2.3	1.8	0.3
	Brazil	3893.9	4162.3	4285.9	5303.0	5896.1	3.4	0.6	2.4	2.1
	Argentina	4806.7	5246.9	5502.4	6596.5	7708.3	4.4	0.9	2.0	3.1
	China	565.6	712.3	1048.3	2415.9	3619.5	12.2	8.0	9.7	8.4
	India	411.9	442.5	560.8	868.6	1164.3	3.7	4.9	5.0	6.0
	Russia	4601.5	3683.1	3503.8	6612.6	6922.8	-10.5	-1.0	7.3	0.9
	United States	33230.5	34628.9	39776.1	44861.4	45660.7	2.1	2.8	1.4	0.4
Urbanization rate (% of total)	World	43.6	44.3	46.2	50.5	52.9	0.8	0.8	1.0	1.0
	Middle-income countries	35.7	36.8	39.4	45.2	48.4	1.4	1.4	1.5	1.4
	Low-income countries	22.7	23.3	24.6	27.4	29.4	1.3	1.1	1.2	1.4
	High-income countries	75.3	75.7	76.7	79.3	80.5	0.3	0.3	0.4	0.3
	Brazil	75.4	76.9	80.5	83.8	85.2	1.0	0.9	0.4	0.3
	Argentina	87.5	87.9	88.9	90.6	91.4	0.2	0.2	0.4	0.1
	China	28.2	30.0	34.9	46.5	53.2	3.2	3.0	3.3	2.7
	India	26.0	26.4	27.5	30.3	32.0	0.8	0.8	1.1	1.1
	Russia	73.4	73.4	73.4	73.6	73.9	0.0	0.0	0.0	0.1
	United States	76.1	76.9	78.7	80.4	81.3	0.5	0.5	0.2	0.2
Total population (million)	World	5453.3	5621.0	6035.5	6759.0	7174.5	1.5	1.4	1.3	1.2
	Middle-income countries	3891.6	4022.4	4344.2	4879.2	5178.5	1.7	1.6	1.3	1.2
	Low-income countries	342.1	362.1	414.7	529.1	605.5	2.9	2.8	2.7	2.7
	High-income countries	1219.6	1236.5	1276.6	1350.6	1390.6	0.7	0.6	0.6	0.6
	Brazil	155.4	160.3	173.2	194.8	204.3	1.6	1.6	1.3	1.0
	Argentina	33.6	34.5	36.6	40.3	42.5	1.3	1.1	1.0	1.0
	China	1165.0	1191.8	1252.7	1324.7	1357.4	1.2	1.0	0.6	0.5
	India	906.5	942.6	1035.0	1197.1	1279.5	2.0	1.9	1.6	1.3
	Russia	148.7	148.3	147.2	142.7	143.5	-0.1	-0.2	-0.3	0.1
	United States	256.5	263.1	279.0	304.1	316.5	1.3	1.2	1.0	0.8

Source: World Bank (2016).

Table 6.3 Economic Indicators for the Agricultural Sector for Several Countries and Regions of the World (1992–2013)

Indicators	Regions and countries	1992	1994	1999	2008	2013	Rate of Geometric Growth			
							1992–1994	1994–1999	1999–2008	2008–2013
Arable land (million hectares)	Brazil	51.8	52.8	57.8	70.3	76.0	0.9	1.8	2.2	1.6
	China	122.9	120.7	119.3	108.1	105.7	-0.9	-0.2	-1.1	-0.5
	India	162.7	162.5	161.0	158.0	157.0	-0.1	-0.2	-0.2	-0.1
	Argentina	26.7	26.9	27.5	35.2	39.6	0.3	0.3	2.7	2.3
	Russia	132.0	128.4	125.0	121.7	122.2	-1.4	-0.5	-0.3	0.1
	United States	184.1	181.9	175.4	161.8	151.8	-0.6	-0.7	-0.9	-1.3
Index of agricultural production (2004–2006 = 100)	World	72.5	74.8	85.9	110.2	125.1	1.6	2.8	2.8	2.6
	Middle-income countries	66.3	69.8	82.6	113.2	131.2	2.6	3.4	3.6	3.0
	Low-income countries	71.0	72.1	82.8	110.9	138.1	0.8	2.8	3.3	4.5
	High-income countries	88.6	87.7	94.6	102.7	108.2	-0.5	1.5	0.9	1.1
	Brazil	63.9	68.1	75.7	121.8	140.3	3.3	2.2	5.4	2.9
	Argentina	59.9	59.6	82.0	113.7	127.9	1.4	6.5	3.6	2.0
	China	57.8	63.4	80.8	114.7	133.6	4.7	5.0	4.0	3.1
	India	77.2	82.3	94.4	117.5	141.9	3.2	2.8	2.5	3.8
	Russia	100.4	78.6	68.4	112.8	115.7	-11.5	-2.8	5.7	0.5
	United States	87.0	93.3	92.1	101.1	108.7	3.6	-0.3	1.0	1.5
Livestock production index (2004–2006 = 100)	World	76.0	79.4	88.1	108.3	117.1	2.2	2.1	2.3	1.6
	Middle-income countries	61.6	67.7	80.6	111.7	125.7	4.9	3.5	3.7	2.4
	Low-income countries	70.1	69.7	83.5	110.3	122.4	-0.3	3.7	3.1	2.1
	High-income countries	94.4	94.4	97.8	104.0	106.2	0.0	0.7	0.7	0.4
	Brazil	51.6	56.5	74.1	111.5	127.5	4.6	5.6	4.6	2.7
	Argentina	81.1	89.4	94.9	107.6	110.6	5.0	1.1	1.4	0.5
	China	48.0	59.3	79.3	111.8	126.5	11.1	6.0	3.9	2.5
	India	63.9	68.4	82.5	114.6	135.2	3.5	3.8	3.7	3.4
	Russia	158.8	137.7	96.0	109.4	122.4	-6.9	-7.0	1.5	2.3
	United States	82.9	87.0	95.8	106.8	107.7	2.4	2.0	1.2	0.2

Land productivity
(kg per hectare)

World	2777.4	2812.6	3105.7	3548.2	3851.3	0.6	2.0	1.5	1.7
Middle-income countries	2530.8	2582.2	2893.1	3383.9	3711.0	1.0	2.3	1.8	1.9
High-income countries	1078.3	1096.6	1195.6	1317.5	1580.6	0.8	1.7	1.1	3.7
	3569.0	3635.7	4025.9	4551.8	4929.9	0.9	2.1	1.4	1.6
Brazil	2142.5	2284.4	2721.0	3830.8	4826.4	3.3	3.6	3.9	4.7
Argentina	3057.3	2816.0	3351.5	3906.8	4724.7	-4.0	3.5	1.7	3.8
China	4362.5	4504.9	4944.9	5547.6	5891.4	1.6	1.9	1.3	1.2
India	2024.8	2115.5	2313.7	2637.9	2961.6	2.2	1.8	1.5	2.3
Russia	1743.2	1457.6	1452.6	2387.3	2240.1	-8.6	-0.1	5.7	-1.3
United States	5360.6	5563.4	5733.0	6620.0	7340.4	1.9	0.6	1.6	2.1

Labor productivity
(constant 2005 US$)

World	837.2	827.7	1037.6	1251.7	1406.3	-0.6	4.6	2.1	2.4
Middle-income countries	587.5	605.9	674.9	886.1	1053.3	1.6	2.2	3.1	3.5
Low-income countries	252.1	242.5	263.9	287.4	309.6	-1.9	1.7	1.0	1.5
High-income countries	..	..	14258.8	20412.5	24508.8	..	..	4.1	3.7
Brazil	1732.5	1902.0	2369.8	4069.9	5296.8	4.8	4.5	6.2	5.4
Argentina	7455.3	8449.8	9861.3	11358.9	12438	6.4	3.1	1.5	1.8
China	333.9	359.5	429.0	602.1	754.1	3.8	3.6	3.8	4.6
India	464.8	487.5	533.8	621.8	714.9	2.4	1.8	1.7	2.8
Russia	3669.2	3305.2	3268.4	5482.3	6342.4	-5.1	-0.2	5.9	3.0
United States	..	..	32977.1	52447.4	69456.8	..	..	5.3	5.8

Source: World Bank (2016).

1999–2008, during the commodities boom, Brazil displayed the highest labor productivity increase, around 6.2 percent. From 2008 to 2013, Brazil achieved the highest land productivity growth rate among the analyzed regions at 4.7 percent.

Technologies significantly affect productivity in the Brazilian agricultural chain. The most important ones are new genetic materials and forage; soil fertility management, biological nitrogen fixation, conservation practices such as no-tillage systems, and expansion of irrigation systems in the field. More recent additions include crop rotation and crop-livestock-forest integration systems.

Brazilian researchers, especially those at Embrapa and the universities, have focused on Brazil's specific characteristics. This perspective created technological packages that are adapted for the country, and production has expanded from the South to the Center-West, North, and part of the Northeast, mainly toward the Cerrado in the region of Matopiba.[7]

Until the mid-1990s, the domestic market primarily drove Brazilian agriculture and livestock. In the last twenty years, Brazil has directed a growing portion of agricultural products to foreign markets.[8] The government's macroeconomic adjustment policies directly influenced agribusiness exports. Brazilian exports were boosted by inflationary control measures implemented in 1994 and the fixed exchange rate regime in 1999.[9] Since 2000, several factors have worked in favor of Brazil's agricultural sector but have negatively affected other sectors when considering the positive trade balance. The government enacted macroeconomic adjustments and changes in agricultural policy while at the same time investing in technology. External factors, such as the increase in GDP per capita and the urban population in middle-income countries, also help to explain this shift.

Brazil directs 80 percent of its production to the domestic market and exports to more than 180 countries, making it a key player in international agriculture. Its largest trading partners are the European Union, China, the United States, Japan, Russia, and Saudi Arabia.[10] An agribusiness chain grew rapidly. In 1994, agribusiness GDP was estimated at R$728 million and in 2013, this amount reached around R$1 billion.[11] The balance of international agribusiness trade (exports minus imports) increased from approximately US$11 billion in 1989 to US$82.9 billion in 2013, corresponding to an annual growth rate of 8.8 percent (figure 6.3).

In 2013, Brazil's overall trade balance was only US$2.6 billion, and it became negative in 2014. For agribusiness, the balance has been positive,

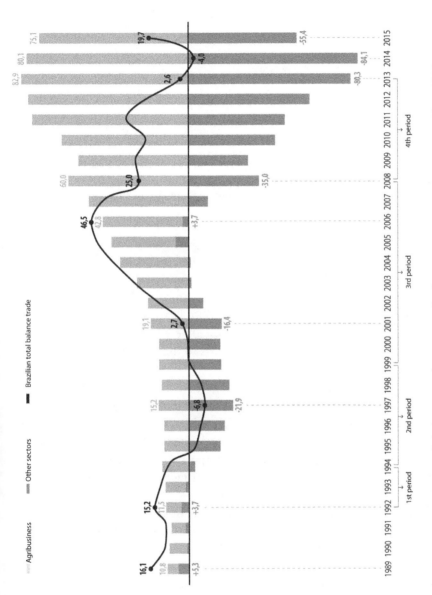

Figure 6.3 Brazilian trade balance, agribusiness, and other economic activity sectors, 1989 to 2015 (in billions of dollars).

Source: Conab (2015).

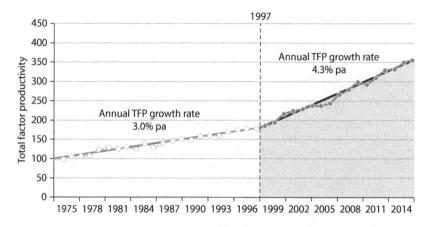

Figure 6.4   Evolution of total factor productivity in Brazil, 1975 to 2014.

Source: José Garcia Gasques et al. (2016).

increasing each year since 2000. It reached a surplus of more than US$80 billion in 2014. At the same time, other sectors of the economy followed an opposite path, with a deficit of approximately US$84 billion. In the domestic economic recession in 2015, Brazil imported less, reaching a surplus of around US$19.7 billion. These numbers highlight the importance of Brazil's agricultural exports to the macroeconomic stability of the country.

There was a structural change in the growth of total factor productivity (TFP) in 1997. These results are shown in figure 6.4. The TFP grew at a rate of 3 percent a year between 1975 and 1997, but 4.3 percent thereafter. From 1997 to 2014, expansion accelerated to 4.3 percent per year. The growth of the Chinese economy, important for all emerging countries, accelerated import of foodstuffs, boosting the demand and, with it, the productivity of agricultural suppliers.

In 2000, China imported only $0.5 billion, or 3 percent, of Brazil's total agricultural exports. In 2018, China imported almost US$20.5 billion, or 22 percent, while becoming the major market. The EU was second in 2013 with US$18.3 billion, or 20 percent. The United States imported only $4.6 billion. Brazilian agricultural exports are expected to increase in the future, probably with lower rates. With the recovery of developed countries in recent years, the Brazilian real depreciated, thereby assisting exports.

BRAZIL'S POSITION IN WORLD AGRICULTURAL
PRODUCTION AND EXPORTS

Table 6.4 shows Brazil's ranking in global production as well as exports. In 2013, Brazil was the global leader in the production of coffee, sugarcane, sugar, and oranges. In the same year, Brazil became a world leader in exporting soybeans, coffee, sugar, orange juice, and beef and chicken.

Brazil surpassed the United States as the world's largest soybean exporter in 2013. To illustrate this growth, the export value of soybeans was about US$808 million in 1992, and in 2013 this value rose to US$22 billion.[12] China is the leader in soybean imports.

In addition, demand for vegetable oils for human consumption, biofuels, and animal feed is increasing in emerging countries. North Africa, the Middle East, and Asia have been investing in raw material processing equipment. This region is likely to import a greater volume of soybeans in the future.

In 1992, Brazil ranked fifty-second among corn-exporting countries. In 2013, Brazil moved up to second position. Over the past thirty-five years, this crop has undergone major changes, with production increasing by 66.9 million tons, equivalent to an increase of 478 percent from 1977 to 2013 harvests. This increase in corn production was made

Table 6.4 Brazil's Position in the World Ranking of Agricultural Production and Exports (1992–2013)

Products	Production					Exports				
	1992	1994	1999	2008	2013	1992	1994	1999	2008	2013
Soybeans	2°	2°	2°	2°	2°	2°	2°	2°	2°	1°
Corn	3°	3°	3°	3°	3°	52°	39°	31°	4°	2°
Cotton	6°	7°	8°	5°	5°	25°	56°	48°	2°	4°
Coffee beans	1°	1°	1°	1°	1°	2°	1°	1°	1°	1°
Roasted coffee	-	-	-	-	-	21°	37°	34°	20°	30°
Wheat	28°	32°	29°	22°	23°	-	73°	50°	22°	17°
Sugarcane	1°	1°	1°	1°	1°	-	-	-	-	-
Raw sugar	2°	1°	1°	1°	1°	5°	3°	1°	1°	1°
Refined sugar	-	-	-	-	-	6°	6°	2°	1°	1°
Oranges	1°	1°	1°	1°	1°	14°	13°	17°	20°	26°
Orange juice	-	-	-	-	-	1°	1°	1°	1°	1°
Boneless beef	2°	2°	2°	2°	2°	8°	9°	10°	1°	1°
Poultry meat	4°	3°	3°	3°	3°	4°	4°	2°	1°	1°
Pork	12°	7°	5°	5°	5°	12°	11°	27°	11°	16°

Source: Faostat (2015).

possible by growing two different crops in the same year, a practice introduced by farmers in the late 1970s. Initially, the second corn crop was modest. Thanks to a genetic improvement in soybeans, which shortened that crop's life cycle, the second harvest season lengthened. In some Brazilian regions, corn production in the second crop exceeded the volume of the first crop.

Brazil's position in cotton has also improved over time. In the 1990s, this sector experienced difficulties. A U.S. credit program for cotton consumers and exporters led to lower international prices. In 2009, Brazil won its case against the United States at the WTO and was permitted to retaliate against American products. In 2010, the United States signed a compensation agreement that allocated US$147.3 million to the Brazilian Cotton Institute. This institution was created to manage the proceeds of the agreement to promote and strengthen the segment. In 2013, the sector ranked fourth among the largest exporters, but Brazilian cotton exports between 2013–14 and 2023–24 are expected to more than double,[13] making Brazil the country most likely to increase exports over the next ten years.

Coffee production has been an important part of the Brazilian economy since the nineteenth century. Brazil is a leader both in production and exports, and coffee's contribution to the trade balance is significant. Exports of roasted coffee fell short of the desired level and ranked only thirtieth in 2013. Germany re-exports much of the imported Brazilian grain in the form of fine, industrialized coffee with greater added value.

In the wheat market, Brazil is the twenty-third producer and the seventeenth exporter in the world. Cereals are one of the main raw materials of Brazilian industry and remain the second-largest item among imports, behind only the petroleum chain. Brazil has not yet achieved self-sufficiency, and Argentina has continued to be a major supplier. Limits to domestic wheat production include the fragility of production, storage bottlenecks, and high production costs. In 2013, wheat imports reached US$17.1 billion and accounted for 7.3 million tons.

Brazil is a major producer of sugarcane, thanks to a favorable climate with sufficient rainfall, and is the main producer and exporter of sugar. During the 2012–13 harvest, 588.5 million tons of sugarcane, 38.2 million tons of sugar, and 23.2 billion liters of ethanol were produced. Most of the ethanol produced is consumed in the domestic market. Ethanol exports are residual, varying with the global price of sugar.

Brazil is also the largest producer of oranges and the largest exporter of orange juice in the world. The export of ready-to-drink juices represents

43 percent of the sector's business. The industrial sector is made up of modern and advanced factories, and production is almost totally directed at the foreign market. Export of oranges, however, are less competitive. Fresh fruit exports depend on low price and high quality, requirements that most Brazilian exporters do not meet. From 2008 to 2011, the volume of fresh fruit exports declined at an average rate of 7.2 percent.

Brazil's participation in the global meat market is also quite high. Beef production remained in second place in the worldwide ranking in the period. As of 2008, Brazil ranked first in boneless beef exports. The availability of land, which makes it possible to enlarge production, is one of the competitive advantages for Brazil. Genetic engineering has also contributed to increased productivity.

In poultry production, Brazil ranked fourth in 1992. In following years, the country moved up to third place. Exported chicken output accounted for US$436 million in 1992, and by 2013 exports reached US$6 billion, making Brazil the largest exporter of chicken in the world. Large companies and several cooperatives have invested in this sector since 1998, generating surplus production. As a result, Brazil has become the world's main supplier of poultry to more than 140 countries. Brazil has been able to sustain its position due to the quality of the national product and its strict sanitary control program.

Brazil has been increasing its production of pork in the global market. In 1992, Brazil was the twelfth-largest producer, but it reached fifth place in 2013, earning its place among the world's largest producers. Pork exports, however, are just sixteenth in the ranking. Barriers on pork exports are due to sanitary requirements and these other factors: (1) a concentration of Brazilian exports in markets that until recently were still signing unilateral or short-term contracts (Russia and China), and (2) competition with the United States and the European Union, both with diversified markets and stable long-term markets in Japan and South Korea.

DETERMINANTS OF BRAZILIAN AGRIBUSINESS EXPORT GROWTH

The constant market share (CMS) method analyzes the factors that contribute to the export performance of a country or economic bloc in relation to the rest of the world or to specific foreign markets in a given period.

In its simplified and general form, the CMS[14] method defines a country's market share as the quantity exported divided by total global exports (variables expressed in monetary values), which is, in turn, a function of relative competitiveness.

$$\frac{dq}{dt} \equiv S\frac{dQ}{dt} + Q\frac{dS}{dt} = S\frac{dQ}{dt} + Qf'\left(\frac{d(c/C)}{dt}\right)$$

The total variation of the exported quantity from country $(\dot{q})$ is described by the effect of global export growth $(S\dot{Q})$ and by the competitiveness effect $(Q\dot{S})$. The first effect represents the change in exports when market share is kept constant, and the second effect provides additional export growth attributed to changes in relative competitiveness.

Accordingly, total trade growth $(\sum_i \sum_j S_{ij}\dot{Q}_{ij})$ can be further decomposed:

$$\dot{q} \equiv S\dot{Q} + \left[\sum_i S_i\dot{Q}_i - S\dot{Q}\right] + \left[\sum_i\sum_j S_{ij}\dot{Q}_{ij} - \sum_i S_i\dot{Q}_i\right] + \sum_i\sum_j Q_{ij}\dot{S}_{ij}$$

$$\quad\quad\quad\quad (i) \quad\quad\quad\quad (ii) \quad\quad\quad\quad (iii) \quad\quad (iv)$$

There are four effects on the right side of the identity: (i) growth in world trade, (ii) commodity effect, (iii) market effect, and (iv) a residual effect representing competitiveness. It is possible to rewrite the previous equation as follows:

$$\Delta q \equiv gq^0 + \sum_i (g_i - g)q_i^0 + \sum_i\sum_j (g_{ij} - g_i)q_{ij}^0 + \sum_i\sum_j \left(q_{ij}^1 - q_{ij}^0 - g_{ij}q_{ij}^0\right)$$

$$\quad (i) \quad\quad\quad (ii) \quad\quad\quad\quad (iii) \quad\quad\quad\quad\quad\quad (iv)$$

with g the increase in global exports in the period 0 to 1. Comparison is always in terms of rates of growth.

The limitation of this method is interpretation of the competitive effect, which is quantified without identifying the exact explanatory factors. But as Richardson put it, this residual effect reflects several factors affecting a country's ability to sell to foreign markets, such as distinctive quality improvement, trade and financial agreements, changes in trade policy, and others.[15] To evaluate the sources of agribusiness[16] export growth after 1990, we consider four subperiods: (i) 1992 to 1994—a period that includes global and local trade liberalization and elimination of the main nontariff barriers; (ii) 1994 to 1999—characterized by the implementation of the "Real Plan," with its overvalued currency and negative impacts on the export sector; (iii) 1999 to 2008—a period including devaluation of the currency in 1999 and the international financial crisis of 2008; and (iv) 2008 to 2013—which excludes more recent postcrisis years that have seen lower growth in Brazilian agricultural exports.

Table 6.5   Annual Growth Rates of Agricultural and Livestock Exports in Brazil and Worldwide with Specification of Causes (in Percent)

Indicators	1992–1994 (%)	1994–1999 (%)	1999–2008 (%)	2008–2013 (%)
Annual Growth Rates				
World exports	1.9	–0.4	11.0	6.0
Brazilian exports	32.6	5.5	19.0	11.2
Sources of Growth				
Global growth	5.2	–8.5	44.3	48.0
Commodity effect	50.7	7.0	1.0	12.9
Market effect	45.7	55.6	22.1	10.6
Competitive effect	–1.6	45.8	32.5	28.4

Source: Authors' own work; data used was collected from the Food and Agriculture Organization of the United Nations.

Table 6.5 presents the results of this breakdown of Brazilian agricultural sector exports. During the first period (1992 to 1994), worldwide agricultural exports showed a growth rate of 1.9 percent, while the Brazilian growth rate was 32.6 percent, demonstrating export growth well above global rates. The Brazilian economy grew at rates of 4.9 percent in 1993 and 5.9 percent in 1994. Good agricultural output in 1994 also contributed. This result became the "green anchor of the real" because the increase in agricultural supply contributed to stabilization.

The commodity effect in 1992–1994 was 50.7 percent, the highest rate in all periods. Measures to increase the liberalization of Brazilian imports were decisive in stimulating exports in the early 1990s. Attention was paid to the composition of output; specializing in products for which international demand was greater was the secret to success.

Creation of Mercosul in 1991 also helped. Trade liberalization measures included the reduction of agricultural protectionism, and Brazil became a central player in these multilateral negotiations. Major reforms were introduced between 1991 and 1996 to stimulate foreign trade operations. Legislation was enacted to reduce the delay in the analysis of antidumping cases, and taxation on exports, quotas, and export licensing were eliminated. Export licenses were eliminated for sugar and ethanol in 1992.

From 1992 to 1994, the Brazilian economy experienced a negative competitive effect. Macroeconomic policies such as a lack of inflation controls and the absence of an agricultural credit policy were inhibitory. Until mid-1992, Brazilian agriculture suffered a loss of competitiveness.

In the period between 1994 and 1999, there was a drop in the growth rate of world exports of about –0.4 percent. The performance of national exports was slightly positive at a rate of 5.5 percent. This was the lowest rate for all periods. The decline of world trade growth negatively influenced Brazilian exports by -8.5 percent. The economic dynamism of Brazil's main importing countries accounted for 55.6 percent of the total gain, as well as a large positive competitive effect from trade liberalization and stability, about 45.8 percent.

Between the end of 1994 and 1998, the international financial market was shaken by three crises. The first was in Mexico in late 1994, spilling over into emerging markets in the first half of 1995, including Brazil. Following this came the 1997 crisis that originated in Thailand and rapidly spread to South Korea, Indonesia, and Malaysia. The third was the Russian crisis of 1998. Brazil was seriously affected by the "contagion effect" associated with the reduction of financial loans to emerging countries and the decrease in domestic foreign currency reserves, which occurred after international difficulties. The commodity effect presented a positive rate of only 7 percent.

Despite these crises, agroindustry in Brazil remained strong, boosted by an appreciation of the Brazilian currency. This led to lower import costs for agricultural technology. Real prices of agricultural inputs declined, especially those of fertilizers, pesticides, medicines, and machinery, which contributed to modernization of the sector.

Another boost was the National Program for Strengthening Family Agriculture (Pronaf), created in 1996, which placed family agriculture on the country's political agenda. The program consisted of three types of intervention: rural infrastructure improvement, credit support for family farming, and technical training for farmers. The 1996 Kandir Law benefited the export of raw materials at zero rates and became a subsidy for fresh grain exports at the expense of processed products. The intent was to lower the product's final price in the international market.

In the third period studied (1999–2008), Brazilian exports grew well above global export rates. A breakdown of the growth rate showed that world trade was the main component. In 2000, the federal government created a new program called Moderfrota to stimulate the modernization of tractor fleets and agricultural machinery. Its grants subsidized credit through the Brazilian Development Bank (BNDES) to increase the demand for agricultural machinery. Playing an important role in updating the tractor and harvester fleet in Brazilian agriculture, the program increased credit volume in the last fifteen years.

Global economic demand, driven by the growth of the Chinese economy, permitted an increase in the price of agricultural commodities, and the global export growth rate was around 11 percent. Growth of world trade has contributed 44.3 percent of the total.

Market and competitive effects were positive and significant: 22.1 percent and 32.5 percent, respectively. There was a higher concentration of exports in primary products. The argument that Brazilian agriculture produces items with low value added is somewhat incorrect. Brazilian agriculture experienced a significant leap in productivity due to increased inputs and advanced machinery, together with investments in R&D that spurred decades of genetic development and new techniques in grain production and meat processing. This "re-primarization" of the Brazilian commodity factor was associated with China. After entering the WTO in 2001, China boosted its international trade to meet growing industrial demands for raw materials.

In the latest period (2008–2013), the international financial crisis did not greatly affect the dynamics of Brazilian exports. The growth rate of national exports was higher than the global average but lower than in the previous period. Brazilian exports grew at a rate of 11.2 percent, and the world figure was around 6 percent. In terms of the breakdown, the performance of global trade was the main effect of growth, at 48 percent (its largest share among all periods).

The market effect was positive between 2008 and 2013. This measure played a lesser role than in previous periods. The 2008 global financial crisis altered the destination of exports as South-South trade flows gained in importance. That was a new source of demand for Brazilian agriculture. After 2008, this demand expanded corn, cotton, beef, and chicken production.

The competitive factor was important, with growth of 28.4 percent, but this was lower when compared to 1999–2008. Given Brazil's logistical problems and structural inefficiencies, sales to the international market require more investment. Planning should promote intermodal routes and expand storage and delivery networks, reducing costs and increasing international competitiveness.

FINAL REMARKS

Agribusiness will continue to account for a large part of Brazilian export earnings over the coming years. There will be variations, of course, dependent on weather conditions. Brazil has played an important and cooperative role as international policies continue to evolve. Climate warming may produce large negative consequences for Brazil. That is a subject we take up in the next chapter.

CHAPTER 7

Agricultural Expansion and Low-Carbon Emissions

The relationship between increased food production and the environment is now central. There is a connection between a growing world population and the efficient use of natural resources. This has become more evident since 1992, when the first United Nations Conference on Environment and Development took place in Rio de Janeiro, discussing global warming and climate change.[1]

The Kyoto Protocol, the first addition to the United Nations Framework Convention on Climate Change, was discussed and negotiated in 1997. This agreement featured strict commitments to reduce greenhouse gas (GHG) emissions. The principle adopted was a common, but differentiated, responsibility among countries based on both level of economic development and historical responsibilities for atmospheric pollution. The agreement was ratified in 1999 and implemented in 2005, following the signatures of a group of countries responsible for more than 55 percent of global GHG emissions.

As discussed earlier, Brazil's agricultural frontier has been expanding in the Cerrado biome, advancing toward the Center-West, Matopiba, and the Amazonian transition zone. Did this geographic shift harm the environment? Agriculture is responsible for emissions (mainly through enteric fermentation and nitrogen fertilization of the soil), and the ability of the sector (including livestock) to mitigate the problems of climate change is significant. Technological capacity for intensified use of resources permits continuing gains.

FOOD PRODUCTION, POPULATION GROWTH, AND THE ENVIRONMENT

With the growth of emerging economies in the 2000s, there has been a rapid expansion of per capita output and increases in household income.

Middle-income countries achieved a rate of advance of 5 percent in GDP per capita between 2002 and 2013, higher than the world average of 1.7 percent. China, India, Argentina, and Brazil recorded growth rates of 9.6 percent, 6.1 percent, 4.2 percent, and 2.6 percent, respectively. World population has been growing as well. Total population has reached 7 billion and is expected to increase to more than 9 billion by 2050. This growth comes from expansion in the world's poorest regions, where the birth rate remains high. In the last two decades, the population growth rate of low-income countries has been around 3 percent; at that rate, the population in these regions would double in size in twenty-three years.

Future trends suggest that more people will live in major urban centers, per capita income will increase, the middle class will expand, and the emerging economies will play a larger role in world production. These factors increase the demand for food and industrial products. As a consequence, concerns about the environment and sustainable development continue to mount.

Brazil has become one of the main agriculture-producing countries. Total factor productivity (TFP) has grown sharply since the 1970s, with a higher rate beginning in the late 1990s. In relation to livestock production, an increase in the exports of bovine meat followed the Agreement on the Application of Sanitary and Phytosanitary Measures of 1995, after the creation of the WTO. In 2016, Brazil accounted for about 20 percent of the world's beef exports and was among the world's leading exporters along with India.

With increased productivity, Brazilian agricultural production has expanded to the Cerrado biome. First, the Center-West was incorporated into the productive frontier in the 1980s. Subsequently, from 1990 to 2016, consolidated production in the Center-West was the goal. Production in the northeastern Cerrado was also expanded, especially in the region called Matopiba, through the accumulation of knowledge in areas already exploited. This expansion of production occurred in the agricultural and livestock sectors, which drew attention to productive practices that had an environmental impact.

Environmental discussions gained momentum by linking growth to deforestation. Brazilian President Cardoso raised requirements for protected areas (legal reserves) from 50 percent to 80 percent in rural properties located in the Legal Amazon in 1996. He used a provisional measure to do so. This measure was reissued in 2012 and defined a legal reserve as a proportion of the total area that borders forest land, corresponding to (i) 80 percent of the property located in a forest area; (ii) 35 percent of the property located in the Cerrado; (iii) 20 percent of the property located in areas of vast plains (or general fields); and in other regions of the country (iv) the legal reserve covers 20 percent of the property's area.

Brazilian livestock expansion has been occurring near regions of the Amazon biome due to intensive use of knowledge and technology. Brazilian agriculture has intensified since 2005, but deforestation has fallen sharply and has not been associated with agricultural production growth. Reduction of approximately 40 percent in national GHG emissions and a potential cooling of the local climate have been the result.

Changes in land use reinforced inequality in ownership. This contributed to rural-urban migration that fuels expansion of urban areas. Resolution of conflicts over land rights would be an important step forward.

According to the annual estimates in Brazil, the agricultural sector has been the main sector responsible for GHG emissions, recording 32 percent of total emissions in 2010. This percentage is related to cattle enteric fermentation (18.4 percent, produced by methane) and the application of synthetic fertilizers (11 percent, due to nitrous oxide emissions). These estimates are based on average indicators of agriculture and livestock productivity, and they do not consider recent technological advances that conserve natural resources.

In this chapter, we examine productive expansion, measuring land-saving effects achieved by modern technology and comparing these results with GHG emissions. In addition, we estimate TFP, as shown in Appendix D, by incorporating GHG emissions arising from livestock production.

DEFORESTATION AND AGRICULTURAL EXPANSION IN BRAZIL

Agricultural production in the Brazilian Cerrado has expanded, especially in grain production. Livestock assembly has also intensified in traditional regions in the southern states with the inclusion of the border areas between Center-West, Pará, and the Amazonian biome (bovine farming).

Figure 7.1 identifies Brazilian biomes by geography (Amazon, Cerrado, Caatinga, Atlantic Forest, Pantanal, and Pampa) and the Legal Amazon region. Figure 7.2 shows deforestation rates from 1990 to 2016.[2] The region with the greatest expansion of livestock occurred in the Legal Amazon, encompassing three biomes: the Amazon, the Cerrado, and a smaller portion of the Pantanal.

Tax incentives that dominated expansion in the past, but since the 1990s, expansion of the agricultural frontier in the Amazon has been based

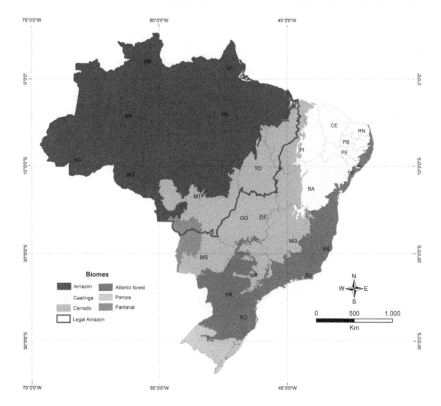

Figure 7.1 **Brazilian biomes by geography.**

Source: Developed by the authors, with data from INPE, IBAMA, MCTIC, and SOSMA.

on logging and livestock profits and lower land prices. With creation of the Plan for Prevention and Control of the Legal Amazon Deforestation (PPCDAM) in 2004, a prominent decline in deforestation was achieved, from an annual average of approximately 18,309 km² in the 1990 to 2004 to almost 9,035 km² in 2005 to 2016, with the lowest rate, 4,571 km², in 2012. Pastures for beef production continue to occupy 60 to 80 percent of deforested land, with the cattle herd count in the North region reaching about 47 million head.

In the Cerrado, agricultural land totals 1 million square kilometers. Cattle raising is a major economic activity. Nevertheless, in the last fifteen years, intense substitution of pasture by large-scale mechanized production of soybeans, corn, cotton, and sugarcane has pushed livestock production to the edge of the Amazon biome. The Cerrado is the most important

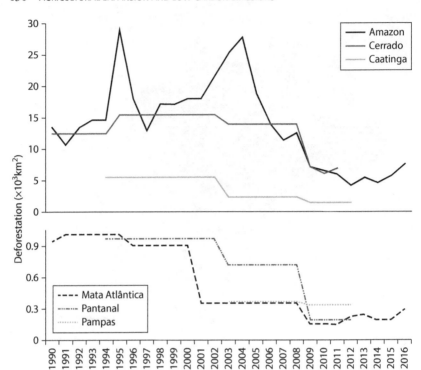

Figure 7.2   Annual deforestation rates in Brazil and Legal Amazon, 1990 to 2016.

Source: Developed by the authors, with data from INPE, IBAMA, MCTIC, and SOSMA.

region of Brazil for meat production, accounting for about 50 percent of Brazil's national herd. This is despite the region's geographic characteristics, which favor large-scale mechanized agriculture.

In the Pantanal, silviculture, hydroelectric construction, and access to navigation increased land use. About 15 percent of its original extension is utilized, mainly for livestock. This region experienced a decline in deforestation over the last decade, following national trends, from 962 km² in 1994 to 2002 to 189 km² in 2009 to 2012. Environmental concerns about uncontrolled expansion of sugarcane plantations into neighboring biomes led to a legal ban on this type of crop in the Pantanal and Amazon areas.

Since 2014, Brazil as a whole has seen a moderate increase in deforestation rates, which raises concerns. Land-saving is very important, be it at the frontier of the Amazon forest or in the transformation of land use within the Cerrado. The Cerrado biome has the greatest potential for future deforestation because it lacks the monitoring and surveillance programs that exist in the Amazonian forest. Barreto and Araújo[3] argued for increased public oversight emanating from social pressure. They wanted a moratorium on soybeans and proposed actions holding the meat-producing chain accountable for environmental management of rural properties. These restrictions were essential to reduce the deforestation rate in all biomes, including in the Legal Amazon.

To analyze the spatial dynamics of cattle herd by state between 1990 and 2015, table 7.1 shows the number of heads by federative states, as well as the variation (in percentage) for the periods from 2000 to 2015 and 1990 to 2015. The states with the largest bovine animal population in 2015 were Mato Grosso (13.65 percent of the national total), Minas Gerais (11.05 percent), Goiás (10.17 percent), Mato Grosso do Sul (9.92 percent), and Pará (9.42 percent). Over the entire period, from 1990 to 2015, the highest positive percentage changes occurred in the states bordering the Amazonian biome: Rondônia, Acre, Pará, Mato Grosso, Roraima, and Amazonas, in that order. In Brazil, bovine herds were estimated at around 147 million head in 1990, increasing to around 215 million head in 2015, a change of 46.3 percent.

Figure 7.3 shows an increase in the size of the cattle herd along with a reduction of pasture area. According to the Agricultural Census of 2006, crops represented around 19 percent of total area, forests and jungle areas accounted for about 31 percent, and pasture areas were almost 50 percent. Interpolation of data from the last two agricultural censuses (1995–96 and 2006) show a reduction in pasture area, which was probably taken over by agricultural crops. An increase was also observed in the number of animals per hectare, indicating an intensification of livestock production.

Three thematic maps were developed to analyze the spatial dynamics of the cattle herd in the years 1990, 2000, and 2015. The darkest shade represents the highest concentration of animals (figure 7.4). By comparing the three moments, the 1990s are distinct from the years 2000 and 2015. In 1990, the state of Mato Grosso do Sul showed the greatest concentration, although the states of Goiás, Mato Grosso, and Pará were also highly concentrated. When the years 2000 and 2015 are observed, the higher concentrations are intensified on the edges of the Amazon forest, near the states of Mato Grosso, Pará, Goiás, and Rondônia, in addition to Maranhão. These maps show greater competition for land on the border

Table 7.1   Total Cattle Herd by State, from 1990 to 2015 (in Millions of Heads)

States	1990	1995	2000	2005	2010	2015	2015 (%)	2000–2015 (%)	1990–2015 (%)
Rondônia	1.72	3.93	5.66	11.35	11.84	13.40	6.23	136.5	679.5
Acre	0.40	0.47	1.03	2.31	2.58	2.92	1.36	182.2	628.9
Amazonas	0.64	0.81	0.84	1.20	1.36	1.29	0.60	53.4	102.9
Roraima		0.28	0.48	0.51	0.58	0.79	0.37	65.4	181.8*
Pará	6.18	8.06	10.27	18.06	17.63	20.27	9.42	97.4	227.9
Amapá	0.07	0.09	0.08	0.10	0.11	0.08	0.04	-4.0	14.2
Tocantins	4.31	5.54	6.14	7.96	7.99	8.40	3.90	36.8	95.0
Maranhão	3.90	4.16	4.09	6.45	6.98	7.64	3.55	86.7	96.0
Piauí	1.97	2.14	1.78	1.83	1.68	1.65	0.77	-7.3	-16.4
Ceará	2.62	2.27	2.21	2.30	2.55	2.52	1.17	14.1	-4.0
Rio Grande do Norre	0.96	0.72	0.80	0.98	1.06	0.92	0.43	14.3	-3.9
Paraíba	1.35	1.05	0.95	1.05	1.24	1.17	0.54	22.9	-13.0
Pernambuco	1.97	1.36	1.52	1.91	2.38	1.95	0.91	28.5	-0.9
Alagoas	0.89	0.83	0.78	0.99	1.22	1.26	0.58	61.2	40.9
Sergipe	1.03	0.80	0.88	1.01	1.12	1.23	0.57	39.9	19.5
Bahia	11.51	9.84	9.56	10.46	10.53	10.76	5.00	12.6	-6.5
Minas Gerais	20.47	20.15	19.98	21.40	22.70	23.77	11.05	19.0	16.1
Espírito Santo	1.66	1.97	1.83	2.03	2.20	2.22	1.03	21.8	33.6
Rio de Janeiro	1.92	1.91	1.96	2.09	2.16	2.35	1.09	20.0	22.2
São Paulo	12.26	13.15	13.09	13.42	11.20	10.47	4.86	-20.0	-14.6
Paraná	8.62	9.39	9.65	10.15	9.41	9.31	4.33	-3.4	8.1
Santa Catarina	2.99	2.99	3.05	3.38	3.99	4.38	2.04	43.6	46.4
Rio Grande do Sul	13.72	14.26	13.60	14.24	14.47	13.74	6.38	1.0	0.2
Mato Grosso do Sul	19.16	22.29	22.21	24.50	22.35	21.36	9.92	-3.8	11.4
Mato Grosso	9.04	14.15	18.92	26.65	28.76	29.36	13.65	55.2	224.8
Goiás	17.64	18.49	18.40	20.73	21.35	21.89	10.17	19.0	24.1
Federal District	0.11	0.12	0.11	0.10	0.10	0.10	0.04	-13.9	-8.5
Brazil	147.10	161.23	169.88	207.16	209.54	215.20	100.00	26.7	46.3

Source: IBGE, Municipal Livestock Research.

*1995–2015

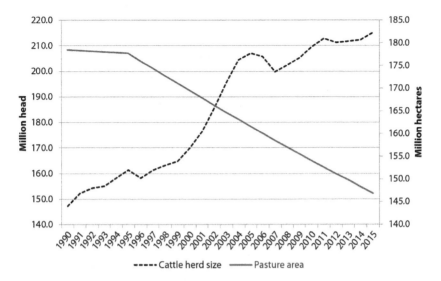

Figure 7.3   Cattle herd size and pasture area, 1990 to 2015.

Source: Developed by the authors.

between the Cerrado and Amazon biome, raising concerns about the use of natural resources, deforestation, and an increase in GHG emissions.

In figure 7.4, the most densely shaded municipality in the state of Pará was São Félix do Xingu in 2015, whose main source of income is cattle raising. This municipality has the largest cattle herd in the whole country, about 2.2 million head. São Felix do Xingu is bordered to the west by the Altamira region (with a herd of 629,000 head) and has been the focus of attention since construction of the Belo Monte hydroelectric power plant. However, the municipality has not invested in infrastructure to deal adequately with the increase in population. This problem has aggravated disputes over land and the rational use of natural resources because the region lies on the banks of the Xingu River, a major river with many tributaries.

In Pará, we also highlight Marabá, which has the fifth-largest herd in the country (1.07 million head), as well as Novo Repartimento, host to the eighth-largest herd (930,000 head). In the state of Mato Grosso, the most densely shaded municipality is Cáceres, the fourth-largest herd in Brazil (1.08 million head), followed by Vila Bela da Santíssima Trindade, the sixth-largest herd (986,000 head), and Juara, which has an economy based on timber extraction and livestock production and has the country's

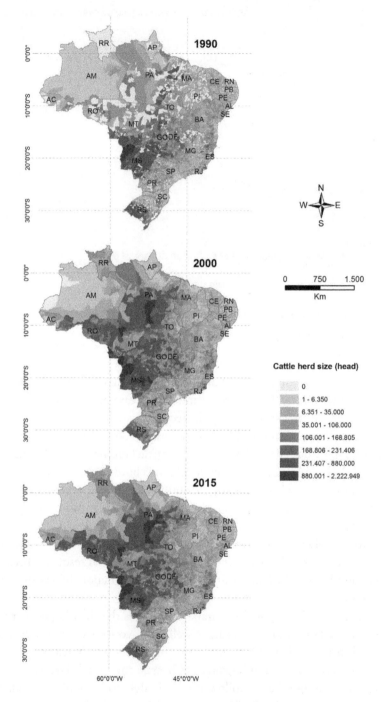

Figure 7.4   Distribution of beef cattle in Brazil, 1990, 2000, and 2015.

Source: IBGE, Municipal Livestock Research.

seventh-largest cattle herd (946,000 head). Meat and dairy production are important economic activities in both Pará and Mato Grosso.

The environmental impact of this livestock farming merits attention. Part of the criticism stems from the assertion that expansion is related to deforestation; however, the main reason is inadequate pasture management. Cattle and dairy production systems in Brazil have low zootechnical indexes of management, whereas modern production requires the use of improved genetics, for both animals and forage crop plants, as well as investments in management.

Some areas of pasture are not very productive (low-support capacity), which leads to high GHG emission levels per kilogram of supplied meat. The potential of pastures to store carbon is influenced by the intensity of use and management of the soil. The higher the stocking rate without proper investment in pasture recovery, the greater the carbon loss. Various recovery techniques exist, such as liming and fertilization, physical-mechanical treatments, and crop-livestock integration. Kichel et al.[4] showed that meat productivity in degraded pasture reaches around 30 kilograms per hectare per year, whereas in a pasture restored by crop-livestock integration, the output reaches 450 kilograms per hectare per year. The zootechnical indexes of recovered pastures are well above those of degraded pastures (table 7.2). Recovery of a small percentage of degraded area (with low productivity) can increase production and efficiency in livestock undertakings. It is necessary to increase birth rates while reducing mortality rates. Keys to doing so involve investment in improvement of the herd and the infrastructure of agricultural properties and in the recovery of pastures.

A balanced diet contributes to increased carcass weight, reducing the time to slaughter and lessening GHG emissions. Almeida and Medeiros[5]

Table 7.2 Characteristics of Cattle Production in Brazil, 1990 to 2015

Zootechnical Indexes	Low Productivity (degraded pastures)	Improved System (recovered pastures)
Birth rate (%)	60	85
Preweaning mortality rate (%)	4	2
Age at first calving (years)	4	2.5
Slaughter age (years)	4.5	2.5
Stocking rate (head per hectare)	0.7	2.5

Source: Dias Filho, Moacyr Bernardino, "Congresso Brasileiro de Zootecnia," in *Sustentabilidade e Produção Animal: Anais Das Palestras* (Palmas: Universidade Federal de Tocantins, 2010), 131–45.

showed that, in an experimental setting, animals with higher daily gains in weight emit lower amounts of methane with a diet of better quality. Rapidly digested animal feed yields lower methane emissions per unit of food intake than low-quality diets. In addition to improved cattle feed, well-managed pastures accumulate carbon at similar or higher levels than that of native vegetation. Degraded pastures promote accumulated carbon loss and impaired animal performance. Adequate management and balanced feeding are assets.

International agreements on climate change have already made profound changes in patterns of consumption and production. Yet economies (usually more developed) that emit greater emissions have opposed the agreed-upon targets. Although it is difficult to implement the carbon market at the global level, increasing voluntary commitments and legislation between and within countries can make a difference. These factors are essential to satisfy medium and long-term carbon reduction.

LAND-SAVING EFFECT IN BRAZILIAN AGRICULTURE AND LIVESTOCK

To calculate the land-saving effect,[6] table 7.3 presents data on the Brazilian agricultural and livestock sectors. There is an increase in both agricultural and livestock productivity, with a simultaneous increase in production from 1990 to 2015. The area for agricultural production occupied by temporary and permanent crops has increased, but there has been a reduction in pasture area. This can be observed by analyzing the stocking rate, which shows the number of animals per unit area.

Figure 7.5 shows the evolution of productivity growth for agriculture and livestock production in Brazil from 1990 to 2015.[7] Agricultural productivity growth was unstable, with relative progress in the 1990s and in the second half of the 2000s. In 1998 and 2005, agricultural productivity declined. There has even been a decrease in the land's net yield in recent years.

Brazil maintained its leadership in the export of soybeans, coffee, sugar, and orange juice and became important in the corn and cotton markets. The grain harvest, in general, has attained successive records every year, and national production has proved extremely competitive, even with the many political, structural, and logistical problems.

Evaluation of cattle ranching productivity, which is based on stocking rate and animal performance, shows a more linear pattern. Productivity has grown quickly, going from 15.9 kilograms per hectare to about

Table 7.3 Characteristics of Agricultural and Livestock Production in Brazil, 1990 to 2015

Sectors	Variables	Nomenclature	Calculation	1990	1995	2000	2005	2010	2015
Agriculture	Production (million tons)	P	1	467.4	548.6	590.7	614.8	950.2	1039.1
	Area planted (million hectares)	L	2	53.2	51.9	51.8	64.3	65.4	76.8
	Productivity (ton/hectare)	A	(1/2)=3	8.793	10.580	11.400	9.558	14.535	13.530
Livestock	Slaughtered animals (million head)	An	4	13.4	17.2	17.1	28.0	29.3	30.7
	Pasture area* (million hectares)	L	5	178.4	177.7	169.4	161.6	154.1	146.9
	Carcass weight (kg / head)	G	6	212.0	215.9	228.2	226.3	238.3	244.5
	Stocking rate (head / hectare)	S	(4/5)=7	0.07	0.10	0.10	0.17	0.19	0.21
	Productivity (kg / hectare)	A	6.7	15.9	20.9	23.0	39.3	45.3	51.0
	Production (million kilograms)	P	4.6	2835.8	3707.5	3899.1	6344.2	6976.4	7494.0

Source: IBGE, "Municipal Agricultural Research, Municipal Livestock Research and Agricultural Census," 1990–2015.
*Interpolation of data from the Agricultural Census 1995–96 and 2006.

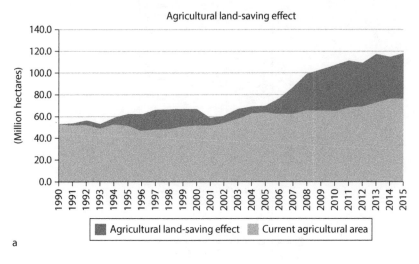

a

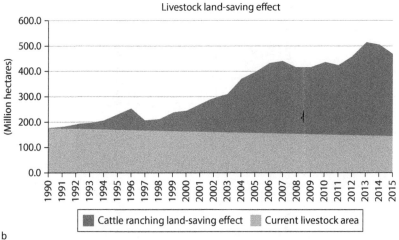

b

Figure 7.5   Evolution of land-saving growth for agriculture (a) and livestock (b) production in Brazil, 1990 to 2015.

Source: Developed by the authors.

50 kilograms per hectare. In 1992, Brazil was the world's eighth-largest beef exporter, and by the early 2000s it was the largest exporter.

Table 7.4 presents the results of calculations on the land-saving effect in both agriculture and cattle ranching. The calculation of this measure uses a comparative static approach to determine the area saved by use

Table 7.4   Land-Saving Effect on Brazilian Agriculture and Cattle Ranching for Different Periods (in Million Hectares)

	Land-Saving Effect		
Period	Agriculture	Cattle Ranching	Total
1990–2015	41.4	324.7	366.0
1995–2015	21.4	212.3	233.7
2000–2015	14.4	178.8	193.1
2005–2015	31.9	43.9	75.9
2010–2015	–5.3	18.6	13.3
1990–1995	10.5	55.6	66.1
1995–2000	4.0	17.4	21.5
2000–2005	–10.4	114.1	103.7
2005–2010	34.0	23.6	57.7

Source: Authors' own work.

of past technology to produce the present quantity. There was no land saving in the most recent period, a time when productivity was reduced. For agriculture, as noted earlier, these negative periods were from 2010 to 2015 and from 2000 to 2005. For the full period, the land-saving effect on agriculture alone was around 41.4 million hectares, practically an area 1.6 times greater than the state of São Paulo. The period from 2005 to 2015 showed the land-saving effect on agriculture of about 31.9 million hectares.

For cattle ranching, the land-saving effect is much higher than it is for agriculture in almost all time periods. There was an exception from 2005 to 2010, when the savings generated in agricultural production were higher than those observed in livestock. Land saving in cattle ranching alone was around 324.7 million hectares, an area 5.5 times the size of the state of Minas Gerais. The total saving effect from 1990 to 2015 was around 366.0 million hectares, or about 43 percent of national territory. Even in the most recent period, livestock production was able to save 18.6 million hectares. This result will reduce GHG emissions, providing an increase in production per unit of emission. The potential for a positive carbon balance is greater in livestock than in agriculture.[8]

Figure 7.6 shows livestock production growth in different periods for animal performance (carcass weight), stocking rate, and pasture area. With the reduction of pasture area over time, a negative contribution of land was observed. However, there is a positive contribution of stocking

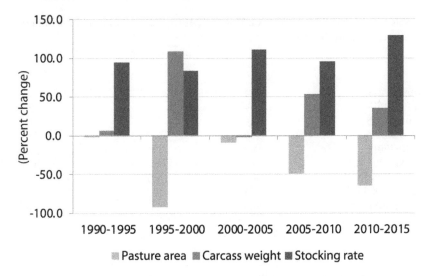

Figure 7.6   Breakdown of livestock production growth rate by pasture area, carcass weight, and stocking rate in different periods.

Source: Developed by the authors.

rate, which reflects an intensification of production, caused by either an increase in the number of slaughtered animals per hectare or an increase in the slaughter rate.[9] With the exception of the period from 2000 to 2005, animal performance was positive. From 2005 to 2015, the factors responsible for the growth in production were the increase in the stocking rate and more productive animal performance.

Room for further improvement remains. For an international comparison, in 2015 the slaughter rate of the main producing countries of the world was 23.7 percent for Argentina, 32.3 percent for the United States, and 33.3 percent for Australia. The Brazilian percentage is similar to that of India, 12.3 percent.

AGRICULTURAL PRODUCTION PER GHG EMISSION UNIT

At the Fifteenth Conference of the Parties (COP15) held in 2009 in Copenhagen, Denmark, a consensus response to global warming was reached. Brazil was the first country to submit a target emission level to the United Nations Framework Convention on Climate Change

(UNFCCC). This policy set out voluntary commitments to reduce GHG emissions between 36.1 percent and 38.9 percent of projected emissions in 2020, a reduction in billion tons of CO_2 equivalent (see Appendix E).[10] To this end, the following commitments were reached:

1. To reduce the rate of deforestation in the Amazon by 80 percent, and by 40 percent in the Cerrado.
2. To pursue degraded pasture recovery, promote productive integration systems (crop-livestock-forest), increase the use of no-till and intensify biological nitrogen fixation; to increase energy efficiency by the use of biofuels, hydroelectric power (including small power plants), biomass energy production, and wind power generation.

In the agricultural sector, a National Plan for Low Carbon Emission in Agriculture (ABC Plan) was organized between 2010 and 2011. Table 7.5 shows the commitments by the agricultural sector from 2010 to 2020. Among the goals are the recovery of 15 million hectares of pastures through appropriate management and fertilization; better integration of crop-livestock-forest (CLF) areas in 4 million hectares; the use of no-till practices in 8 million hectares; the expansion of biological nitrogen fixation by 5.5 million hectares; the promotion of tree planting in the fiber, wood, and pulp sectors totaling 3 million hectares; and greater use of technologies on animal waste treatment for power generation and organic compost production of 4.4 million m³.

Table 7.5   Goals and Commitment of the ABC Plan, 2010 to 2020

Subprograms—Technological Processes	Current Area (million hectares)	Agricultural Commitment 2010–2020	
		Area (million hectares)	Potential Mitigation (million tons of CO_2 eq.)
Recovery of degraded pastures	40	15	83–104
Integration of the crop-livestock-forest system	2	4	18–22
No-till	25	8	16–20
Biological fixation of nitrogen	11	5.5	10
Tree planting	6	3	—
Treatment of animal waste	—	Management of 4.4 million m³	6.9
Total	94	—	133.9–162.9

Source: Brazil, Ministry of Livestock and Agriculture, *Plano Agrícola e Pecuário 2012/2013* (Brasília: Mapa, 2012).

In 2015, the Twenty-First Conference of Parties (COP21) was held in France, and the Paris Agreement[11] was approved by 195 countries that are parties to the UNFCCC. This outlined actions to reduce GHG emissions to achieve sustainable levels. The goal was to assure a maximal global increase of a 2.0°C threshold while aiming for 1.5°C above preindustrial levels. Developed countries were supposed to take the lead in absolute emission reduction. The poorest developing countries, reflecting their special circumstances, were to prepare strategies, plans, and actions to achieve lower GHG emissions.

Brazil again assumed a central role and designed more ambitious goals. According to Gurgel and Laurenzana,[12] the commitment to cut 2020 GHG emissions was 37 percent by 2025 and 43 percent by 2030, different from the targets adopted at COP15. The COP21 objectives were more pragmatic and less dependent on hypothetical projections of an emissions baseline.

Brazil specifically agreed to (i) end illegal deforestation; (ii) restore 12 million hectares of forests; (iii) maintain the commitment to recover 15 million hectares of degraded pasture; (iv) integrate 5 million hectares of crop-livestock-forest; (v) guarantee 45 percent of total energy sources to be renewable: 66 percent hydroelectric and 23 percent wind, solar, and biomass; (vi) increase energy efficiency by 10 percent; and (vii) increase ethanol production to 16 percent of total energy. Efforts to reduce GHG emissions were thus significant.

With the commitments redefined at COP21, the agricultural sector took on a central role in reducing GHG emissions. Altered agricultural production is part of the solution, it is not the problem. Increased productivity, modernization of agricultural and livestock production, and continuing environmental supervision are requisites. Although emissions data point to a significant agricultural impact, there is potential to deal with the problem. In a survey of the 2015–16 harvest, Brazil had an estimated 11.5 million hectares, 83 percent with crop-livestock integration, 9 percent with crop-livestock-forest integration, 7 percent with livestock-forest integration, and 1 percent with crop-forest integration. With these percentages, Brazil would have fulfilled its commitments as agreed at COP15 and COP21.

Guimarães Júnior et al.[13] demonstrated the potential of this integration compared to a traditional livestock system to mitigate GHG emissions. The traditional system, with a stocking rate of 1.0 head per hectare per year, presented a negative carbon balance (-0.4 t CO_2 eq/ha/year), whereas the integrated systems had stocking rates of 3.0 and 1.7 head/ha/year with a positive carbon balance of 1.3 and 23.0 t CO_2 eq/ha /year, respectively. The integrated systems yield greater carbon sequestration. Embrapa developed the concept of "carbon neutral meat," with guidelines for meat production based on neutralization of GHGs through carbon sequestration by trees in the pasture.

Following the national GHG emissions registry, table 7.6 shows the sector emissions estimates from 1990 to 2014. The share of the agricultural sector increased over the period, from 21.4 percent in 1990 to 33 percent in 2014. Emissions were divided into five sectors, energy (by burning fuels), industrial processes, agriculture (mainly through enteric fermentation), land use (related to deforestation), and the treatment of waste.

Deforestation rates fell drastically after 2004, causing the category land use to drop from 59 percent in 1990 to 18.2 percent in 2014. In 2014 enteric fermentation accounted for 18.7 percent of total emissions, or more than 56 percent of emissions from agriculture and livestock.

For methane emissions, 89 percent were associated with raising cattle (beef and dairy), with the remaining percentage associated with other husbandry (such as pigs, poultry, and goats). Agricultural land was responsible for 11.9 percent of all emissions, and 36 percent of agricultural emissions were from the nitrogen fertilization processes of cultivated areas. A smaller share is also highlighted from the management of animal waste, rice cultivation, and the burning of sugarcane and cotton during harvests.

Figure 7.7 shows GHG emissions from the agricultural sector and, in particular, the enteric fermentation of cattle (beef), along with overall cattle productivity from 1990 to 2014. The growth of productivity increases faster than GHG emissions, a trend that persisted after 2010.

Another way to evaluate the contribution of technological change to GHG emission is to measure increases in production per unit of gas emission. Table 7.7 measures these values in both agricultural and livestock production. For agricultural production, changes were positive in the three periods. Overall, from 1990 to 2014, production output per unit of emission in the agricultural sector rose 46.4 percent. For livestock, the equivalent gain was 104.8 percent.

Sugarcane and cotton burning pollutants declined due to restrictions and legislation prohibiting this practice. This indicator can increase in two ways, either by reducing emissions in the respective sector or by

Table 7.6 Estimation of GHG Emissions by Sectors, from 1990 to 2014 (Gt CO_2eq. × 10^3)

Sectors	1990	%	1995	%	2000	%	2005	%	2010	%	2014	%	1990–2010 (%)	1990–2014 (%)	2010–2014 (%)
1. Energy	185.8	13.8	223.7	8.7	284.3	14.3	312.7	11.4	371.1	29.2	469.8	36.6	99.7	152.9	26.6
2. Industrial processes	52.1	3.9	65.6	2.6	75.6	3.8	80.5	2.9	89.9	7.1	94.3	7.3	72.8	81.1	4.8
3. Agriculture and livestock	287.0	21.4	316.7	12.3	328.4	16.5	392.5	14.3	407.1	32.0	424.5	33.0	41.8	47.9	4.3
• Enteric fermentation	172.7	12.9	188.1	7.3	196.3	9.9	235.5	8.6	234.3	18.4	239.8	18.7	35.7	38.8	2.3
• Management of animal waste	12.0	0.9	13.5	0.5	13.6	0.7	15.4	0.6	17.4	1.4	17.8	1.4	45.2	48.7	2.4
• Agricultural soils	90.1	6.7	100.9	3.9	105.9	5.3	127.9	4.7	140.3	11.0	153.0	11.9	55.6	69.8	9.1
• Rice cultivation	9.1	0.7	10.7	0.4	9.4	0.5	9.7	0.4	9.7	0.8	9.7	0.8	7.1	6.7	-0.4
• Sugarcane and cotton burning	3.1	0.2	3.4	0.1	3.0	0.2	4.0	0.1	5.4	0.4	4.2	0.3	74.1	36.4	-21.6
4. Change in land use	792.0	59.0	1931.5	75.2	1265.6	63.5	1904.7	69.6	349.2	27.5	233.1	18.2	-55.9	-70.6	-33.2
5. Waste treatment	26.0	1.9	31.4	1.2	38.7	1.9	45.5	1.7	54.1	4.3	62.8	4.9	108.1	141.4	16.0
Total (net emissions)	1342.9	100.0	2568.9	100.0	1992.5	100.0	2735.9	100.0	1271.4	100.0	1284.5	100.0	-5.3	-4.3	1.0

Source: Sirene—MCTIC (third inventory, 2016).

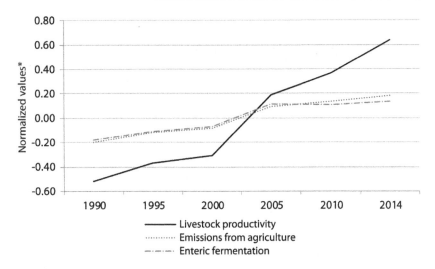

Figure 7.7   Productivity versus emissions, 1990 to 2014.

Source: Developed by the authors.

Note: *Normalized value = [(observation - mean) / average].

increasing overall output. Normally this increase has been due to productivity gains over time.

PRODUCTIVITY AND SUSTAINABILITY

We have discussed the expansion of the agricultural frontier in Brazil between 1990 and 2015 and provided data on GHG emissions. We emphasized livestock production because it is one of the sectors that most contributes to GHG emissions. The objective was to present an overview of livestock productivity over time, identifying the land-saving effect, which traditionally has been underestimated. We sought to compare land-saving gains with data on GHG emissions in Brazil, calculated using average productivity. Emissions measure the contribution of each sector of economic activity.

GHG emissions were estimated from 1990 to 2010 by several economic indicators. From 2010 onward, estimates are extrapolated, with technology held constant. These emissions projections are overestimated given the current technological advances in Brazilian livestock production. Between 1990 and 2015, land saving of livestock production was around 324.7 million hectares, much higher than that for agricultural

Table 7.7 Agricultural and Livestock Production Per Unit of GHG Emission by Sectors, from 1990 to 2014 (Tons Per Gg CO$_2$ eq.)

Activities	Emissions/Sectors	1990	1995	2000	2005	2010	2014	1990–2010 (%)	1990–2014 (%)	2010–2014 (%)
Agriculture	Agriculture and livestock	1629	1732	1799	1566	2334	2385	43.3	46.4	2.2
	Enteric fermentation	2706	2917	3009	2611	4055	4222	49.8	56.0	4.1
	Management of animal waste	39070	40740	43321	39929	54700	56919	40.0	45.7	4.1
	Agricultural soils	5185	5436	5576	4806	6775	6616	30.7	27.6	-2.4
	Rice cultivation	51333	51148	62776	63136	97492	104244	89.9	103.1	6.9
	Sugarcane and cotton burning	151210	159109	193744	155319	176626	240112	16.8	58.8	35.9
	Total (net emissions)	348	214	296	225	747	788	114.7	126.4	5.4
Livestock	Agriculture and livestock	10	12	12	16	17	19	73.4	92.2	10.8
	Enteric fermentation	16	20	20	27	30	34	81.3	104.8	13.0
	Management of animal waste	237	275	286	412	402	453	69.4	91.2	12.9
	Agricultural soils	31	37	37	50	50	53	58.1	67.5	5.9
	Rice cultivation	311	346	414	652	716	830	129.8	166.6	16.0
	Sugarcane and cotton burning	917	1075	1279	1603	1297	1912	41.3	108.5	47.5
	Total (net emissions)	2	1	2	2	5	6	159.9	197.3	14.4

Source: Authors' own work.

production. From 2010 to 2015, livestock contributed land saving of 18.6 million hectares.

In measuring production per unit of emissions, productivity growth exceeded emissions growth. This evaluation is preliminary. The goal is to show how the agricultural sector, through the incorporation of technology, contributed to the reduction and mitigation of GHG emissions. Brazil has every reason to take credit for this performance.

CHAPTER 8

The Structural Heterogeneity of Family Farming in Brazil

Brazil's agricultural productivity continued to increase after the country moved to democracy, despite the absence of incentives, lack of coordinated planning, and inadequate infrastructure. Production has increased year after year, even in an environment with little stimulus. However, progress has been uneven. Although there is a modern rural sector, some regions remain in acute poverty. This problem is prevalent in Brazil's northeastern region.[1]

Some of the issues can be traced to public policy. In Brazil, misguided public policies distort relative prices and access to technology and credit, discouraging entry of small farmers into the technological race. Climate and regional factors affect productivity differentials across different crop types. Less innovative producers are more vulnerable to fluctuations and context-specific risks.

Family agriculture in the Northeast suffers from greater inequality in technological innovation than does the southern region. Structural inequality prevents marginalized farmers from even trying to modernize. The basic hypothesis is that technological innovations can lead to greater inequality in agricultural production and growth. This favors more dynamic and innovative regions and contributes to stagnation for those on the margin.

The politics and economics of fiscal responsibility are now radically distinct from the more centralized and less land-generous government decisions of the past. We must ask: is it possible today to establish medium- and long-term priorities that are also feasible to implement? In other words, what role could the state and public policies play in promoting the agricultural sector? How can the country work with both a modern and competitive agriculture and an underdeveloped small-scale farming sector that needs mechanisms for labor training programs and rural extension? What is the role of Embrapa in the Northeast, in the incorporation of new agricultural frontiers concentrated in the Cerrado, and in the mitigation of rural poverty in the semiarid region? Finally, how does public policy contribute to attenuating market imperfections in sectors where the participation of multinationals is as intense as it is in the seed, fertilizer, and pesticides industries? These questions serve as strong motivation to rethink the future of the agricultural sector.

INNOVATION AND TECHNOLOGY IN SMALL-SCALE AGRICULTURE

Agricultural modernization can lead to regional and productive inequality because some economic agents are able to incorporate and absorb technological content, and others remain excluded from the innovative environment, learning processes, and dissemination of new techniques. Producers adopt pioneering technological inputs to increase productivity and reduce production costs. Small-scale farmers have little incentive to adopt these techniques because the higher cost involved in incorporating technology is not offset by the expected yield. Farmers who lag behind are living in poverty and need other sources of nonfarm income to survive.[2]

A producer's investment decision has two basic functions: generation of innovation and greater access to new knowledge. Empirical analysis of family farming in Brazil's southern region verifies this point. This has been Brazil's most dynamic region, and it has the best economic development indicators—an achievement that reflects an institutional and technological foundation developed over time. This kind of productive environment that fosters innovation does not exist in the Northeast. To benefit regions that are less advanced, a better understanding of the structural heterogeneity of family farming is needed that is aimed at proposing solutions.

Alves and Souza[3] showed the possibility of an increase in the incomes of small farmers. They determined that market imperfections were the main obstacle and had resulted from the federal government's past top-down public policies that invited little participation from local institutions. A counterexample is the state of Rio Grande do Sul, which allowed participation of farmers as well as municipal and state government in the development of public policies. This model was also followed in Paraná and Santa Catarina. In contrast, the nonirrigated areas of the northeastern semiarid region depended heavily on income transfer policies rather than on productivity advances. Some crops are integrated into modern value chains that encompass the private sector and public research organizations (universities and rural extension services). Others, however, are not targets of such investment.

In this chapter, we investigate the smallest family-run farms or enterprises that account for the vast majority of producers in Brazil (84 percent of all establishments). This group is also the most vulnerable in accessing technology. Although the term "family farming" is not entirely appropriate, the analysis is restricted to this group because there is a legal criterion defining public policies to promote this sector. Pursuant to these legal guidelines, a rural family entrepreneur is someone with the following characteristics: (i) does not legally own a land area larger than four fiscal modules; (ii) predominantly uses family labor to run the economic activities of the establishment; (iii) has a household income that originates mainly from economic activities linked to the establishment or enterprise; and (iv) operates the establishment or enterprise with his or her family.

METHODOLOGICAL TAXONOMY AND PRODUCTIVE INEQUALITY INDEX

The methodology in this study classifies family farms into groups defined by their technological efficiency and institutional environment. We constructed a taxonomy of high, medium, and low technological and institutional efficiency based on both economic and qualitative criteria. The economic criteria are linked to total factor productivity (TFP), and the qualitative measure has two categories of economic agents: high technological/institutional content (HT) and low technological/institutional content (LT).

TFP is the value of gross income generated per unit of cost. Both the production function chosen and the input mix affect this measure. A TFP less than 1 means that gross income is less than total cost, a negative net income. The reverse is also true; when the TFP is greater than 1, net income is positive. TFP cannot be decoupled from temporal change because annual fluctuations in production can be caused by exogenous shocks such as climate changes, crop failures, the emergence of new pests, or changes in international price levels. The analysis covers a single year, 2006, so qualitative criteria were added to the study to offset this variability.

We formulated twenty-two yes/no questions on the use of different technologies and the agents' degree of institutional organization. To divide the properties into high and low technological and institutional content, the proportion of establishments was grouped according to the frequency with which they responded yes to the questions posed. Values that exceed the average of the distribution were classified as HT, and values below average were classified as LT.

A taxonomy of productive establishments was obtained by blending the economic and qualitative criteria. Table 8.1 shows the resulting technological-efficiency groupings. Several variables were also calculated to compare the different groups. Data are available for gross income, total cost, investment (capital, labor, and technologies), the value of capital, net income, and labor productivity.

The production function is described by Leontief fixed proportions between two forms of capital. Agricultural growth depends on capital growth. To obtain land-saving and labor-saving technologies, fixed capital growth is restricted to the growth of variable capital, and vice versa. To quantify the land-saving technologies (linked to variable capital), a proxy variable was created from the sum of expenditures on seeds and seedlings, products to correct soil chemistry, fertilizers, agrochemicals, animal feed, and veterinary medicines.

Labor-saving technologies (related to fixed capital) were represented by an estimate of the value of vehicles, tractors, machinery, and implements (with a depreciation of 6 percent and an average life span of fifteen years), plus machinery rental.

Labor productivity—measured by dividing value added per person employed in each productive establishment—is the variable that determines structural heterogeneity in the Economic Commission for Latin America and the Caribbean (ECLAC) studies.[4] The greater the dispersion in labor productivity, the greater diversity of production and the higher structural inequalities observed. The gross production value (GPV value

Table 8.1 Taxonomy by Technological-Efficiency Group

Economic criterion—economic efficiency	TFP > 1		TFP < 1	
Qualitative criterion—technological/ institutional content	HT	LT	HT	LT
Technological groups	Group 1	Group 2	Group 3	Group 4
Taxonomy—technological efficiency	High		Medium	Low

Source: Authors' own work.

of production including consumption) was stratified into four income brackets defined by the minimum wage equivalent:

- $0 < MWE \leq 2$ times the minimum wage or "extreme poverty";
- $2 < MWE \leq 10$ minimum monthly wages or "low income";
- $10 < MWE \leq 200$ minimum monthly wages or "middle income" and
- $MWE > 200$ times the minimum wage or "high income."

The next step was to calculate the Gini coefficient of gross income for each group based on technological efficiency and comparing Brazil's different agricultural regions. Finally, a comparison is made between the productive inequality index (PII) and labor productivity measured as the value added per person employed (VA/PE). Both are standardized indicators (obtained by subtracting the mean and dividing by the standard deviation). In this comparison, four categories are identified, as shown in the quadrants of figure 8.1:

1. High productivity with low inequality (best-case scenario, or homogenization of income);
2. Low inequality and low productivity (worst-case scenario, or socialization of poverty);

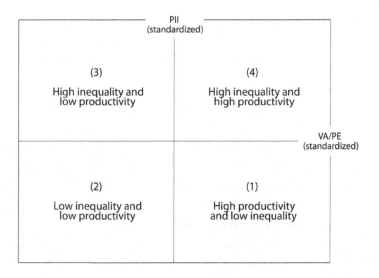

Figure 8.1   Inequality compared to labor productivity.

Source: Developed by the authors.

Table 8.2   Stratification of Reported Income from Family Farming (2006)

Income groups	Minimum Wage Equivalent (MWE)*	Share of Family Farms in Brazil (%)	Share of Family Farm Production (%)	Number of Family Farms (thousands)	%	Annual Gross Production Value (R$ billions)	%
Extreme poverty	(0–2)	89.5	87.3	2900	74.2	5.7	10.2
Low income	(2–10)	81.0	79.4	778	19.9	14.7	26.3
Middle income	(10–200)	53.8	41.3	224	5.7	24.7	44.1
High income	>200	15.7	13.3	4	0.1	10.9	19.5
Brazil		84.4	33.6	3,906**	100	56.0	100

Source: IBGE, 2006 Agricultural Census.
*MWE = gross production value per month/monthly minimum wage.

3. High inequality and low productivity (heterogeneity in poverty); and

4. High inequality and high productivity (heterogeneity in income).

Table 8.2 presents information on agricultural production classified by income levels as previously defined. At the upper end, including middle- and high-income groups, 5.8 percent of farms generated 63.6 percent of gross product value. At the lower end, consisting only of the extreme poverty group, 74.2 percent of farms contributed around 10 percent to gross product value. These results are even more concentrated when all agricultural units are taken into account (see chapter 4). The extreme poverty group—consisting of 2.9 million establishments—is on the fringes of agricultural production due to the almost universal lack of innovation.

Figure 8.2 compares family agricultural production to that of Brazil as a whole. The differences are apparent. While 84 percent of the establishments belong to families, they generate only 34 percent of gross income. There are two reasons: differences in technological sophistication and the crops produced. Large units are committed to production of soybeans, corn, sugar-cane, cotton and the like. These crops are inputs into increasing exports. Thus, corporate enterprises utilize more than three-quarters of the land, utilizing advanced technology requiring much higher ratios of capital to labor inputs.

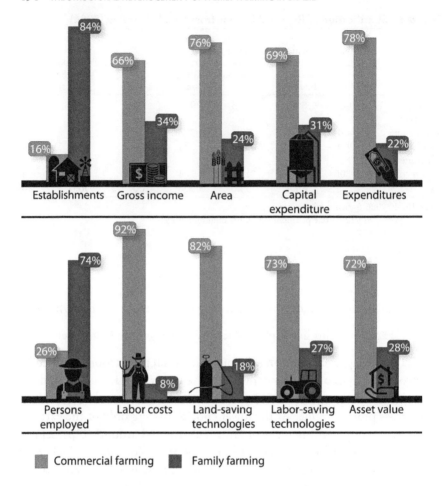

Figure 8.2   Family agricultural production in Brazil compared to that of Brazil as a whole.

Reducing this concentration is complex, requiring comprehensible long-term policies. These include educational reform, improvement in provision of health services, and provision of infrastructure. The population working on the land is more likely to migrate to urban areas, so short-term measures are also required, including direct income transfer.

Government should assist the low-income group through measures to reinvigorate small-scale family-based production. These producers operate with low levels of technology and have limited capacity to absorb advances. Better access to credit is required, as well as new technologies. The government should provide technical assistance that reaches the grassroots level and place research in the public domain when the market fails to do so. In family farming, this low-income group consists of 778,000 farms, most of which are located in the southern region (about 41 percent).

Finally, we turn to another part of the income spectrum. The country's agricultural profile also includes middle- and high-income groups. The South has the largest absolute number of medium- and high-income family farms, consisting of around 100,000 establishments, or 44 percent of the national total. The Center-West region has the fewest (11,600), representing 5 percent of establishments in the family farming universe. For this group, the macroeconomic environment is essential; absorptive technological capability is secondary. Public policies should focus on stimulating market competitiveness, export promotion, and agricultural insurance as well as improving logistics.

Figure 8.3 displays the TFP criterion. Of the 4.4 million family farms in the Brazilian agriculture sector in 2006, about 42 percent had a gross income exceeding total costs. Not surprisingly, the majority of establishments (58 percent) faced financial difficulties and had a TFP below 1, a negative net income.

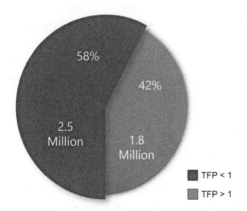

Figure 8.3   Classification of family farms under the TFP economic criterion in Brazil, 2006 (by millions and percentage).

Source: 2006 Agricultural Census.

Family farmers earned less than half of the national average income of the entire agricultural sector. Family farming establishments with a TFP greater than 1 and high technological content have a gross income exceeding the Brazilian average. Therefore, there are also highly productive establishments in family farming. Distinguishing between family and commercial farming is essential.

When studying technology in agriculture, land availability is a key factor. Better technology can generate savings on land intensity and increase production. If technology has this capacity, the land (since it is a given) becomes secondary. Bringing more land into use may increase final output, but productivity grows only by incorporating more technology. Agents with high technological intensity have a smaller average farm area than their low-intensity counterparts. Technology is more important than land area to obtain a higher income.[5]

Family firms with high technological content have lower costs than the country average. Nonetheless, their expenses are higher than the average for family farming (table 8.3). Because those establishments use above-average technological inputs, their expenditures exceed average results of family farming. If future increases in production fail to compensate for prior investment in technological inputs, costs rise and establishments risk financial difficulties. Farmers with medium technological efficiency are 20 percent of all establishments. At the other extreme, low technology and high productivity farms have a positive net income, a situation pertaining to 19 percent.

In general, family farms invest less in technology and generate slightly less value added per worker. Labor productivity in family farming is R$2,000 per person compared to an estimated R$2,100 for the Brazilian agriculture sector as a whole. Nonetheless, family farming with positive net income is efficient from the TFP standpoint and represents 35 percent of total establishments. Family farms that are profitable and have low technological content have the highest TFP, owing to the relatively high productivity of the land. Family production reporting positive net income shows productivity indices above the national average.

The low technological efficiency group consists of unproductive establishments. The weak performance of this group is partly due to greater use of land, usually associated with a smaller share in gross income. Public actions should encourage the efficient use of resources. Equally, the government should set higher productivity targets, giving priority to assist those with the greatest potential for success. Lack of dynamism creates

Table 8.3 Comparison of Family Farming by Technological-Intensity Group and Selected Economic Indicators, 2006

		Family Farming				
		TFP > 1			TFP < 1	Total Family Farming	Brazil
Economic and Qualitative Criteria		HT	LT	HT	LT		
Taxonomy—Technological Intensity		High	Medium	Medium	Low		
Indicators by Establishments — Thousands of Reais	Gross income (GI)	39.7	13.6	6.6	1.7	12.8	32.2
	Total cost (TC)	11.8	2.5	14.9	5.7	8.3	32.5
	Capital expenditure (CE)	1.0	0.1	1.2	0.2	0.6	1.6
	Labor cost (LC)	0.6	0.1	0.9	0.3	0.5	4.5
	Expenditure on land saving technologies	3.8	0.3	4.3	0.5	2.0	9.5
	Expenditure on labor saving technologies	0.6	0.0	0.8	0.1	0.4	1.1
	Value of capital (VC)	99.0	24.0	132.9	65.8	78.3	239.7
	Net income (NI)	27.9	11.1	-8.3	-4.0	4.5	-0.3
	Employed population (EP)	3.2	2.9	2.9	2.5	2.8	3.2
	Area (Ha)	15.5	12.6	19.1	23.1	18.3	64.5
Derived Variables	TFP	3.4	5.5	0.4	0.3	1.5	1
	Productivity of land (GI/ha) [reais]	2571.7	1077	343.1	73.4	699.8	499.4
	Productivity of capital (GI/CE)	39.5	130.2	5.4	6.9	21.9	20.4
	Productivity of labor (GI/LC)	63.9	107.4	7.6	5.6	28.1	7.1
	Share of land-saving and labor-saving technologies by total cost (%)	37	14	34	11	28	33
	Capital-labor ratio	1.6	0.8	1.4	0.8	1.3	0.3
	Rate of return on capital (NI/VC)	0.3	0.5	-0.1	-0.1	0.1	0
	Productivity of labor (GI/EP) [Thousands R$]	8.9	3.9	-2.3	-1.0	2.0	2.1
	Establishments (thousands)	837	993	1022	1515	4366	5176
	Share of establishments (%)	16	19	20	29	84	100

Source: 2006 Agricultural Census.

Notes: Monetary amounts expressed in reais at 2006 prices; HT: High technological/institutional content; LT: Low technological/institutional content.

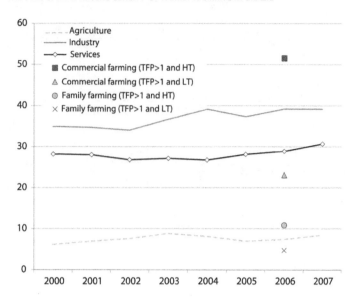

Figure 8.4 **Labor productivity by economic activity sector in Brazil, 2000 to 2007 (thousands of reais).**

Source: Prepared by the authors based on the Brazilian Geographical and Statistical Institute's (IBGE) 2006 Agricultural Census.

Note: Amounts corrected according to the National Consumer Price Index (IPCA) at December 2010 prices.

rural poverty. This group can, and should, be assisted by structural policies, as mentioned earlier in this chapter.

Figure 8.4 compares labor productivity in the agricultural sector with that in other sectors of the economy. IBGE national accounts data were used for value added per person employed between 2000 and 2007. By stratifying technology groups within agriculture, it is possible to compare heterogeneity in the Brazilian agricultural sector.

These data indicate that Brazilian agriculture remains far less productive than the industrial and service sectors. Yet there is a high degree of variability in labor productivity across productive establishments. Productive agents have different abilities to absorb technological knowledge. The most productive farmers have a labor productivity nearly 7 times the national average, even surpassing averages in the industrial and service sectors.

Labor productivity in family farming varies much less than in commercial agriculture. Unfortunately, family farming is homogeneous in terms of "socialization of poverty" and requires much more attention if better income distribution is to be realized.

DISAGGREGATED REGIONAL ANALYSIS OF PRODUCTIVE INEQUALITY

Labor productivity varies considerably across sectors and regions. Comparing sectors, labor productivity in industry was about 1.2 times that of services, but close to 4.5 times that in agriculture. In regional terms, the industry/agriculture labor productivity ratios were 6.5 in the Northeast and 1.2 in the Center-West region. The highly productive Center-West farming region, with extensive soybean and livestock breeding and where few workers are employed, stands in stark contrast to farming in the Northeast.

Table 8.4 compares regional family farming by technological-intensity groups. In the Northeast, the production pattern is more varied, as both modern and backward sectors coexist. In contrast, production in the South is more uniform and concentrated in the highest income brackets, yielding totals above the national average. The South is considered the most dynamic for family farming, with the lowest rate of rural poverty (around 47.4 percent of farms) and the lowest PII (0.73). In the Center-West, high and medium technological-intensity groups display a better distribution of gross income in the highest income brackets. Nonetheless, compared to the other regions, the low technology-intensity group displays a high level of inequality.

Focusing on the Northeast region, high technology-intensive agriculture produces greater inequality. There is heterogeneity even within the most advanced segments. However, in the Center-West, Southeast, and South, there is a more uniform distribution of production. In the Northeast, the higher the level of technological and institutional intensity, the higher the PII.

This pattern of duality can also be seen in other regions. Both the high and low technological-intensity groups recorded much lower variability than regional totals; this suggests homogeneity at the extremes.

The "socialization of poverty" thus coexists with a "heterogeneity of wealth." In the latter case, 0.11 percent of farms in the Center-West region generate income 23.2 percent of gross product value. In the Northeast, half of that percentage of establishments is responsible for more than 25.2 percent of production. The gross value produced by the high-income bracket in the Northeast was R$3,400 million, and that in the Center-West region came to only R$726.4 million. This comparison shows how unequal family farming is within the Northeast.

Socialization of poverty features low technology-intensive family farming, where 98.3 percent of farms generate income in the range between

Table 8.4 Family Farming by Technological-Intensity Group, Minimum Wage Equivalent (MWE) income bracket, and PII, 2006

Taxonomy		Establishments (thousands) and GPV (millions of Reais)	MWE Income Brackets (0–2)	(2–10)	(10–200)	>200	Total	Percentages (0–2)	(2–10)	(10–200)	>200	PII
TFP > 1 HT	High	N°	11.2	12.2	3.1	0.1	26.6	42.3	45.8	11.6	0.2	0.71
		GPV	50.2	202.2	343.3	114.1	709.8	7.1	28.5	48.4	16.1	
TFP > 1 LT	Medium	N°	104.6	46.0	15.2	0.5	166.3	62.9	27.7	9.2	0.3	0.79
		GPV	302.0	750.3	1736.7	788.1	3577.2	8.4	21.0	48.6	22.0	
TFP <1 HT		N°	28.1	2.8	0.2	0.0	31.1	90.4	9.0	0.6	0.0	0.40
		GPV	71.9	38.8	16.0	0.0	126.7	56.7	30.6	12.6	0.0	
TFP <1 LT	Low	N°	113.7	19.4	0.9	0.0	133.9	84.9	14.5	0.7	0.0	0.48
		GPV	293.6	306.3	53.5	1.8	655.3	44.8	46.8	8.2	0.3	
North		N°	257.6	80.4	19.4	0.6	357.9	72.0	22.5	5.4	0.2	0.76
		GPV	717.7	1297.6	2149.5	904	5069	14.2	25.6	42.4	17.8	
TFP > 1 HT	High	N°	207.5	69.2	19.6	0.7	297.0	69.9	23.3	6.6	0.2	0.82
		GPV	628.5	1170.2	2166.1	2445.7	6410.5	9.8	18.3	33.8	38.2	
TFP > 1 LT	Medium	N°	596.2	74.5	24.4	0.4	695.4	85.7	10.7	3.5	0.1	0.78
		GPV	986.4	1290.5	2449.7	936.8	5663.3	17.4	22.8	43.3	16.5	
TFP <1 HT		N°	306.7	11.5	0.4	0.0	318.6	96.3	3.6	0.1	0.0	0.29
		GPV	453.4	159.6	35.3	0.0	648.4	69.9	24.6	5.4	0.0	
TFP <1 LT	Low	N°	657.5	11.1	0.4	0.0	669.0	98.3	1.7	0.1	0.0	0.27
		GPV	490.9	163.7	23.8	0.9	679.2	72.3	24.1	3.5	0.1	
Northeast		N°	1767.9	166.3	44.8	1.1	1980.0	89.3	8.4	2.3	0.1	0.78
		GPV	2559.2	2784.0	4674.9	3383.4	13401.4	19.1	20.8	34.9	25.2	
TFP > 1 HT	High	N°	42.8	78.1	34.4	0.7	156.0	27.5	50.1	22.0	0.4	0.72
		GPV	189.2	1548.9	3811.3	2319.1	7868.5	2.4	19.7	48.4	29.5	
TFP > 1 LT	Medium	N°	42.0	20.2	7.5	0.1	69.9	60.1	28.9	10.8	0.2	0.79
		GPV	113.8	378.1	771.1	366.3	1629.1	7.0	23.2	47.3	22.5	
TFP <1 HT		N°	164.2	47.4	6.4	0.0	218.0	75.3	21.7	2.9	0.0	0.63
		GPV	428.6	803.1	479.8	8.4	1720.0	24.9	46.7	27.9	0.5	
TFP <1 LT	Low	N°	137.4	17.3	1.2	0.0	155.9	88.2	11.1	0.7	0.0	0.60
		GPV	184.7	296.3	70.8	0.0	551.7	33.5	53.7	12.8	0.0	

Southeast			N°	386.4	163.0	49.5	0.8	599.8	64.4	27.2	8.3	0.1	0.79
			GPV	916.3	3026.4	5133.0	2693.8	11769.3	7.8	25.7	43.6	22.9	
TFP >1	HT	High	N°	58.5	196.0	79.1	1.0	334.6	17.5	58.6	23.6	0.3	0.64
			GPV	289.2	4091.5	9093.0	2866.5	16340.2	1.8	25.0	55.6	17.5	
TFP >1	LT	Medium	N°	23.4	9.3	3.3	0.1	36.0	64.9	25.8	9.1	0.2	0.79
			GPV	67.8	174.1	374.1	168.4	784.4	8.6	22.2	47.7	21.5	
TFP <1	HT		N°	211.5	105.1	16.1	0.0	332.8	63.6	31.6	4.8	0.0	0.63
			GPV	660.2	1879.5	1185.5	15.9	3741.0	17.6	50.2	31.7	0.4	
TFP <1	LT	Low	N°	82.3	6.7	0.3	0.0	89.2	92.2	7.5	0.3	0.0	0.50
			GPV	109.6	104.8	22.4	0.0	236.9	46.3	44.2	9.5	0.0	
South			N°	375.7	317.1	98.8	1.1	792.6	47.4	40.0	12.5	0.1	0.73
			GPV	1126.8	6249.9	10675.0	3050.8	21102.5	5.3	29.6	50.6	14.5	
TFP >1	HT	High	N°	5.4	12.3	4.7	0.1	22.6	23.8	54.7	20.9	0.5	0.74
			GPV	28.3	227.2	607.8	442.5	1305.8	2.2	17.4	46.5	33.9	
TFP >1	LT	Medium	N°	9.1	11.6	4.1	0.0	24.9	36.6	46.8	16.4	0.2	0.73
			GPV	34.7	233.8	383.5	265.9	917.9	3.8	25.5	41.8	29.0	
TFP <1	HT		N°	37.7	9.5	1.5	0.0	48.7	77.5	19.5	3.1	0.0	0.65
			GPV	109.5	150.2	139.5	17.9	417.2	26.3	36.0	33.4	4.3	
TFP <1	LT	Low	N°	60.3	17.2	1.1	0.0	78.7	76.7	21.9	1.4	0.0	0.59
			GPV	132.0	292.6	68.9	0.0	493.4	26.7	59.3	14.0	0.0	
Center-West			N°	112.5	50.7	11.4	0.2	174.8	64.4	29.0	6.5	0.1	0.77
			GPV	304.5	903.8	1199.7	726.4	3134.4	9.7	28.8	38.3	23.2	
TFP >1	HT	High	N°	325.5	367.9	140.9	2.5	836.7	38.9	44.0	16.8	0.3	0.74
			GPV	1185.4	7239.9	16021.5	8187.9	32634.8	3.6	22.2	49.1	25.1	
TFP >1	LT	Medium	N°	775.2	161.7	54.5	1.1	992.5	78.1	16.3	5.5	0.1	0.81
			GPV	1504.7	2826.7	5715.1	2525.5	12571.9	12.0	22.5	45.5	20.1	
TFP <1	HT		N°	748.3	176.2	24.7	0.0	949.2	78.8	18.6	2.6	0.0	0.64
			GPV	1723.6	3031.3	1856.1	42.2	6653.2	25.9	45.6	27.9	0.6	
TFP <1	LT	Low	N°	1051.1	71.7	3.8	0.0	1126.6	93.3	6.4	0.3	0.0	0.51
			GPV	1210.7	1163.7	239.4	2.7	2616.5	46.3	44.5	9.1	0.0	
Brazil			N°	2900.1	777.5	223.9	3.6	3905.1	74.3	19.9	5.7	0.1	0.80
			GPV	5624.4	14261.6	23832.1	10758.3	54476.4	10.3	26.2	43.7	19.7	

Source: 2006 Agricultural Census.

zero and 2 times the minimum wage. The percentage of establishments compared to GPV shows a larger number of producers in the higher income strata in the more modernized regions. Establishments in backward regions are concentrated in lower income strata. The PII of the average technology-intensive group displays greater inequality.

Comparison of the PII with labor productivity, measured using standardized indicators, is shown in figure 8.5.

Labor productivity data for commercial agriculture is more dispersed, whereas the corresponding figures for family farming are more concentrated. The bottom quadrant to the right identifies low productive inequality combined with high productivity (homogenization of wealth) and contains only three observations. Two of them are commercial farming and one is family farming.

The upper quadrant to the left, representing high inequality combined with low productivity, consists predominantly of commercial farming. In that group, which requires specific policies to raise productivity, inequality levels are high because it can be affected by seasonal fluctuations and other external shocks to the market. With regard to the heterogeneity of wealth (represented by the upper-right-hand quadrant), commercial and

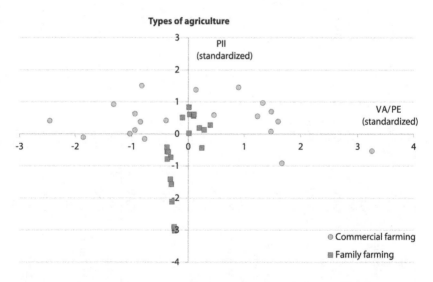

Figure 8.5 PII compared to labor productivity (standardized indicators) by type of farming (commercial and family), 2006.

Source: 2006 Agricultural Census.

family farms are present, with the latter concentrated close to the PII axis. The lower-left-hand quadrant (typical of the socialization of poverty) is populated by family farming. There are many establishments with low productivity and low levels of inequality.

Figure 8.6 focuses exclusively on family farms and adds regions. High and medium technology-intensive farms are concentrated on the right-hand side, representing higher labor productivity. The left-hand portion contains low and medium technology-intensive establishments. Structural heterogeneity is found in all regions, but at varying degrees. This is to be expected. In the low-inequality/high-productivity quadrant on the lower right (homogenization of wealth), the South offers the sole observation. Family farming can combine high technology, high labor productivity, and low productive inequality when an institutional environment exists that encourages growth and technological innovation.

The category of low productive inequality combined with low productivity (socialization of poverty) is dominant. The Northeast and North are at the very bottom left-hand side. The more dynamic regions are found to the right.

THE CHALLENGE OF INCLUSION AND MARKET ACCESS

In recent decades, the Brazilian agricultural sector has undergone changes that promote greater technological progress and higher productivity. Nonetheless, small family farms with low technological content and low productivity still exist. Agriculture cannot simply be divided into modern and backward producers. Structural problems create inefficiency, and management of this situation is still lacking.

We have identified and quantified the structural heterogeneity found in family farming. Backward segments do not participate in dynamic markets. However, the distinction between family and commercial farming can be overstated. Results reveal the coexistence of modern productive agents and backward ones within similar groupings. The internal diversity of family farming requires special attention to these specifics. Equally, regional differences are important. As a policy strategy is formulated, both region and type of farms are relevant.

Introducing crop-specific analysis will also help, and many studies have appeared in recent years. Public policies must take these into account. Brazil needs clear intent to assure technology absorption. Access to rural extension and better education is essential. More closely integrated

Technological and institutional content

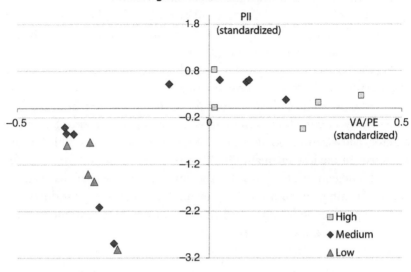

Regions

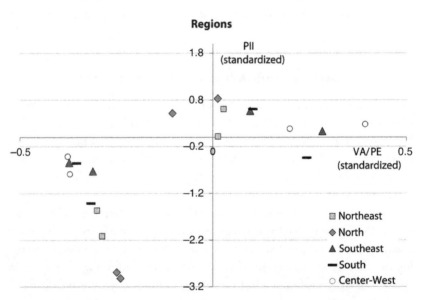

Figure 8.6   PII compared to labor productivity (standardized indicators) by family farming technology intensive group and by region, 2006

Source: 2006 Agricultural Census.

policies across federal, state, and municipal levels are necessary to reach out at a grassroots level, spreading new techniques and knowledge to producers. Transforming market-based family farming will be the main challenge for agricultural planning and policy in Brazil in the coming years. This includes a redefinition of public research institutions. Embrapa will undoubtedly play an important role in the extension of agricultural frontiers and in alleviating rural poverty.

CHAPTER 9

Is the Oil Ours?

OIL INDUSTRY AND PETROBRÁS: DEEP-WATER OIL EXPLORATION AND TECHNOLOGICAL GUIDEPOSTS

A handful of late-industrializing countries demonstrated the emergence and development of global competitiveness based on technical change. Studies of the learning process explain what is involved in moving from imitation to innovation. Imitation relies on the assimilation of embodied knowledge, whereas problem-solving skills are needed to create knowledge.

In Brazil, the offshore oil production industry is an example of development of a firm-centered knowledge network. As studied by Dantas and Bell,[1] Brazilian oil production has evolved to create knowledge to the point of shared offshore technologies.

Domestic oil exploration can be divided into two eras: *before* and *after* the founding of state-owned Petrobrás in 1953.[2] Pioneering explorations were made by small private initiatives in the first decades of the twentieth century, and these early attempts were successful in supplying oil for residential use. Further incentives for expansion emerged after discovery of mineral resources in several Latin American countries. Government agencies and private companies continued exploration activities in the 1930s, but with disappointing economic results. At the same time, the automotive and chemical industries increased their demand for petroleum-based products. In 1934, the National Department of Mineral Production (DNPM) was launched and has been responsible for directing exploration in Brazil since then. In 1938, the National Petroleum Council (CNP) was created to intensify investments. In 1939, the first oil field, though non-commercial, was discovered in the *Lobato* field, in the state of Bahia. The first commercial oil discovery was drilled near *Candeias* in 1941.

Imminent expectations of larger-scale production, which was occurring elsewhere in Latin America, led to the creation of Petrobrás in 1953. At that time, the Brazilian government imposed state monopolization for production, refinement, and bulk transport of oil, but not for its distribution to consumers.

Following this change, Brazilian oil production can be segmented into three stages. From 1950 to 1970, oil production was dominated by an effort to reduce external dependency on imports and to begin research and development activities. In 1955, the share of national production in total domestic consumption was just 7.3 percent. In this stage, several oil fields were discovered in the Northeast, but these onshore discoveries were not enough to meet expanding Brazilian demand. In 1966, a formal research and development center was established. This permitted investment to be redirected for exploration along the coast. In 1968, initial exploration occurred in the *Recôncavo*, *Espírito Santo*, and *Sergipe-Alagoas* basins. In the same year, Petrobrás first drilled offshore in the *Guaricema* field, located in 30 meters of water off the São Francisco River delta. Discovery of this well confirmed the existence of oil reserves beneath the continental shelf. Later, in 1971, exploration returned to the *Campos* basin.

The second stage covers the period from 1974 to 2006. During this time, Brazil actively pursued self-sufficiency. The 1970s were marked by the first oil crisis, which was created by newly founded OPEC. World supply was drastically reduced to generate a significant increase in oil prices. With this change, Brazil created two new paths: (i) replace oil with other energy sources, and (ii) intensify offshore exploration, mainly in the Campos basin.

The federal government implemented the National Alcohol Program (Pró-Álcool) in 1975 to encourage the use of ethanol fuel based on sugar as a replacement for gasoline. The price of imported oil had risen from about US$3 to US$12 per barrel, representing an increase in import expenditures from US$469 million to US$2.8 billion. Furthermore, the global sugar industry went through a major decline that encouraged the biofuel market. The price of sugar dropped sharply from US$1,200 per ton in 1974 to roughly US$172 per ton in 1978.

In the 1970s, Brazil still relied largely on imports, which represented about 70 percent of Brazil's domestic oil consumption. Consequent price increases adversely affected the balance of payments and gave rise to a looming debt crisis. In 1979, this situation was aggravated by a second oil shock, which was caused by a regional conflict in the Middle East and the Iran-Iraq War. This second rise in prices was an increase from US$12 to US$18 per barrel. This shock was magnified by rising prices and recession in the developed countries, which was related to the rise in U.S. interest rates. This, in turn, led to a default on Brazilian public debt, and Brazil was soon joined by many other developing economies. (For the story of the country's economic decline over the next decade, see chapter 2.)

These two oil shocks encouraged investment in deep-water oil exploration. High oil prices spurred innovation in new offshore discoveries, and deep-water exploration promoted domestic production in the following decade. After several attempts, Petrobrás discovered the first oil fields through a series of drillings at the Campos basin in the *Garoupa* field in 1974. This represented an important turning point for offshore Brazilian efforts. The drilling of a 120-meter well opened the way for intensive exploration of the Campos basin in the next two years as well as successive discoveries in the *Pargo, Badejo, Namorado*, and *Enchova* fields.

Over the next two decades, production increased, Petrobrás was beginning to be an exporter of offshore oil drilling technology in the late 1970s. By the 1980s, import dependence was reduced. In 1984, the *Albacora* field was drilled to a depth of 293 meters.

Although exploration had started in the *Santos* basin around 1970, it wasn't until 1984 that a Shell Oil affiliate discovered gas in shallow waters up to 150 meters. By 1985, production reached more than 31 million cubic meters, and the share of national production in total domestic consumption rose to roughly half.

Four years later Petrobrás also achieved success at the *Tubarão* oilfield, followed by the *Estrela do Mar* in 1990. In 2000, Petrobrás shifted its focus to deep and ultra-deep-water drilling. The result was the discovery of the *Mexilhão* basin, Brazil's largest natural gas field. By expanding its offshore drilling operations in the 1990s, Petrobrás discovered giant fields in progressively deeper waters. Larger discoveries were made in the tertiary sandstone reservoirs in deep waters at depths of more than 500 meters, including the *Marlim, Barracuda*, and *Roncador* fields.

Evidence indicated that privatization and greater market competition (entry of new firms) could increase productivity of public enterprises. National pride may have played a role in averting that fate in Brazil. Petrobrás's own productivity rose sharply after a legal monopoly on oil exploration and production ended with creation of the National Petroleum Agency (ANP) in 1997. That doubled the company's performance within six years. Although Petrobrás was neither privatized nor faced competition, the mere threat of privatization altered previous results. A change in the competitive environment can lead to improved performance.

In 1992, Petrobrás was awarded a prize for its offshore activity, the Distinguished Achievement Award of the Offshore Technology Conference.[3] The award recognized innovative engineering technologies in the Marlim field, including the use of wet valves with flexible pipes at water depths exceeding 700 meters, the installation of the world's deepest mono-buoy (405 meters), the floating production systems based on semisubmersible platforms, and the establishment of a scientific partnership to share deep-water expertise.

In 2001, Petrobrás received a second award recognizing its performance in ultra-deep waters. This was related to innovations to reduce development and operational costs in the Roncador field. In 1999, Petrobrás set a world record for the shortest time frame, just twenty-seven months from discovery to first oil production, drilling more than 1,800 meters. This achievement used a production structure that incorporated several incremental innovations in subsea control systems (steel catenary exporting risers, taut-leg polyester mooring, and subsea production hardware).[4]

The third stage of the Brazilian oil industry is associated with self-sufficiency. In 2006, a giant oil accumulation in the pre-salt layer was found at *Tupi*, a reservoir located 2,000 meters off the coast and 5,000 meters below the ocean's surface. A new era had begun. Petrobrás was considered a major participant in ultra-deep-water oil exploration, designing technologies and building capabilities as a firm centered in innovation networks. In the same year, oil production reached almost 100 million cubic meters, and the share of national production within total domestic consumption approached 100 percent. The oil found in the pre-salt zone was of greater economic value and lighter than the heavy crude that had earlier dominated most of Brazil's production.

In 2007, based on estimates of fifteen wells, Petrobrás announced the full extent of the pre-salt frontier, covering an area 800 km long and 200 km wide in the Espírito Santo, Campos, and Santos basins. Following this, Petrobrás developed a strategic plan to explore the Tupi, *Iara*, and *Guará* fields. The development strategy started with extensive well tests followed by exploration and production projects. This included redesign of floating platforms, storage systems, and offloading facilities. For a geographic overview of oil production in Brazil's main basins, including the pre-salt polygon, see figure 9.1.

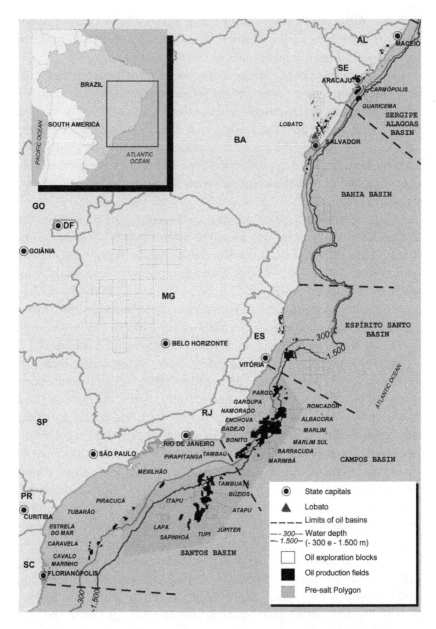

Figure 9.1 Brazilian offshore oil production in the main basins, including the pre-salt polygon.

Source: Developed by the authors.

Offshore oil exploration is extremely costly, creating barriers to entry for new competitors. Rental of drilling platforms became necessary, which can equal or exceed US$600,000 per workday. In the Campos basin, the average cost of drilling an exploratory well is about US$20 million, reaching a ceiling of US$60 million for fifty to one hundred days of operations. In the case of pre-salt exploration, the total operating cost of the first oil well in *Parati* in 2006 reached US$240 million, the world's most expensive at the time. In 2009, pre-salt wells cost around US$80 million.

Despite these successful exploratory efforts in the Santos basin, development of the Tupi field and other nearby areas faced a number of new challenges. The presence of a thick salt border created favorable conditions for facilitating exploration. However, drilling through this border, with extreme high pressure and low temperature, presented an extensive list of operational problems. Extraction of oil was much more complicated. The development of new materials and equipment was necessary, as well as new production units such as adapted platforms, more resistant and flexible pipes, and technologies to drill through salt layers. For an overview of the depth involved in pre-salt exploration, see figure 9.2.

PROBLEMS AND TECHNOLOGICAL SOLUTIONS

During this period, and since Petrobrás's founding, technology developed in response to production needs. Brazilian performance evolved, moving from onshore to offshore, and then from shallow to deep and ultra-deep waters.

Incentives to develop new technologies increased as production reached greater water depths. But the collapse of oil prices in 1986 limited ongoing investment in deep-water facilities. This was a different era, unlike the 1970s when oil prices were elevated. New ways of thinking about the regional geology and the local environment, as well as novel responses to drilling and production challenges, were required. Such efforts involved different institutions and national and foreign partners such as research centers, universities, and other firms.

A strategic innovation network allowed for R&D in a variety of technologies. Deep-water exploration flourished in Brazil during this period. Petrobrás became a world leader in advancing the frontier of international production. Petrobrás's greatest success was structuring an international network beyond the firm's boundaries (figure 9.3).

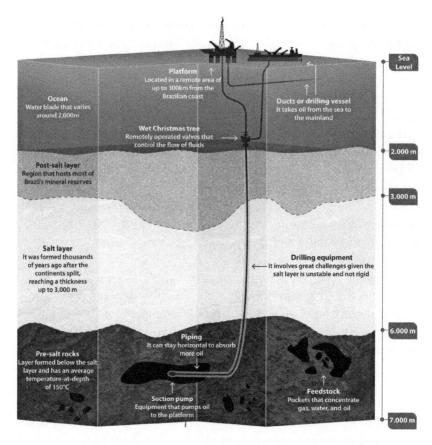

Figure 9.2   Depth involved in pre-salt exploration and associated challenges.

Source: Developed by the authors.

Petrobrás's innovation process related challenges like marine environment, long distances, operational invisibility, and oil density and contaminants to technical solutions. Extreme pressure and temperature demanded new materials. Seismic and modeling techniques were required to analyze the evolution of sedimentary basins and to calculate their productive potential. As humans cannot dive deeper than 300 meters, remotely operated vehicles and unmanned submarines were needed. With the increased distance between platform and well, devices became necessary to manage and control subsea equipment. Systems for carrying data, signals, and power between well and platform, such as an umbilical, were developed. Flexible flow lines and risers were created to

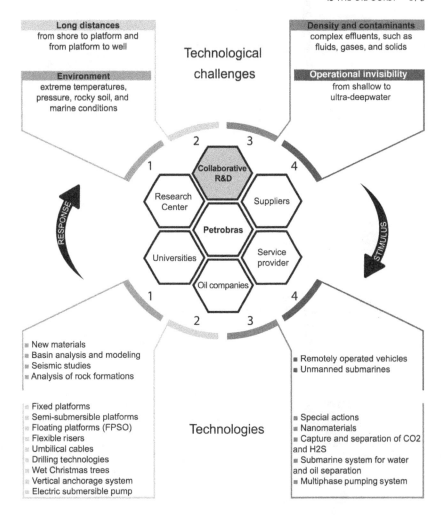

Figure 9.3 **Structure of innovation process and problem solving as a firm centered in the knowledge network.**

Source: Adapted from José Mauro de Morais, *Petróleo Em Águas Profundas: Uma História Tecnológica Da Petrobras Na Exploração e Produção Offshore* (Brasília: Ipea, 2013).

carry oil and gas to the surface and inject materials (mainly contaminants and CO_2) into the well, boosting productivity. To control oil flow, a system of valves and other instruments (known as wet Christmas trees) was installed at the wellhead.

Different platforms addressed complexities such as coastal distance versus drilling depth (table 9.1). Until the early 1990s, when depth was

Table 9.1 Different Types of Platforms Used by Petrobrás

Types	Fixed	Jack-Up	Semisubmersible	FPSO (Floating Platform, Storage, and Offloading Production)	FPSO Monocolumn	TLWP (Tension Leg Wellhead Platform)	Drilling Vessel
Water depth	Up to 300 meters	Up to 150 meters	More than 2,000 meters	More than 2,000 meters	More than 2,000 meters	Up to 1,500 meters	More than 2,000 meters
How it is used	Works as a rigid structure, fixed on the seabed by a system of driven piles.	Has self-elevating legs. Upon arriving at the location, a mechanism lowers the legs and sets them on the seabed.	Floating platform, stabilized by columns. Can be anchored on the seabed or equipped with a dynamic positioning system that automatically maintains the platform's position.	Floating platform, in most cases converted from oil tankers. As is the case with the semisubmersible platform, it is anchored to the seabed.	This platform has the same characteristics as an FPSO, but its hull is cylindrical.	Floating platform, with a hull similar to a semisubmersible's. It is anchored to the seabed by cables or tensioned steel tendons.	Floating platform with a ship-shaped hull and is used for drilling wells. These vessels can be anchored to the seabed or equipped with dynamic positioning systems, which maintain the vessel's position.
Drilling activity	Yes	Yes	Yes (some may be only for production)	No	No	Yes (only for well maintenance)	Yes

Production activity	Yes	No	Yes (some may be only for drilling)	Yes	Yes (units are usually for drilling or production)	Yes	No
Where well control takes place	Surface	Surface	Seabed	Seabed	Seabed	Surface	Seabed
Storage capacity	No	No	No	Yes	Yes	No	No
Production flow	Pipelines	No	Pipelines or storage vessels and subsequent offloading at terminals.	The oil is offloaded to tankers, which, in turn, offload it at the terminals.	The oil is offloaded to tankers, which, in turn, offload it at the terminals.	The oil is offloaded to a production platform (FPSO), which undertakes the processing and offloads it by ship.	No
Advantage	Installation is straightforward and allows for well control on the surface.	How easy it is to change the fixed structure's location and behavior, which allows well control to take place from the surface.	Designed specially to have little movement.	The storage capacity allows them to operate at great distances from the coast, where building pipelines is not feasible.	Smaller movements than those of an FPSO-type vessel.	It has a rigid anchoring system and reduced movements, which allow for well control to be done from the surface.	Greater autonomy to drill at great distances from the shore.

Source: Petrobrás

shallower, fixed platforms equipped with production facilities in the sea-bed were preferable to floating structures. Over time, and with oil drilling at greater depths, use of semisubmersible structures, floating platforms, and vessels increased, including for production, storage, and drilling activities.

To boost offshore production and highlight Petrobrás's pioneering activities in the international market, research on technological programs was essential. Based on post-1986 expectations of deep-water oil explora-tion, the company invested 1 percent of its revenue in R&D, creating what was considered to be the largest technological program in Brazilian history. The Technological Capability Development Program on Deep Water Production Systems (PROCAP) developed knowledge for large depths and reduced dependence on foreign technology. PROCAP was applied in three modalities.

First, PROCAP 1000 was created at the beginning of offshore explora-tion from 1986 to 1991. The goal was to enable the company to produce oil and gas in water at depths up to 1,000 meters. Many technologies were available in the market, and most had to be acquired and adapted to local conditions through incremental innovations. Over six years, 109 projects were undertaken, with 80 percent focused on the extension of existing technology and 20 percent focused on technological inno-vation. The program cost US$68 million and involved collaboration among 132 research organizations, 400 internal staff members, and 1,000 technical personnel.

To promote scientific and applied research, the company financed the creation of the Center for Petroleum Studies (CEPETRO) in 1987 as part of the Department of Mechanical Engineering at the State University of Campinas (UNICAMP). More than 250 patent applications were filed by Petrobrás and Cenpes from 1987 to 1992, 140 of which were registered in the domestic market and 111 abroad. The annual average of patent appli-cations compared to previous years (1981–1986) increased from twenty to forty-two. The main outcome was installation of floating and early pro-duction systems in the Marlim field at 1,027 meters. Floating platforms became the main technological trajectory toward greater technical and economic viability for future use.

Second, PROCAP 2000 was created to improve learning processes and internal research between 1993 and 1999. Existing technology was inad-equate, giving rise to efforts to generate new knowledge. The immediate goal was to extend applied research to explore at 2,000 meters. With a budget of US$750 million, twenty projects were approved, with 80 percent of the funds dedicated to innovation and the rest to extension, the opposite of the previous phase. In 1996, discovery of a giant oil deposit (132 km^2) in the Roncador field led to incorporation of several new technologies, and these advances and discoveries led to increased offshore production.

Finally, between the years 2000 and 2006, PROCAP 3000 provided technical support to the Campos basin production project. It fundamentally supported potential fields in ultra-deep water up to 3,000 meters. This program's R&D component was budgeted at US$130 million and involved 350 researchers working on nineteen different projects. This phase followed the sequence of previous programs but focused on generating technologies that minimized costs in field production and enabled exploration in ultra-deep waters, as in the case of pre-salt reserves. Among these three PROCAP modalities, the return on investment increased from US$4.30 to US$8.20 per barrel in 2004.

Between 1990 and 2006, Petrobrás filed 733 patent applications, more than any other company in Brazil, 70 percent were national and 30 percent international. In an Ipea survey conducted from 1992 to 2009 with a database provided by Cenpes, Petrobrás invested around R$3.3 billion in science and technology.[5] The Southeast region accounted for three-quarters of this total value, predominantly from the states of Rio de Janeiro and São Paulo. This investment grew exponentially from 2004 to its peak in 2006 at R$1 billion. In addition, resources were allocated mainly for production (24.4 percent), development (20.6 percent), exploration (11.9 percent), and refinement (9.7 percent), creating contracts with more than 196 science and technology institutions.

The five most important partner institutions in these efforts were the Federal University of Rio de Janeiro (UFRJ), the Pontifical Catholic University of Rio de Janeiro (PUC-Rio), the University of São Paulo (USP), UNICAMP, and the Federal University of Rio Grande do Norte (UFRN), in that order. The main research programs focused on chemistry, geosciences, mechanical engineering, chemical engineering, computer science, and materials engineering, allowing broad interdisciplinary research.

TECHNOLOGICAL TRAJECTORY BASED ON SIZE AND STRUCTURE REQUIREMENTS

These programs established guideposts for the offshore oil industry. Development of new technology depends on the size and structure of the challenges. A given technology is developed to become larger (like the evolution of platforms, flexible risers, or drilling devices) or smaller (such as nanomaterials that help to build more resistant pipes for exploration).

The relationship between size and structural requirements can shape and define technological trajectories. Its evolution is best characterized as a process of learning by scaling. Change in size of a technology requires development of appropriate construction material. Three types of innovation can be distinguished: (i) *structural innovations* that come from the design process where the parts and the whole system do not function integrally; (ii) *material innovations* required in the construction process as a consequence of variations in the scale of new technology; and (iii) *systems innovations* that arise from integration of two or more symbiotic technologies, simplifying the overall structure.

Through the process of learning by scaling, promoted during all modalities of PROCAP, the decision to explore offshore oil resulted in higher economic risks. It was necessary to invest in adapted platforms, drilling and storage vessels, seismic research, logistic production, and management of people. Figure 9.4 illustrates the technological efforts of Petrobrás over time. In 1979, the first record[6] in shallow waters was set in the *Bonito* field, at a depth of 189 meters. In 1985, that record was broken, with a new one established in deep waters (383 meters) in the *Marimbá* field. Petrobrás dominated world records for deep-water drilling, ranging from 300 to 1,500 meters except in 1988 (when Placid Oil was the victor). The ultra-deep-water records (above 1,500 meters) varied among the principal competitors in the market (Shell, Marathon, Adarko, and Petrobrás). Petrobrás set the most recent record in 2012 in the *Cascade* field, at a depth of 2,500 meters. This sequence of events is associated with cumulative complexity of technological challenges, with learning determined by the technical scale.

Since the creation of Petrobrás, Brazil's target for oil exploration has been defined by reduced dependence on oil imports. As shown in figure 9.5, national production compared to domestic consumption increased in the early years, but fell in the 1960s and 1970s. In the late 1970s, the decision to invest in offshore production once again stimulated national production. This expansion phase was associated with efforts undertaken by Petrobrás to build capacity and develop technology. Investments increased as the importance of strategic innovation networks and organizations intensified. Since 2006, Brazil has maintained oil self-sufficiency, and Petrobrás has become a market leader in producing cutting-edge technology worldwide.

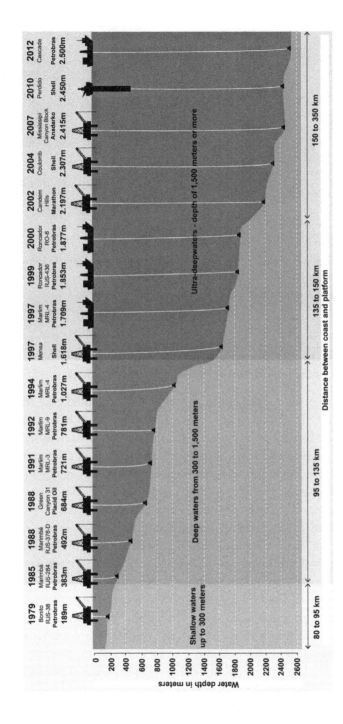

Figure 9.4 Worldwide progression of water depth capabilities for offshore drilling and production, 1979 to 2012.

Source: Adapted from José Mauro de Morais, *Petróleo Em Águas Profundas: Uma História Tecnológica Da Petrobrás Na Exploração e Produção Offshore* (Brasília: Ipea, 2013).

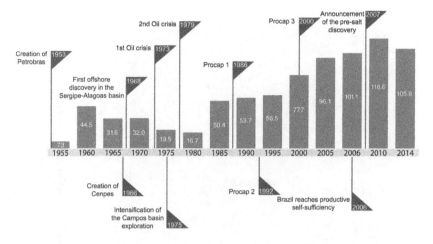

Figure 9.5   National production and total domestic consumption, 1955 to 2014 (in percent).

Source: Ipeadata (2015) and ANP (2015).

EFFECTS OF THE LAVA JATO (CAR WASH) INVESTIGATION: IS INSTITUTIONAL RESTRUCTURING POSSIBLE?

These improvements suggested that Brazil could and would take advantage of the rapid rise in oil prices experienced after 2003. In early 2011, global oil prices peaked at more than US$150 a barrel. Petrobrás seemed to be on the verge of assuring Brazil's future with its pre-salt discoveries.

Congress accordingly turned to restructuring Petrobrás's capital to permit greater state control and to have the company play a dominant role in the development of these resources. Through an equity transfer to the federal government, Petrobrás gained full control of exploration rights for 5 billion barrels of oil. With this, the public stake rose from 40 to 49 percent, as well as almost two-thirds of voting shares. Moreover, the government changed the rules for future exploration of the pre-salt area. Petrobrás was required to have a minimum 30 percent stake in all contracts, exploration, and production. Firms could bid for the right to coparticipate with Petrobrás, and winners were granted exploration rights for up to thirty-five years. This change reduced the rate of return for private firms, but there was less uncertainty about finding oil in the sections auctioned.

Under the agreement, net resources were allotted to a social fund similar to the system in Norway. In theory, all of the country's states and municipalities would benefit from the estimated profits and thereby accelerate social progress. Domestic firms could charge as much as 25 percent more than external competitors for the necessary inputs to develop the pre-salt fields. This advantage meant more opportunity to participate in the production of ships, oil platforms, and other needs. This forecast of large and immediate profits was flawed, even with positive estimates. Costs were presumed to be favorable despite the continuing unknowns of oil drilling at a depth of more than 7 kilometers through pre-salt deposits. Initially, the cost of each drilled well was estimated at approximately US$60 million. Petrobrás required external help to resolve all the technological problems associated with a project of this size. This option of seeking investment from partners was set aside.

Second, the first exploration phase was not expected to yield negative returns. Initially, fixed costs prevailed. Greater expenditure was required during the first years, allowing the deficit per unit of output to decline gradually. The net result would not be equal to the expected steady-state gains. However, with oil at an all-time high price, this was considered a minor matter.

Third, forecasts failed to consider alternative production techniques that were already under way. Fracking,[7] especially in the United States, was coming online, switching demand to much less expensive natural gas. Record high oil prices also influenced the rapid growth of shale, largely produced in Canada but increasingly within the United States, which now serves as an antidote to historical peak prices.

Finally, Petrobrás encountered unanticipated and mushrooming hidden costs. The cost estimates of the Abreu & Lima Refinery eventually were 4 times higher than originally predicted. Hugo Chavez, former president of Venezuela, did not fulfill a promise to pay half of the investment. At the Rio de Janeiro Petrochemical Complex (Comperj), located in the municipality of *Itaboraí* in the east of Rio de Janeiro state, construction ceased altogether. Technical issues were partially responsible for the continual delay, but a greater problem emerged. Only now are discussions occurring with China about joint investment to complete the project.

Then came Lava Jato. It all began with the arrest of Alberto Youseff on March 17, 2014, a black-market money dealer and businessman. He was indicted on charges of money laundering and previously had been involved in the Banestado scandals.[8] This was the beginning of what would become the largest corruption investigation in the country, led by federal judge Sérgio Moro.[9] Youseff admitted that he received bribes for working as an intermediary of fraudulent transactions, including those involving Petrobrás. Through a plea bargain, he confessed to the crimes, shortened his jail time, and implicated many others.

Just three days after Youseff's arrest, a Petrobrás director was arrested. He was Paulo Roberto Costa, former director of supply from 2004 to 2012, appointed to his post by the Progressive Party (PP). With this, the corruption scheme was reported in detail to the federal police. Indictments showed that Petrobrás had paid an exorbitant, artificially high price for the Pasadena refinery located in Texas. This international purchase occurred under Dilma Rousseff, the chair of the company's board prior to her first presidential election in 2010. In November of 2014, the investigation led to the preventive detention of several presidents and directors of large contractors such as the engineering firms OAS, IESA Óleo & Gás, Camargo Corrêa, UTC Engenharia, Engevix, and Construtora Queiroz Galvão.

After Rousseff's reelection, several Petrobrás directors were arrested and convicted at the end of 2014 and in early 2015. High-profile cases included that of Renato Duque (former director of services between 2003 and 2012), appointed by the PT, and Nestor Cerveró (former director of the international area between 2003 and 2008), appointed by the PMDB. In plea-bargain testimony, the defendants revealed the complexity of the scheme. Meanwhile, a lobbyist named Fernando Soares (nicknamed the *Baiano*) and João Vaccari Neto (treasurer of the PT party) were also arrested for acting as intermediaries within the PMDB and PT parties, respectively.

Soon after the elections, in February 2015, Maria das Graças Foster, president of Petrobrás (appointed by Rousseff in 2011), was replaced by Aldemir Bendine, the former CEO of Banco do Brasil. (He himself was later convicted for illicit receipts from Odebrecht.) In March, Rodrigo Janot, the federal prosecutor since 2013, presented twenty-eight petitions to the Federal Supreme Court for the opening of criminal investigations into fifty-five people, forty-nine of whom benefited from executive privilege. These individuals were cited in the plea-bargaining testimonies and had been appointed to Petrobrás's high-level positions by Brazilian lawmakers.

The scheme had become clear. It revolved around the company's overpriced billion-dollar contracts, in which contractors, organized as cartels, paid bribes (varying from 1 to 5 percent) to Petrobrás's senior executives and other public officials. The bribes were distributed through the

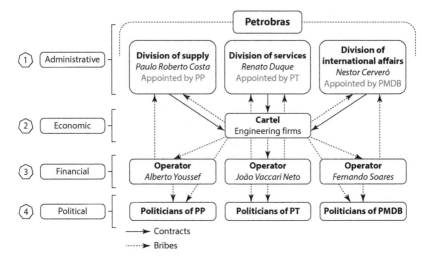

Figure 9.6   Lava Jato (Car Wash) operation, a Petrobrás corruption scheme.

Source: Adapted from the Brazilian Federal Prosecutor (MPF) (2016).

financial operators to all who had been involved: employees, business-men, and, of course, to numerous politicians, including the Speaker of the House of Representatives. This was not difficult to accomplish with high oil prices, and many of those investigated sought plea bargains.

Figure 9.6 diagrams the bribery scheme organized in four areas: administrative, economic, financial, and political. In a normal bidding process, the contract is awarded to the lowest bidder. With the cartel, fake competition was created throughout the bidding process. The contractors organized themselves into a "club" and selected the bid winner and the final price to be offered in secret meetings, leading to illegitimate personal gains and state losses. To ensure the exclusive entry of the group of con-tractors, public agents were encouraged to restrict the entry of legitimate competing firms. Some of the practices that benefited the whole group involved unjustified contracts, unnecessary additive terms with excessive prices, nonenforcement of the contract's relevant steps, and leaking of confidential information.

The financial area operators engaged in money laundering through international financial transactions and fake contracts. The resources were distributed to the beneficiaries through international wire transfers or illegal payment of goods. The investigations widened beyond Petrobrás.

The federal police played a central role. More and more began to be uncovered, relating back to the World Cup and the Olympics. As Lava Jato widened and the recession deepened, pressure increased to remove Dilma and replace her with Michel Temer, the vice president.

Dilma was impeached by the House, and Petrobrás became a principal target for restructuring. Prices of its shares had fallen sharply, and foreign resources were available only at disadvantageous rates. According to the 2014 financial reports, the company had a R$6.2 billion loss due to corruption and a net loss of R$21.6 billion. In a more recent 2016 estimate, Petrobrás's gross debt reached a record level of R$506.5 billion, whereas in 2003 it was only R$31 billion, which is an increase of 24 percent per year.

Pedro Parente, who had served in the Cardoso government as minister of mines and energy and earlier as chief of staff, took over in May 2016. His task was to disassemble and recreate a new Petrobrás. New leadership, free from political meddling, was only the beginning. Cases were pending in the United States, and investors claimed that losses were caused by the false information regarding the company's financial situation. These cases required time for resolution, meanwhile contributing to net losses. Only later in 2018 were they finally all settled.

Internally, there were changes in structure. An Audit Committee was created, and new internal structures were established to assure integrity and valid reporting. Prices were allowed to vary internally, reflecting international price movements. There was an effort to reduce the immense size of the enterprise by selling off components, thereby reducing debt. At one point, Petrobrás had become the largest company in the world in the petroleum sector. In an attempt to return to Petrobrás's technocratic tradition, expenses were reevaluated, reflecting smaller investments in the short term. Although the concession of exploration rights remained restricted, Petrobrás managed to increase the rate of return for foreign companies, with Petrobrás no longer required to hold 30 percent of all contracts.

These actions resulted in a progressively better financial performance. Operational results improved. Total profits began to turn positive in 2017 and improved even more in 2018. There was talk of sales of stock to diminish the large federal presence, while maintaining the strategy of a smaller, more profitable firm. Holdings of various subsidiaries were sold off.

Then another problem arose. As a means of settling the truckers' strike in mid-2018, Temer agreed to subsidize prices of diesel, inflicting unanticipated losses on Petrobrás. This resolved one matter, but provoked another. This was political interference once again, and Parente resigned in protest.

After an immediate fall in stock prices, the situation rapidly improved. Petrobrás experienced the largest gain in value within the petroleum sector over recent months. Many analysts have suggested Petrobrás as a stock to be purchased. Foreign firms have responded by indicating great interest in future participation under the new rules that continue to require unity. There is also talk of Chinese interest in participating in a joint effort to bring Comperj to completion.

Petrobrás has continued to show gains in productivity in recent years, but caution should be exercised. Market prices for petroleum products have settled into a favorable range, although they continue to be volatile. The current moment is an extremely serious time for the company due to fear of renewed political interference in business management. Petrobrás can only change course if the changes resulting from the Car Wash investigation are proven to be institutional changes, and not mere temporary rearrangements.

Technical-based management without political interference is central to the future of the company. This is the only way for Petrobrás to regain its former international position. Continuous acquisition and generation of technology is key. The company must return to research and management based on market principles to resume growth and continue on its disrupted path of innovation.

CHAPTER 10

The Technological Evolution of Embraer

Technological innovation plays a critical role in aircraft development, an enterprise dependent on systems engineering, an interdisciplinary field of knowledge that focuses on the modeling and organization of complex systems. Solutions for problems relating to the entire range of operations—performance, cost escalation, testing, manufacturing, training, and distribution—are essential. Innovation by development of new materials, the improvement of aerodynamics, the propulsion of the motors, built-in electronics, and integrated command systems are key.

Since the 1930s, the aircraft industry has been an extremely competitive sector for newcomers worldwide. Many aircraft manufacturers emerged after 1945. Moving forward four decades, the 1980s ushered in a period mergers and acquisitions. In this chapter, we trace the history of Embraer since its founding in 1969. The story is emblematic of a company from a developing country that succeeded in a global competitive environment.

THE EMERGENCE OF AN AIRCRAFT MANUFACTURING INDUSTRY

Brazil entered the global market in the late 1960s. Embraer appeared in the United States market in 1978, with the first Brazilian aircraft to fly through American airspace. The company was privatized in the 1990s, a decade in which the sector became extremely competitive. Embraer had achieved success designing aircraft for regional aviation—a market niche relatively unexplored by major international manufacturers.[1]

An intense transformation over the last seventy years has led to a complete restructuring and consolidation of aircraft production. At the end of the day, only four major competitors remained, and they were divided into two markets: continental and regional aviation. The continental aviation market now consists of Boeing (a U.S. company) and Airbus (a European conglomerate). This concentration resulted from progressively fewer competing firms seeking innovation through scaled-up production to manufacture aircraft with more seating and longer flight ranges. Embraer and Bombardier (Canadian) focused on regional aviation. These two companies competed to innovate smaller-scale aircraft. Several firms initially pursued long-distance aviation, linking large urban centers (usually equipped with adequate infrastructure), but firms in regional markets specialized in products for short-haul flights. These were designed to interconnect medium-sized urban centers whose infrastructure was limited.

Two major breakthroughs revolutionized the civil aviation industry. The first was production of the U.S. DC3 by Douglas Aircraft Company in the mid-1930s. Its success relied on mass production with a dominant design for the manufacture of piston engines.[2] The second involved the introduction of jet engines and Boeing-powered wings in the 707 model in the late 1950s, radically transforming aircraft technical standards by increasing seating and cargo capacity, cruising speed, and flight range.[3]

Evolution of the DC3 to the DC7 in 1956 was made possible by incremental innovations. The power of a propeller engine with increased wing-span size and fuselage length doubled the maximum take-off weight and permitted a flight range 5 times greater. Douglas, in an attempt to be more competitive, replaced the propeller engine with a jet engine in the DC8. In 1968, competition with Boeing jets and financial difficulties led Douglas to merge with McDonnell, the U.S. manufacturer of military aircraft. In the 1960s, McDonnell Douglas succeeded in producing jet airplanes at competitive prices. From then on, there was competition between two engine standards, turboprop and jet. The turboprop engine had been the only available solution, but entry of jet engines progressively reduced the share of turboprops in the continental market.

Turboprops had an advantage in aircraft markets with smaller capacity; jet engines evolved on larger scale aircraft. From 1948 to 1997, the turboprop engine industry witnessed few changes and had a small number of producers. This oligopoly did not result from the exit of small manufacturers but was due to the existence of one dominant technology with variable strategies. This contrasts with the jet engine scenario, in which the entry and exit of firms was more intense.

After the two oil crises in the 1970s, many aircraft manufacturers experienced difficulty. Financial viability depended on the cost per available seat-kilometer.[4] Production of ever-larger aircraft boosted competition among manufacturers. In Europe, several companies dissolved or left the civil aviation market. Aeronautical manufacturers in the United Kingdom, Germany, and France withdrew. In 1967, these countries began negotiations on a joint production arrangement for the Airbus A300. Airbus had been created in 1970 by Aerospatiale and Deutsche Aerospace (the latter being a group of German companies). Fokker (Dutch) and Hawker Siddeley (British) joined soon after. In 1972, the contract to build part of the project's tail was awarded to Construcciones Aeronáuticas S.A. (Spanish).[5]

The situation was similar in the United States. Several companies failed or left the market, such as North American, Convair, and Lockheed. In 1997, to compete with Airbus, Boeing bought McDonnell Douglas, strengthening its position in the European continental aviation market.

INTERNAL MACROECONOMIC ENVIRONMENT: INSTITUTION BUILDING

Brazilian success in an activity in which a few countries dominate was based on three characteristics: investment in knowledge, innovation in management, and institution building over time.

The process of industrialization in Brazil, including the nascent aeronautical sector, accelerated in 1930.[6] The Vargas era, beginning with the 1930 Revolution, lasted until the end of *Estado Novo* in 1945. National aviation policy began to be designed and implemented during this era. The National Air Mail and the Department of Civil Aviation (DAC) were created in 1931. The Naval Air Mail was created in 1934, and finally, in 1941, the Brazilian Air Force (FAB) and the Ministry of Aeronautics were created. Ventures in the national aviation industry also moved forward. Examples in the private sector include Ypiranga Aeronautics Company (1931), National Air Navigation Company (1935), and Paulista Aeronautics Company (1942). In the public sector, innovation rarely went beyond inputs to the military.

With the end of World War II in 1945, Brazil's nascent aircraft industry faced a crisis. This resulted from two principal factors. First, the administration of president Eurico Dutra was more liberal and less interested in market intervention. Second, a supply of military aircraft was obtained at very competitive prices. As a result, the domestic aircraft market virtually collapsed.

Despite efforts made to foster the domestic industry, Brazil relied on the import of manufactured goods, particularly for the most sophisticated sectors. A shift occurred when the Ministry of Aeronautics began to define a strategic project. This project sought to incorporate technological knowledge from other countries to develop Brazil's aviation industry. Professor Richard Smith from MIT was invited to Brazil in 1945 to establish a teaching and research center in São José dos Campos (São Paulo state). This consisted of two coordinated but autonomous scientific institutes: one for higher technical education and the other for research and industrial development.

In 1946, the government launched the Technological Center of Aeronautics (CTA). In 1950, the Technological Institute of Aeronautics (ITA) engineering school was created to expand human resources. In 1953, a Research and Development Institute (IPD) was created, developing experimental projects like the Convertiplane,[7] the Beija-flor helicopter, and the Bandeirante airplane.

With the return of Getúlio Vargas to the presidency in the early 1950s, and his support of the aeronautical sector, foreign competition was welcomed. The Dutch aircraft company Fokker began producing in Brazil, benefiting from local facilities. The Dutch received capital provided by Brazilian and Dutch investors, as well as help from the government. Fokker committed itself not only to the delivery of several aircraft but also to the transfer of information. That undertaking was interrupted with the end of the Vargas government in 1954.

The Sociedade Construtora Aeronáutica Neiva (Neiva), an aircraft manufacturer, was also founded in 1954 to build planes for a newly purchased aircraft carrier. In the next year, Neiva obtained a license to manufacture the Paulistinha CAP-4,[8] an aircraft produced until 1948 by Paulista Aeronautics Company. With several modifications to the original design, the Paulistinha P-56 was the only aircraft to be completely designed and produced in Brazil until the end of the 1960s. During this time, ITA-trained engineers launched private initiatives, such as the Avibras in 1961 (later specialized in military armaments) and Aerotec in 1962. ITA and Brazil's CTA collaborated in these projects and disseminated knowledge and technology.

THE GENESIS OF EMBRAER

Early failure to achieve a domestic aircraft industry can be explained by a single factor: none of the preliminary models captured any market share. Embraer's founding in 1969 was to alter that result. Development of Embraer's first plane is illustrative of the company's trajectory. The experimental project IPD-6504, developed by the IPD, was the prototype of Embraer's first airplane, the Bandeirante.[9] Embraer was founded with a clear objective: to produce a series of planes with national technology and to conquer a significant portion of the market. This effort depended on international competitiveness when other Brazilian initiatives had failed. Ten years after Embraer's founding, its plane entered the North American market, where demand was rising in smaller cities.

Following the company's entry into the U.S. market, sales to American customers soared. Embraer soon accounted for a third of the U.S. market in the less than twenty-seat aircraft category, despite the fact that the Bandeirante was nonpressurized, less fuel-efficient, slower, and had a more limited flight range than its direct competitors, Beech and Fairchild. Brazilian bank interest rates of around 9 percent, when market rates ranged from 15 to 18 percent, played a role in the plane's international success. In addition, the Bandeirante had lower maintenance costs, and after-sales service was oriented to local needs.

The Bandeirante was a versatile turboprop with capacity for eight to twenty-one passengers, ideal for medium-sized urban centers, and an advantage over its direct competitors. Embraer sought to simultaneously license projects and establish international agreements, with the objective of gaining industrial maturity. For a summary of Embraer's evolution over time, including specification of the evolving market, see table 10.1. Here we focus on commercial production, not forgetting, however, the wide range of additional aircraft primarily produced for the local market.

Later, in the 1980s, as Bandeirante's reputation was established in the United States, the U.S. airline industry underwent deregulation. Embraer launched its second successful product, the Brasília. This model secured a significant portion of the U.S. market in the twenty- to forty-seat aircraft category. More Embraer aircraft were operating in the United States than in Brazil, so production of larger planes became the priority. By focusing on this niche market, Embraer enhanced its global insertion.

In production for military purposes, some manufacturing techniques proved essential to the development of Embraer aircraft in the 1990s. Three commercial aircraft defined the output of the firm in the late 1980s. The first was the EMB 120 Brasília (twin turboprop, pressurized, with low cabin noise). The second was the CBA 123, developed through a partnership between the Brazilian and Argentine governments.

Aircraft	Designation	Marketplace	First Flight–End of Production	Description
Ipanema	EMB 200/201	Agricultural	1970–to present	Most popular and sold agricultural airplane since the creation of Embraer.
Bandeirante	EMB 110/111	Commercial and defense	1972–1991	Redesign of Bandeirante, which proved to be a versatile, economical, and well-accepted airplane in the market. Production ended in 1991.
Xavante	EMB 326	Defense	1971–1981	Manufactured under Italian license.
Piper line (Carioca; Corisco; Tupi; Minuano; Sertanejo; Seneca)	EMB 710/711/ 712/720/ 721/810	Light aviation	1975–2000	Manufactured under license from Piper.
Xingu	EMB 121	Business and defense	1976–1987	Pressurized twin turboprop flying at high altitudes that had greater fuel economy, an important feature in the 1970s.
Tucano	EMB 312	Defense	1980–1998	Military training airplane specially produced for the FAB.
Brasília	EMB 120	Commercial	1983–2007	Twin turboprop, pressurized, designed for the regional aviation thirty-seat category.
AMX	A-1	Defense	1985–to present	Military combat fighter designed by a joint venture between Embraer, Aermacchi, and Aeritalia. Also important for technology transfer.
Vector	CBA 123	Commercial	1990 (prototype)	Aircraft built in partnership between Brazil and Argentina with a revolutionary design. It was not a profitable project, but it was important for Embraer's future generation of aircraft.
Super Tucano	EMB 312H	Defense	1993–to present	Redesign and modeling of military training aircraft. In this project, Embraer proved to be a strong competitor in the international defense market.
ERJ 145	ERJ 145/140/135	Commercial and defense	1995–to present	A variant (jet) of the Brasília aircraft with technology from CBA 123, with 145, 140, and 135 versions. By using a series of innovative partnerships involving risk sharing, this project reinstated Embraer in the regional aviation market.
E-Jets	EMB 170/190	Commercial	2002–to present	The E-Jets aircraft family included versions 170, 175, 190, and 195. The project was carried out with risk-sharing partnerships and around 90 percent of the parts were used in various models, enabling a significant reduction in operational costs and training.
Legacy	Legacy 600/650	Business	2001–to present	Midrange and intercontinental range aircraft, built on the ERJ 135 platform.
Phenom	Phenom 100/300	Business	2007–to present	Medium-range business aircraft.
Lineage	Lineage 1000	Business	2007–to present	Large business aircraft, a variant of the EMB 190.
KC 390	KC 390	Defense	2015 (under development)	Military transport aircraft, in-flight refueling, with fly-by-wire technology in its avionics, having a twenty-three-ton load capacity, including heavy vehicles. Project under development since 2009.

Source: Embraer, *Historical Center Embraer* (2015).

The third, the ERJ 145, was a jetliner version of the Brasília expanded to accommodate forty-five passengers but using CBA 123 technology. The Brasília was one of the best-selling aircrafts, but the CBA 123 proved to be extremely expensive due to its modern design and was a financial failure. This project incorporated extremely advanced solutions, systems, and equipment for that time, but these advances were undervalued by the market. In addition, most Argentine counterparts did not meet the agreement requirements. What was learned from the CBA 123 project was important for the design of future generations of Embraer aircraft, notably the Embraer Regional Jet (ERJ) aircraft family.

In the second half of the 1980s, Embraer was still not profitable, despite these technological advances.[10] During that time, the supply of international credit was restricted worldwide, aircraft development costs increased, and competition in the regional aviation market intensified. Despite the variety of earlier partnerships and joint ventures, the industry had fewer independent actors. Companies competed via collaboration, through risk sharing, and by mobilizing common resources.

Embraer's budget was drastically reduced. This scenario was troublesome. Embraer's culture and state management structure were incompatible with the flexibility and acceleration of decisions demanded by substantial market competition. From 1985 to 1994, Brazil also faced a succession of economic problems, increasing uncertainty.

TRADE LIBERALIZATION, PRIVATIZATION, AND CONSOLIDATION

To make matters worse, the administration of President Fernando Collor reversed protectionist industrial policies in 1990, and the economy was reoriented toward less intervention. This meant the end of subsidized export financing for working capital for products requiring more than eighteen months to produce. Embraer's difficulty was also a result of its strong dependence on government and defense contracts. The end of the Cold War led to reduced military spending worldwide, and the First Gulf War (1991) aggravated this with an increase in oil prices, which affected civil aviation. These internal and external difficulties contributed to an acceleration of Embraer's privatization.

Shortly before privatization in 1994, the company was restructured for development of the ERJ 145 program. Privatization had additional financial effects. In 1990, Embraer had more than 9,000 employees, about 47 percent greater than after 1994. Revenue was US$417 million, with a negative equity of US$281 million. The government was the majority shareholder, with a 93 percent stake.

Immediately after privatization, the government share fell to 40 percent and private finance entered for the first time. Few foreign firms were interested. One U.S. company won a sizable share, but reneged thereafter. The Bozano Group was the largest investor with something on the order of 30 percent, followed by Previ and Sistel, pension holders for Bank of Brazil and telephone employees. Together they accounted for the remaining shares.

Over time additional modifications took place. In 1999, the French group Dassault entered with about 20 percent, reflecting sales by the government and the Bozano Group. As the company did well, the government eventually held only one "golden share," which enabled strict government control over Embraer. The firm began to attract a large number of foreign groups, led by the Oppenheimer Fund from the United States and the Barilli Group of Scotland. The two initial pension investors continued, but the Bozano Group and Dassault had minimal participation.

The solution to the restricted supply of credit worldwide was to create innovative partnerships that involved risk sharing. Since its privatization, Embraer has been able to organize a worldwide network of suppliers over more than two decades. At the same time, it had gained international credibility and a reputation for quality. For the production of the ERJ 145, Embraer attracted investment from companies from several countries for the provision of structures and equipment based on the recognized potential of the program.

When Embraer was privatized, an organizational and cultural transformation took place. A number of measures were taken, from reducing operating costs (such as downsizing and increasing productivity) to diversifying production with customized solutions. The company secured economies of scope by using the ERJ 145 platform to manufacture the ERJ 135 and 140 models.

The first years following privatization were complicated because the world was hit by three currency and financial crises: the Mexican (1995), the Asian (1997), and the Russian (1998). Since the ERJ 145 was well rated by the market and had low acquisition and maintenance costs, sales recovered, and Embraer was able to turn a profit in 1997. This recovery was reflected in employee hiring (figure 10.1). The aircraft's low operating cost played a key role. U.S. market deregulation and labor settlements between aircraft unions and airline companies helped as well.

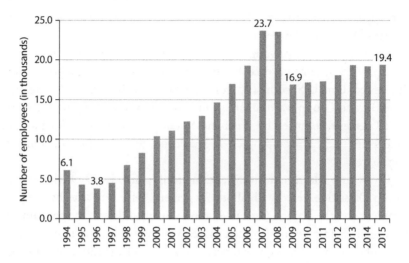

Figure 10.1   Number of Embraer employees, 1994 to 2015.

Source: Embraer (2015), based on several annual reports.

The number of Embraer employees grew from 1996 until the international financial crisis of 2008, falling in 2010 and increasing slightly until 2015. At the same time, rivalry in the regional aviation market between Embraer and Bombardier became more intense.

When Embraer won a contract to provide two hundred jets to the U.S. company Continental Express in 1996, Bombardier filed a complaint with the World Trade Organization (WTO) alleging that the Brazilian company had subsidized its exports through the Export Financing Program (Proex). The Brazilian government argued that Bombardier was also subsidized by a variety of Canadian government agencies. The WTO found irregularity in both cases and requested changes in both programs. In 2001, Brazilian authorities filed a new complaint with the WTO challenging Canada over Bombardier funding; Canada did the same. On both occasions, there were no retaliatory measures by Brazil or Canada. Because of these WTO findings, the Brazilian Development Bank was obliged to modify the mechanism of its financial support to Embraer and to modify the financing mechanisms.

During Embraer's upswing, in 1999 the company decided to invest in the next generation of jets. This new aircraft line was planned to meet aviation demand for short routes but intense passenger traffic. The experience obtained from shared risk management enabled Embraer to

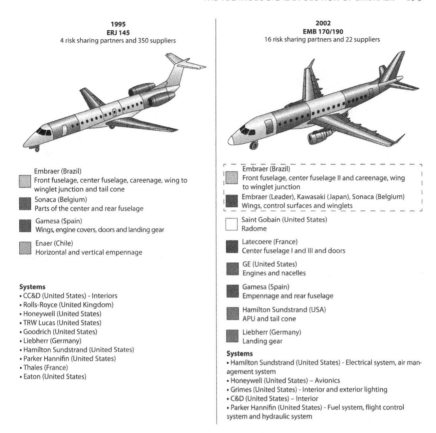

Figure 10.2   Embraer risk sharing in the ERJ 145 and EMB 170/190 programs.

Source: Adapted from Andrea Goldstein, "Embraer: From National Champion to Global Player," *Cepal Review* 77 (2002): 97–115.

leverage partners and resources for the EMB 170/190 aircraft program. The focus was on reducing costs through the development of a common platform, but parts could be tailored to buyers' needs.

Figure 10.2 shows the importance of these partnerships in the production process. In addition, risk sharing increased from one program to another between 1995 and 2002. This demonstrates Embraer's managerial ability to utilize its strategic knowledge.

With its increased presence in the business aviation market (with the launch of the Legacy in 2001 and the Phenom and Lineage jets in 2007), Embraer was in much better shape. Figure 10.3 shows total aircraft delivery since 1996, with reductions in 2001 following the terrorist attacks in

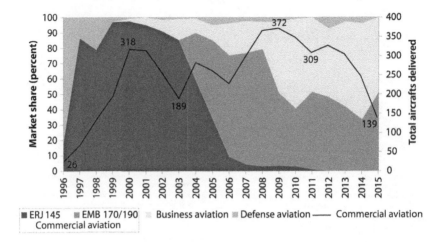

Figure 10.3   Market share of commercial, business, and defense aviation and total aircraft delivered by Embraer, 1996 to 2015.

Source: Embraer (2015), based on several annual reports.

the United States and in 2008 due to the international financial crisis. Until 2000, Embraer's main sales were to the commercial aviation segment, with only a small share of the defense market. However, this situation changed with the launch of business jets in 2001. By 2015, half of total aircraft deliveries were directed to business aviation.

At the end of 2002, Embraer announced a joint venture with the China Aviation Corporation II (AVIC II) to manufacture ERJ 145 aircraft for the Chinese market. The following year, Embraer produced the first aircraft by the partnership. This expanded to production of business jets, with the manufacture of the Legacy and the Phenom. Through this cooperation program, the Chinese aviation industry increased its manufacturing capacity in response to local demand for air transportation. With greater production capacity and knowledge transfer, Chinese companies began to compete directly with Embraer. In 2016, after thirteen years of cooperation, a continuing decline in sales led to a decision by Embraer to end its production in China.

The Chinese partnership was disastrous in competitive terms; it did not achieve Embraer's conquest of the Asian market. However, the ability to centralize resources and manage complex projects such as the KC 390, a military transport, opened up the possibility of broader growth attained only by large manufacturers. Maturation and mastery of technologies applied to the KC 390 are relevant to a broader spectrum of both business and commercial aviation. In 2015, the first KC 390 was launched, exhibiting the technological gains achieved in the interim.

TECHNOLOGICAL GUIDEPOSTS AND INTERNATIONAL LEADERSHIP

The design of an aircraft is composed of three stages: (i) conceptual, i.e., evaluation of candidate alternative projects, including analysis, parametric studies, and configuration; (ii) preliminary, i.e., refining and developing an aerodynamic database; and (iii) detailing and description, component manufacturing, prototype construction, and system testing both in flight and on the ground. Project development usually lasts from five to seven years. Typically, potential customers appear at this stage and may influence the manufacturer's design of the equipment. The life cycle of the product depends on its type. For civilian transport aircraft, the period may vary from thirty to forty years.

Embraer's technological trajectory from the 1970s to the 2000s demonstrates the maximization of the aircraft's market potential (figure 10.4). The evolutionary change of design techniques employed by Embraer for modeling the aerodynamics and wing shape from the Bandeirante to the more modern jets was essential. The company increasingly used advanced testing techniques (such as wind tunnels) to combine complex computational methods with design performance.

Over time, Embraer could take advantage of a market niche, such as turboprops, when the market demanded more economical aircraft and direct competitors could not respond; they were either inefficient or used jet power. Managerial ability to enter strategic innovation networks increased risk sharing in production and improved the ability to combine different types of technologies. In the case of civil aircraft, although jets with swept wings have become dominant, the market for turboprop airplanes with straight wings, operated by short-range airlines, remained. This result is consistent with the idea that technological paradigms exhibit life cycles associated with a specific historical context, as Dosi argues.[11]

The 1970s was a period of adaptation dominated by learning to apply new technology. This process was passive, with manufacturing performed under license. This allowed acquisition of knowledge regarding batch production methods, manufacturing techniques, compliance control, and quality management. All of this had to be learned for the company

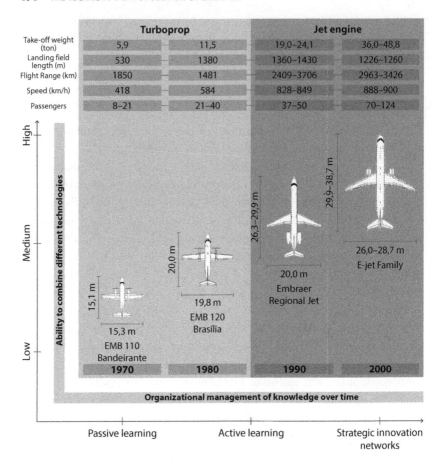

	Turboprop		Jet engine	
Take-off weight (ton)	5,9	11,5	19,0–24,1	36,0–48,8
Landing field length (m)	530	1380	1360–1430	1226–1260
Flight Range (km)	1850	1481	2409–3706	2963–3426
Speed (km/h)	418	584	828–849	888–900
Passengers	8–21	21–40	37–50	70–124

Figure 10.4   Technological progression of Embraer's aircraft production, 1970s to 2000s.

Source: Developed by the authors.

to improve its aircraft technology. But becoming a strategic leader in shifting the knowledge frontier outward was not enough. In the 1980s, aircraft production implemented active learning, and military and government certifications and partnerships took place. The transition from the 1980s to the 1990s was an extremely troubled period, creating uncertainties about the company's future. After privatization, which had been an ultimate hope since inception, a modern managerial culture emerged. Innovation was the only way to survive, and it required strategic networks for the diffusion and sharing of knowledge.

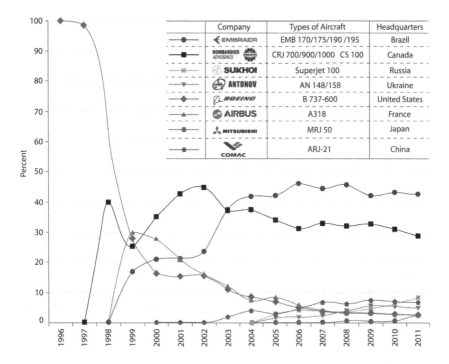

Figure 10.5   Market share in 70- to 120-seat aircraft.

Source: Adapted from ABDI (2014).

Embraer's market share, compared to its main competitors, including Bombardier and new entrants Comac (Chinese), Sukhoi (Russian), Antonov (Ukrainian), and Mitsubishi (Japanese), remained above 40 percent in the commercial aviation market (figure 10.5). Under private management, Embraer became the third-largest manufacturer of commercial jets, continuing as the market leader in aircraft up to 120 seats.

The composition of production has changed in the last decade. With an increase in the production of business jets and a greater number of sales of military aircraft to governments, Embraer has become competitive internationally.

RECENT DEVELOPMENTS IN EMBRAER'S STRATEGY

Financial support has evolved since the company's privatization, including 30 percent financing for the development of the ERJ 145 in 1995;

purchase of R$149 million of debentures in conjunction with warrants (partially converted into IPO shares, a precondition for investment); increased support for R&D for new products and processes; availability of export financing lines of credit; and assistance to abet domestic sales of commercial and business aircraft.

From 1999 to 2006, BNDES financed 50 percent of sold aircraft. In 2007, this percentage was close to zero, but it grew again to 34 percent in 2010. In fact, a large part of BNDES's portfolio in recent years was built on transactions resulting from Embraer's growth.

Interest in the defense area has also been fruitful, with revenues increasing for this segment. In 2010, an Embraer division was created to handle military needs. A first section was for the KC 390. In addition to planned domestic use of thirty-two aircraft by the Brazilian Air Force, partially to combat forest fires, there are explicit export commitments, especially for countries actively involved in the production process.

Second is the partnership between Embraer and Saab (Sweden) to produce advanced military jets. The Swedish company won the competition against the United States and France in 2013. As part of the agreement, a twenty-five-year financing commitment was negotiated at a favorable rate of 2.19 percent per annum. The delivery of thirty-six Gripen aircraft is slated to take place between 2019 and 2024, when new models of the E/F variety become available. An increasing role for Embraer, with greater transfer of technology and more rapid learning, is built into the agreement.

Third is the Brazilian partnership with the French government in French Guiana, where a satellite launch will occur of the Ariadne 5 missile. Originally intended to take place in 2013, the ensuing economic recession curtailed public spending. This commitment was structured to be part of Embraer's future competitive strategy.

Embraer has been profitable virtually since its privatization. It has been a pioneer in competitiveness, allowing introduction of technological advances around the world. Now, as the fifth-largest exporter in Brazil, it is at the same time a leading importer from a variety of countries. In 2015, there was a positive balance of nearly US$3 billion.

Thereafter, in the midst of the Brazilian recession and slower growth internationally, Embraer began to encounter problems. Success had been presumed eternal, but with falling demand, unions called for a return to import substitution. That carried no weight. Instead, management once more responded in an innovative fashion. Embraer has negotiated a contract to divert principal responsibility for passenger jet development to Boeing. Embraer will retain a 20 percent share of this new enterprise and receive US$4.75 billion, thereby assuring needed finance. In turn, another enterprise wholly owned by Embraer will maintain and expand its production of small passenger jets and defense products. Needless to say, there will be opportunity for greater sharing of technology and anticipated cost reductions for both enterprises.

This outcome did not occur by chance. It was preceded by major developments in the fierce competition for aircraft sales. The continuing dispute between Embraer and Bombardier over interest rate subsidies at the WTO goes back to 1996. Each was reciprocally charged for allowing interest subsidies on loans extended to purchasers. Both found ways to satisfy investigative panels while managing to continue to offer credit advantages.

In 2013, Bombardier was able to realize the first flight of its C Series, intended to compete in the range of 100 to 149 seats. A short time later, Brazil returned to the WTO, complaining about illegal subsidies of $3 billion granted by public sources. In 2016, Boeing was the legal complainant, this time in U.S. courts, accusing Bombardier of selling below cost by 40 percent in the U.S. market.

This competitive process flared once again in 2017 when Delta Airlines was able to purchase the new Bombardier C line of jets. Embraer had competed unsuccessfully and brought another case. The U.S. Commerce Department imposed tariffs of around 300 percent on Bombardier imports for five years. The United States International Trade Commission took the case and canceled the duties. More important, Canada decided to forego its planned purchase of billions of dollars of fighter jets from Boeing.

Airbus then entered as a partner with Bombardier for the C-Series program. This involved purchase of a bare majority of equity by Airbus. Moreover, construction of the C line was to take place at Airbus's facilities in Alabama. This time, the U.S. government was quite satisfied and tolerated a subsidized local price.

A situation as serious as this provoked a reaction by Boeing, which earlier had a close relationship with Embraer. It now decided to arrange a deeper commitment. Extensive negotiations occurred before a final agreement was reached in mid-2018. This deal now requires congressional approval in Brazil. Despite efforts by the Temer administration, this matter was not settled. A good reason to hurry was to avoid a postelection negative decision coming from the left, but Bolsonaro has doubts as well. Nationalism is a powerful force.

Further progress will await the new government's decision. The press has been an active participant in publishing short op-eds and articles. Longer articles have likewise been written. This case will test the strategy that may prevail in the new administration. It will equally test the capacity of Embraer to emerge once more as a leader in the global market.

CHAPTER 11

Brazilian Agriculture and Beyond

FINAL CONSIDERATIONS

Throughout this book, we have demonstrated how well-defined innovation policies can leverage available knowledge. The leadership role displayed by Embrapa in institutional and technological transformations is illustrative. The Brazilian agricultural sector played an important role in advancing *aggregate* technological progress; technical change is far more complex than merely importing inputs from industry.

Technological change within agribusiness has led to lower costs and increased efficiency. Many of these benefits have been transferred to the wider society. Industry should not be favored at the expense of the agricultural sector, as so often has occurred in the past. Quite the opposite, these two sectors are increasingly integrated. Taxing agriculture to provide subsidies to manufacturers almost always results in a suboptimal equilibrium.

Our second point is a need for innovation throughout the economy to bolster future Brazilian economic development. We added the cases of Petrobrás and Embraer—other instances of public intervention followed by greater reliance on the private market—precisely to emphasize a cooperative, rather than a competitive, relationship between the state and individual activity.

A BRIEF SUMMARY

Chapter 2 discusses the macroeconomic evolution of Brazil from its late start in the 1890s to more recent difficulties over the last decades. The cyclical variability of growth and inflation influenced the urban demand for food as well as eventually promoting advances in agricultural productivity and output. That, in turn, has provided a backdrop for increasing regional advances as well as a more coherent strategy of exports to the rest of the world. Once a successful BRIC during the commodity boom, Brazil has seen poorer growth emerge, hindered by limited domestic savings, inadequate competitiveness, and an emphasis on the distribution of gains instead of attention to productivity advances.

Chapter 3 offers a theoretical basis for the impressive advance of Brazil's agricultural productivity since the 1960s. For some readers, the content can be a challenge; others may appreciate the didactic approach. The intent is to provide a comprehensive review of changing scholarship, which is needed to modernize and sustain agricultural productivity.

Chapter 4 focuses on the evolution of innovation within the Brazilian agricultural sector since the 1970s. Regional diversity is at the heart of this process. New land areas have been incorporated and productive specialization has changed. Brazil's North and Northeast regions did not immediately benefit. Limited education and little absorption of technology translated into a lag that has only seen improvement in recent years. Restructuring first occurred in the South, and thereafter has expanded westward.

Chapter 5 addresses important institutional changes. There were two principal reasons for success. First came the Green Revolution. That aroused Brazilian interest in utilizing these techniques domestically. Second, and perhaps more critical, was the creation of Embrapa as an agency within the Ministry of Agriculture. This established a platform for continued dissemination of results from experimental research, as well as plans for new research. There was another important contribution: creation and support for agricultural universities, many of whose graduates subsequently became affiliated with Embrapa.

Chapter 6 evaluates Brazil's agricultural trade performance in the international market. The commodity boom from the latter half of the 2000s provided opportunity for growth in export receipts. Although income rose, export quantity did not. Productivity growth, in fact, slowed, especially due to inadequate infrastructure investment and high transportation costs to international markets.

Chapter 7 analyzes Brazilian agricultural expansion since 1990, with a focus on deforestation and environmental sustainability. The productive frontier had advanced toward the Center-West, the northeastern Cerrado, and the edges of the Amazon. This chapter includes an analysis of the land-saving effect from productivity advance and a comparison between production and GHG emissions. The agricultural sector, although responsible for most of these emissions, can also mitigate the effects of climate change through intelligent policies.

Chapter 8 considers the heterogeneity of Brazilian agriculture, focusing on the challenges of small-scale production. Although Brazilian agriculture as a whole has made impressive advances, smaller producers, especially in the North and Northeast, have not. This inefficiency is due to limited technical assistance that is further aggravated by low education levels among farmers. Welfare policies available in the region, such as the Bolsa Família and rural retirement programs, were a partial offset. Over time, rising costs will inevitably result in a declining agricultural workforce and migration to the cities. Only technology and knowledge, not agrarian reform, can provide small farmers with needed access to markets.

Chapters 9 and 10 discuss the cases of Petrobrás and Embraer. The state played an active initial role in both; each was created and operated as a state enterprise. However, each has been able to loosen its ties with the public sector. Oil and aircraft production demonstrate the consequences of continued technical advance. As in agriculture, international collaborative processes and access to foreign markets were significant.

Despite Petrobras's recent problems, there is a basis for optimism. Historical productivity gains accelerated again after recent massive restructuring. Productive earnings will occur only if the return to technocratic competence is sustained and advanced in the future.

Embraer, in turn, is the world's third-largest aircraft production company. It has now moved ahead once more, offsetting recent losses by partially joining Boeing. Embraer will retain full production of defense and smaller aircraft, whose demand is increasing, while retaining a partial share of its commercial production. Marketing will shift to Boeing, which sees the planes as important complements to its continuing expansion of larger, intercontinental aircraft.

INNOVATION POLICIES

Our approach took up the agricultural sector in chapters 3 and 4. In the first of these, the analysis was theoretical, focusing on innovation, diffusion, and generation of new knowledge. This scheme can be seen in figure 11.1: (i) the institutional environment is the basis of search and selection of technology; (ii) the microeconomy activity defines the behavioral relations to create and transmit diversity; and (iii) there is coordination of collaborative networks of external research.

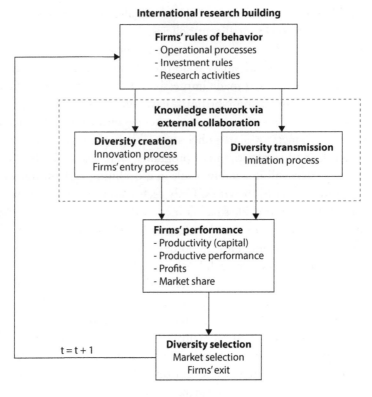

Figure 11.1   Institutional basis of the dynamics of mechanisms for technological search and selection.

Source: Developed by the authors.

Diversity results from technological change—moving from initial imitation to innovation—through the influence of the market. *Imitation* involves utilization of the best technology by domestic firms. *Innovation* introduces local technological diversity. *Selection* leads to the survival of the most dynamic firms, characterized by the best technology. In agriculture, imitation is necessary to assimilate knowledge generated in international research networks. Selection of the most productive technologies for a specific context is a repetitive process. Interactions among these three forces lead to continued technological diversity. This was true of Brazilian agriculture as well as deep water oil production and aircraft manufacturing for the international market.

Successful collaborative research depends on a country's internal capacity to absorb knowledge. Domestic investment not only generates innovations but also expands the capacity to absorb new international knowledge. Embrapa was able to assimilate the knowledge generated by the Green Revolution, apply it locally, and go beyond it. Petrobrás established an extensive research network with various international suppliers. Embraer accumulated knowledge by licensing agreements and was flexible in coordinating strategic risk partnerships. The more developed the sector or region, the greater the ability to share joint interdisciplinary knowledge.

Technological *opportunities* create innovative potential that expands with investments in research. Protection of innovations against imitations involves *appropriability* such as property rights, industrial secrets, and patents. Knowledge is *cumulative*, evolving incrementally. *Transmission* of technological knowledge may be specific or tacit. The first is easily handled, but the second depends on the wishes of the innovative agent.

In the case of agriculture, there is a clear pattern of innovations dependent on learning. This gives rise to greater competition through the entry and exit of firms. Neighbors test and disseminate technology. Producers compete for cost reduction and increases in productivity.

In the case of the petroleum and aircraft industries, innovations have been introduced by innovative firms. Unlike the example of agriculture, these cases are characterized by industrial concentration, creating hierarchical stability among innovative firms. There is less need for patents because the knowledge involved is highly tacit. This pattern, therefore, has high barriers to entry, a characteristic of oligopolistic markets. Table 11.1 provides a comparison of technological regimes in agriculture and industry.

Finally, table 11.2 presents a taxonomy of innovation policies used in the cases studied. The technological policies are grouped into three

Table 11.1 Comparison Between Agriculture and Industry (Oil and Aircraft Production) Technological Regimes

Parameters	Technological Regimes
Degree of knowledge complexity	Agriculture < Industry
Depreciation of knowledge	Agriculture > Industry
Effect of knowledge overflow	Agriculture > Industry
Degree of innovation	Agriculture < Industry
Degree of imitation	Agriculture > Industry
Level of public research	High in Agriculture and Industry

Source: Authors' own work.

Table 11.2 Technological Innovation Policies

Technological policies	Types and Objectives	Scope	Aplications
1. Policies to promote research	Aim to increase investments in R&D of firms	1.1 Financial aid	Improve innovation efficiency by reducing the cost of innovation. An example is crop-livestock-forest integration. However, these are complex systems that require interaction with several areas of knowledge. Payment for environmental services with public and private resources is an important stimulus for the adoption of these systems.
		1.2 Patents	Appropriation and diffusion depend on the cumulative character of innovations. For example, the seed, oil, and aircraft industries rely heavily on property rights. The TRIPS agreement and the Varieties Protection Law provide rules defining these issues.
2. Innovation policies	Aim to increase firms' innovation capacity	2.1 Public research	The various research centers of Embrapa, Petrobrás (Cenpes), and Embraer (ITA) are institutions that expand knowledge. Together, universities and state research institutes play an important role.
		2.2 Technology transfer	This depends on internal R&D and the absorptive capacity of firms. Embraer's risk-sharing partnerships have been decisive in the company's innovative strategy since the 1990s.
		2.3 Promotion of R&D cooperation	Cooperative collaborative research networks
3. Competitive policies	Aim to stimulate technological development through firms	3.1 Competition	Supports competition for the innovative pursuit without letting the market become monopolistic. The export program aimed at serving Embraer exemplifies a policy that enhances international competitiveness. Too much intervention can interfere negatively, discouraging innovation. Maintenance of low gasoline prices was a measure that harmed the Brazilian sugar-energy industry.
		3.2 Technological selection	Choice of technological trajectories and cumulative standards—regulation at different levels, which can be indicated internally or by international demand. This is the case of certifications and adoption of technological standards in specific sectors.

Source: Authors' own work.

axes: policies to promote research, innovation policies, and competitive policies. The first aims to increase the investment in internal R&D of productive units. The second increases capacity for innovation and absorption by agents. The third incorporates technological development through market competition.

WHAT CAN BE LEARNED FROM THE INNOVATION POLICIES IMPLEMENTED IN AGRICULTURE AND BY NATIONAL INDUSTRY?

Clear, long-term objectives that were aligned with state priorities served as the foundation for the success of Embrapa in agriculture, and for Petrobrás and Embraer in the industrial sector. Technological investments accompanied by new institutional structures permitted the growth of these three sectors. An additional and obvious goal was reduced foreign dependence. The issue of "national security" was present in all initiatives, motivating the state to channel public resources for necessary investments.

In the case of Embrapa, population growth, rapid urbanization, and income growth created a risk of a domestic food shortage in the second half of the 1960s. Public attention shifted to discussions about improving domestic food security. For Petrobrás, the goal was energy autonomy with less dependence on oil imports. From the time of its creation in 1953 in the Vargas era, exploration activities and production expanded. As for Embraer, territorial integration via regional aviation and strengthening national defense through military aviation promoted state intervention in this sector.

There is a central role for the state in regulating and fostering a strategic macroeconomic perspective. Petrobrás, when market driven and independently managed, moved from a supporting to a lead role in deep water oil exploration. Embraer was eventually privatized, and its success in international trade has required a managerial capacity for establishing international partnerships. Embrapa invested in research as a public good as opposed to selling technology, and the market and productive agents disseminate the knowledge.

There is also a prior history in these three activities. In the first half of the twentieth century, "research-based transformation" began with the São Paulo coffee industry. The Agronomic Institute of Campinas (IAC) was the key instrument. In Rio Grande do Sul, research on rice cultivation occurred. Such initiatives served as first steps. The establishment of research in agricultural schools and universities was also important. ESALQ, the Lavras Higher School of Agriculture, and UFV, among others, were begun. Technical assistance to farmers, through state associations in the 1960s and later in the 1970s through federal rural extension agencies, likewise was put in place.

Before Petrobrás, there were pioneering explorations based on private initiatives. These were later stimulated by government agencies. This activity generated new knowledge and encouraged exploration. The DNPM was launched in 1934 and the CNP in 1938. Some discoveries preceded the founding of Petrobrás, such as the Lobato field in 1939. In the 1940s, the movement "The oil is ours" (*O petróleo é nosso*) advocated for national sovereignty, arousing debate regarding the exploration of natural resources. Some were ready to rely on free markets for both domestic and foreign companies; others advocated for a state-owned exploration company.

In the 1930s and early 1940s, the state began to organize an institutional and regulatory apparatus for the aviation sector. This included creation of several public institutions such as the National Air Mail, DAC, FAB, and the Ministry of Aeronautics. In addition, a number of private initiatives began: Companhia Ypiranga (1931), the National Air Navigation Company (1942), and Paulista Aeronautical Company (1942). Public initiatives like the Lagoa Santa Factory (1936) and the Galeão Factory (1938), as well as the National Motors Factory (1946), became important as well. The Smith-Montenegro Plan defined a long-term strategic project involving the construction of the CTA in 1946, the ITA in 1950, and the IPD in 1953. These three institutions became responsible for training the workforce and generating scientific knowledge.

These initiatives, both in the private and public spheres, preceded the creation of the three sectors and contributed to later institutional arrangements for their support. Other later similarities exist. The most important were investments in training of the technical staff, exchange with foreign institutions, and the regular application of cumulative knowledge. Embrapa's training project for approximately two thousand researchers (master's and doctorate level) was noteworthy. During its first decade, Embrapa supported researchers in their study abroad to gain expertise in agricultural sciences. Cenpes, the research institute at Petrobrás, developed know-how in offshore exploration. For Embraer, preparation of technical staff was central.

Foreign institutions, professors, and executives also played a role in the founding, training, and partnerships at all of these firms. This included the German researcher Johanna Döbereiner at Embrapa; and executives Heinrich Focke (from Germany), Joseph Kovacs (Hungary), and Max Holste (France) at Embraer. For Petrobrás, there is the geologist Walter Link from the United States. At Embraer and Petrobrás, foreign companies participated through early joint ventures and technological development partnerships, and there were many ties to universities and research centers. In agriculture, Embrapa worked with CGIAR (the world's largest agricultural innovation partnership), which played an important role in research and training scientists in the early years. Other international research centers engaged in effective knowledge sharing for the development of new technologies.

Today, public policies are shaped by a generalized movement toward decentralization. This change has been influenced by greater market globalization. In Brazil, fiscal limitations have hampered needed state investments as well.

What should future policy be? Based on lessons gleaned from the study of these cases, the primary public task is to assure an innovative institutional environment. Once this base is achieved, the state should minimize direct and substantial intervention. That does not exclude diligent regulation by independent agencies or modest subsidies with full public disclosure. Nor does it ignore the continuing obstacles to sustained development such as infrastructure bottlenecks, insufficient attention to science and technology, and quality of education, as well as others we have noted.

Overall, the agricultural and industrial revolutions at Embrapa, Petrobrás, and Embraer serve as examples of public policy, effectively designed and implemented, and enabling long-term increases in productivity. Extremes, whether taken up by the state or by private initiatives, are unlikely to yield better outcomes.

According to the solution of the logistic model, to a discrete interval Δt, the growth of new technology adopters is given by:

$$y(t+1)-y(t)= N\left\{1+e^{-\left[\beta(t+1)+k_s\right]}\right\}^{-1} - N\left[1+e^{-(\beta t+k_s)}\right]^{-1}$$

Rearranging, we have:

$$y(t+1)-y(t)= \frac{Ne^{-(\beta t+k_s)}\left(1-e^{-\beta}\right)}{\left\{1+e^{-\left[\beta(t+1)+k_s\right]}\right\}\left[1+e^{-(\beta t+k_s)}\right]} \tag{a.1}$$

To the same discrete interval Δt, it can be verified that:

$$y(t+1)-y(t)= \theta\frac{y(t)}{N}\left[N-y(t)\right]$$

Substituting $y(t) = N[1+e^{-(\beta t+k_s)}]^{-1}$ in the above equation and rearranging it, we can conclude that:

$$y(t+1)-y(t)= \frac{\theta N}{1+e^{-(\beta t+k_s)}}\left\{1-\left[1+e^{-(\beta t+k_s)}\right]^{-1}\right\} \tag{a.2}$$

Equating (a.1) and (a.2), with β inserted in the open interval $(-\infty, +\infty)$, the relationship between θ and β is given by:

$$\theta = \frac{\left(e^{\beta} - 1\right)\left[e^{(\beta t + k_s)} + 1\right]}{\left(e^{\left[\beta(t+1) + k_s\right]} + 1\right)} \qquad (a.3)$$

Taking the limit of θ as $\beta \to \pm\infty$, θ is within the open interval $(-1, +1)$. However, considering $y(0)$ equal to a positive value in the open interval $(0, N)$, the logistic function is defined only in the positive quadrant and therefore θ assumes values between $(0, 1)$.

Separating the equation[1], it follows that:

$$y'(t)\frac{1}{y(t)\left[N-y(t)\right]}=\frac{\beta}{N}$$

Integrating both sides of equation, we have:

$$\int y'(t)\frac{1}{y(t)\left[N-y(t)\right]}dt=\int\frac{\beta}{N}dt \qquad (b.1)$$

Which can be rewritten as:

$$\left(\int\frac{1}{y(N-y)}dy\right)_{y=y(t)}=\int\frac{\beta}{N}dt$$

To the left side of Equation b.1, the method of partial fractions is be used. Then it can be rewritten as:

$$\frac{1}{y(N-y)}=\frac{A}{y}+\frac{B}{N-y}=\frac{A(N-y)+By}{y(N-y)}$$

Determining the constants A and B and equating numerators,

$$0y+1=1=A(N-y)+By=(B-A)y+AN$$

Therefore, $AN=1$, since $B-A=0$. Then it follows that $A=B=1/N$. In this case, the integral can be expressed by:

$$\int\frac{1}{y(N-y)}dy=\frac{1}{N}\int\frac{1}{y}dy+\frac{1}{N}\int\frac{1}{N-y}dy$$

$$= \frac{1}{N} log|y| + k_1 + \frac{1}{N}\left(\int \frac{-1}{u} du\right)_{\substack{N-y=u \\ dy=-du}}$$

$$= \frac{1}{N} log|y| + k_1 - \frac{1}{N} log|u| + k_2$$

$$= \frac{1}{N} log|y| + k_1 - \frac{1}{N} log|N - y| + k_2$$

$$= \frac{log|y| - log|N - y|}{N} + k_1 + k_2$$

$$= \frac{log\left(\frac{|y|}{|N - y|}\right)}{N} + k_1 + k_2$$

Substituting $y = y(t)$ e $k_1 + k_2 = k_3$:

$$\int y'(t) \frac{1}{y(t)[N - y(t)]} dt = \frac{1}{N} log\left|\frac{y(t)}{N - y(t)}\right| + k_3$$

On the right side of the equality in Equation b.1, the mathematics is more straightforward:

$$\int \frac{\beta}{N} dt = \frac{\beta t}{N} + k_4$$

Equating the two sides, since $y(t) > 0$, $N - y(t) > 0$ and defining $k_5 = (k_4 - k_3)N$, it means that:

$$log\left(\frac{y(t)}{N - y(t)}\right) = \beta t + k_5$$

$$\frac{y(t)}{N - y(t)} = e^{\beta t + k_5}$$

$$y(t) = e^{\beta t + k_5}[N - y(t)]$$

$$y(t) = e^{\beta t + k_5} N - e^{\beta t + k_5} y(t)$$

$$y(t) + e^{\beta t + k_5} y(t) = e^{\beta t + k_5} N$$

$$y(t) = \frac{e^{\beta t + k_5} N}{1 + e^{\beta t + k_5}}$$

In order to analyze agriculture over time, the advance of technology is central. Below, we calculate the land-saving effect on agricultural and livestock production in Brazil.

In the case of agriculture, production, P, is defined as

$$P = A \times L, \tag{c.1}$$

where A is land productivity and L is the harvested area.

In the case of livestock activity, production can be defined similarly. Livestock production is given by (c.2):

$$P = G \times S \times L, \tag{c.2}$$

where land productivity is $A = G \times S$ with G equal to carcass weight, (P/An) and S the stocking rate, the number of animals per land unit (An / L). We used the number of animals slaughtered instead of herd size.

Agricultural productivity growth occurs as a result of applied agricultural research, use of better fertilizers, phytosanitary control, high-yield varieties, as well as process innovations. The growth of harvested area is related to the location of the biome, the regional logistics, the availability of mechanization, the relative price of inputs and the product's final price.

In livestock production, the improvement in productivity is correlated with genetic improvement, balanced nutrition, pasture quality and innovations in management. The growth of the stocking rate is associated with soil fertility and the genetic improvement of new forage varieties.

Finally, the growth of pasture areas reflects the opportunity cost, such as the relative price of meat, competition with food production, and terms of trade for modern inputs.

When production is divided by productivity, the amount of land used is determined. A simple study is to calculate the area used in a situation where technological advance remains constant. It is possible to calculate this effect without technical progress by dividing current production by past productivity. To discover the saved amount, one need only deduct the land used in the current period. Thus, the land-saving effect (LSE) in the present is given by (c.3):

$$LSE_1 = (P_1 / A_0) - L_1,$$ (c.3)

where 1 and 0 are the final and initial periods, respectively.

This measure assesses the effects of technological change on agricultural and livestock output.

We present a way to calculate the consequences on total factor productivity from GHG emissions—an indicator that is useful for the design of public policies financing sustainable development.

Cattle production (P) per GHG emissions (E) can be expressed as in Eq.1, as the product of animal performance (G), stocking rate (S) and pasture area (L):

$$P/E = G.S.L \qquad \text{(d.1)}$$

Therefore, the production growth rate (G_P), excluding the growth rate of emissions (G_E), is determined by the sum of the growth rates of the animal performance (G_G), the stocking rate (G_S) and the pasture area (G_L):

$$G_P - G_E = G_G + G_S + G_L \qquad \text{(d.2)}$$

Livestock production per unit of emission is a function of the use of productive factors, such as pasture area (L), labor (W), tractors (T), animals for fattening (An), animal feed (F) and drugs (M):

$$P/E = f(L, W, T, An, F, M) \qquad \text{(d.3)}$$

The production growth rate, excluding the growth rate of emissions, can be defined as the weighted sum of the costs (Sh_i; $i = L, W, T, An, F, M$) of each of the productive factors multiplied by their respective growth rates, adding to the value a residual term that refers to the growth of total factor productivity (G_{TFP}):

$$G_P - G_E = \left(\sum_{i=L}^{M} Sh_i G_i \right) + G_{TFP}$$

where ($\sum_{i=L}^{M} Sh_i G_i$) = G_I, is the growth rate relative to productivity factors.

Thus total factor productivity can be measured by the production growth rate minus the sum of input growth and emissions rates. So, we have:

$$G_{TFP} = G_P - \left(G_I + G_E \right)$$ (d.4)

If there is no technological change or efficiency improvement, the total factor productivity is the residual component. The production growth rate is an average of efficient use of factors.

To implement this methodology, there are two problems. The first is to create a database for calculations. This is not a simple task, even if the goal is to provide proxies. The second is to specify a base period of emissions for carbon pricing. From that year forward, the increase (or decrease) of the emission rate will be attributed to changes in total factor productivity. Between the current period and the year of carbon pricing, there will be a technical change in the combination of productive factors, which is underestimated in this evaluation.

Technology and knowledge are a means of increasing food production that can meet growing demand from a larger global population. They are also relevant for environmental sustainability, necessary for an efficient agriculture over time.

This is a contribution to the debate about climate change. Brazil is one of the few countries that can preserve its biodiversity through the use of natural resources in a sustainable way, thereby assuring a positive result from the trade-offs among sustainability, economic growth and social development.

GHG and Corresponding Value of Global Warming Potential (CO_2 eq.)

Gas	Symbol	Global Warming Potential
Carbon dioxide	CO_2	1
Methane	CH_4	21
Nitrous oxide	N_2O	310
Hydrofluorocarbons	HFC-23	11,700
	HFC-125	2,800
	HFC-134a	1,300
	HFC-143a	3,800
	HFC-152a	140
Perfluorocarbons	CF_4	6,500
	C_2F_6	9,200
Sulfur hexafluoride	SF_6	23,900

Source: Ministry of Science, Technology, Innovation and Communication, *Modelagem Climática e Vulnerabilidade à Setoriais* (Brasília, 2016).

NOTES

FOREWORD

1. Edward Schuh (with R. Alves), *The Agricultural Development of Brazil* (New York: Praeger, 1970), 339.

2. DEVELOPMENT STRATEGIES IN BRAZIL: A CONTEMPORARY VIEW

1. This section's content is discussed in more detail in Albert Fishlow, "Some Reflections on Post-1964 Brazilian Economic Policy," in *Authoritarian Brazil*, ed. Alfred Stepan (New Haven, CT: Yale, 1973), 69–118.

2. For an extended discussion, see Albert Fishlow, "A Tale of Two Presidents," in *Democratizing Brazil*, ed. Alfred Stepan (New York: Oxford University Press, 1989), 83–119.

3. Mario Henrique Simonsen, *Inflacao: Gradualismo x Tratamento de Choque* (Rio de Janeiro: APEC Editora, 1970), 192.

4. Roberto Campos as quoted in Octavio Ianni, *Crisis in Brazil* (New York: Columbia University Press, 1970), 189.

5. Heterodox policies sought to control inflation by acting on prices in a direct way (for example, market price controls and government-administered price management), whereas orthodox policies indirectly attempted to stabilize the inflationary problem through instruments that operated at the level of economic activity, such as an increase in the interest rate.

6. Persio Arida and Andre Lara Resende, "Inertial Inflation and Monetary Reform," in *Inflation and Indexation*, ed. John Williamson (Washington, DC: Institute for International Economics, 1985), 27–55.

7. For a more elaborate treatment, also with coverage of the period since 1985, see Albert Fishlow, *Starting Over: Brazil Since 1985* (Washington, DC: Brookings Institution, 2011).

3. THE ROLE OF AGRICULTURAL INNOVATION: FROM THE TRADITIONAL APPROACH TOWARD A THEORY OF TECHNICAL AND INSTITUTIONAL CHANGE

1. This chapter is largely based on an earlier article with many more references excluded in this text. José Eustáquio Vieira Filho and José Maria Ferreira Jardim da Silveira, "Mudança Tecnológica Na Agricultura: Uma Revisão Crítica Da Literatura

e o Papel Das Economias de Aprendizado," *Revista de Economia e Sociologia Rural* 50, no. 4 (2012): 721–42.

2. Willard W. Cochrane, *Farm Prices: Myth and Reality* (Minneapolis: University of Minnesota Press, 1958).

3. Zvi Griliches, "Hybrid Corn: An Exploration in the Economics of Technological Change," *Econometrica* 25, no. 4 (1957): 501–22.

4. The mathematical model explanations are based on José Eustaquio Vieira Filho, "Difusão Biotecnológica: A Adoção Dos Transgênicos Na Agricultura." Discussion Paper, 1937 (Brasília: Ipea, 2014).

5. Note that the interpretation of θ and β is different. See appendix A for details.

6. Richard R. Nelson and Sidney Winter, *An Evolutionary Theory of Economic Change* (Cambridge, Mass.: Harvard University Press, 1982).

7. W. Arthur Lewis, "Economic Development with Unlimited Supplies of Labour," *The Manchester School* 22, no. 2 (May 1954): 139–91, https://doi.org/10.1111/j.1467-9957.1954.tb00021.x.

8. Ruy Miller Paiva, "Modernização e Dualismo Tecnológico na Agricultura," *Pesquisa e Planejamento Econômico* 1, no. 2 (1971): 171–234.

9. John Hicks, *The Theory of Wages* (London: Macmillan, 1963).

10. Sidney G. Winter, "Schumpeterian Competition in Alternative Technological Regimes," *Journal of Economic Behavior and Organization* 5 (June 1984), 287–320.

11. Paul David, "Clio and the Economics of Querty," *American Economic Review* 75 (May 1985): 332–37; Brian Arthur, "Competing Technologies, Increasing Returns, and Lock-In by Historical Events," *Economic Journal* 99 (March 1989): 116–31.

12. José Eustaquio Viera Filho and José Silveira, "Modelo Evolucionário da Aprendizado Agrícola," *Revista Brasileira de Inovação* 10 (2011): 265–300.

13. Armen Alchian and Harold Demsetz, "Production, Information Costs, and Economic Organization," *American Economic Review* 62 (December 1972): 777–95.

4. BRAZILIAN AGRICULTURE: A HISTORICAL PERSPECTIVE

1. This chapter was adapted from a text developed by José Eustáquio Ribeiro Vieira Filho, as part of an extensive collection of studies on Brazilian agriculture, that included participation of several researchers from a group of Brazilian research institutions. The work, "O Mundo Rural no Brasil do Século 21: A Formação de um Novo Padrão Agrário e Agrícola," was organized by Antônio Márcio Buainain, Eliseu Alves, José Maria da Silveira, and Zander Navarro.

2. Roberto Esposti, "Public Agricultural R&D Design and Technological Spill-Ins: A Dynamic Model." *Research Policy* 31, no. 5 (2002): 693–717.

3. Francesca Chiaromonte and Giovanni Dosi, "The Micro Foundations of Competitiveness and Their Macroeconomic Implications," In *Technology and the Wealth of Nations: The Dynamics of Constructed Advantages*, ed. Giovanni Dosi, 107–34 (London: Pinter, 1992).

4. Marcus Peixoto, "A Extensão Privada e a Privatização Da Extensão: Uma Análise Da Indústria de Defensivos Agrícolas" (PhD diss., Ufrrj, 2009).

5. Brazilian farmers long referred to this region as the "closed" or "inaccessible" Cerrado because inadequate soil characteristics made it unsuitable for agricultural production. The expansion of the agricultural frontier to the Cerrado made it one of the most productive and attractive marginal lands in the world.

6. A more productive African species, Brachiaria, was crossbred with a native variety, achieving a size 3 times larger than the African plant.

7. For a broad overview of Brazilian agriculture from different perspectives and approaches, see José Garcia Gasques, José Eustáquio Ribeiro Vieira Filho, and Zander Navarro, eds., *Agricultura brasileira: desempenho, desafios e perspectivas* (Brasilia: Ipea, 2010); Antônio Márcio Buainain et al., eds., *O mundo rural no Brasil do século 21: a formação de um novo padrão agrário e agrícola* (Brasilia: Embrapa, 2014); and José Eustáquio Ribeiro Vieira Filho and José Garcia Gasques, eds., *Agricultura, transformação produtiva e sustentabilidade* (Brasilia: Ipea, 2016).

8. Eliseu Alves, Geraldo da Silva e Souza, and Antônio Salazar P. Brandão, "Por Que Os Preços Da Cesta Básica Caíram?", *Revista de Política Agrícola* 19, no. 2 (2010): 14–20.

9. José Eustáquio Ribeiro Vieira Filho and Armando Fornazier, "Productividad Agropecuaria: Reducción de La Brecha Productiva Entre El Brasil y Los Estados Unidos de América," *Revista Cepal* 118 (2016): 215–33.

5. EMBRAPA: A CASE OF INDUCED INSTITUTIONAL INNOVATION

1. José Eustáquio Ribeiro Vieira Filho, Antônio Carvalho Campos, and Carlos Maurício de Carvalho Ferreira, "Abordagem Alternativa Do Crescimento Agrícola: Um Modelo de Dinâmica Evolucionária," *Revista Brasileira de Inovação* 4, no. 2 (2005): 425–76.

2. José Eustáquio Ribeiro Vieira Filho and José Maria Ferreira Jardim da Silveira, "Modelo Evolucionário de Aprendizado Agrícola," *Revista Brasileira de Inovação* 10, no. 2 (2011): 265–300.

3. Smita Srinivas and José Eustáquio Ribeiro Vieira Filho, "Farm Versus Firm: Learning and Technical Linkages of Agriculture and Industry," Discussion Paper 207 (Brasília: Ipea, 2015).

4. Roberto Esposti, "Public Agricultural R&D Design and Technological Spill-Ins: A Dynamic Model," *Research Policy* 31, no. 5 (2002): 693–717.

5. Theodore William Schultz, *The Economic Organization of Agriculture* (New York: McGraw-Hill, 1953).

6. José Roberto Mendonça de Barros and Lídia Goldenstein, "Avaliação Do Processo de Reestruturação Industrial Brasileiro," *Revista de Economia Política* 17, no. 2 (1997): 11–31.

7. Geraldo Murtha, Eliseu Alves and Elisio Contini, "Land-saving Approaches and Beef Production Growth in Brazil," *Agricultural Systems* 110 (2012): 173–77.

8. Eliseu Roberto de Andrade Alves, "Embrapa: A Successful Case of Institutional Innovation," *Revista de Política Agrícola* (2010): 64–72.

9. Paulo Correa and Cristiane Schmidt, "Public Research Organizations and Agricultural Development in Brazil: How Did Embrapa Get It Right?," *World Bank Economic Premise* 145 (2014): 1–10.

10. José Eustáquio Vieira Filho and Adriana Vieira, "A Inovacao na Agricultura Brasileira: uma Reflexão a partir da Analise dos Certificados de Proteção de Cultivares," *Texto para Discussao* 1866, (2013), IPEA.

6. THE COMPETITIVENESS OF AGRIBUSINESS IN INTERNATIONAL TRADE

1. Carol Deitos Fries and Daniel Arruda Coronel, "A Competitividade Das Exportações Gaúchas de Soja Em Grão (2001–2012)," *Pesquisa & Debate* 25, no. 1 (2014): 163–89.

2. Luiz A. Martinelli, Rachael Garrett, Silvio Ferraz, and Rosamond Naylor, "Sugar and Ethanol Production as a Rural Development Strategy in Brazil: Evidence from the State of São Paulo," *Agricultural Systems* 104, no. 5 (2011): 419–28.

3. Brazil and the United States are the world's main producers of biofuels (clean energy) worldwide. Since the 1990s, Brazil has had a favorable cycle of sugar-alcohol production with little state intervention. In fact, ethanol production increased significantly in Brazil in 2003 with the production of a vehicle with a flexible engine adjusted to the fuel mix. In the United States, ethanol is made from corn and enjoys large government subsidies. The U.S. model based on corn is not as efficient as Brazil's model.

4. José Garcia Gasques, Gervásio Castro de Rezende, Carlos Monteiro Villa Verde, Mario Sergio Salerno, Júnia Cristina P. R. da Conceição, and João Carlos de Souza Carvalho, "Desempenho e Crescimento Do Agronegócio No Brasil," Discussion Paper 1009 (Brasília: Ipea, 2004).

5. Emiko Fukase and Will Martin, "Who Will Feed China in the 21st Century? Income Growth and Food Demand and Supply in China," *Journal of Agricultural Economics* 67, no. 1 (2016): 3–23.

6. Eliana Valéria Covolan Figueiredo and Elisio Contini, "China: Gigante Também Na Agricultura," *Revista de Política Agrícola* 22, no. 2 (2013): 5–29.

7. This area includes the Brazilian states of Maranhão, Tocantins, Piauí, and Bahia.

8. Geraldo Martha Júnior, Eliseu Alves, Elisio Contini, and S. Ramos, "Estilo de Desenvolvimento Da Agropecuária Brasileira e Desafios Futuros," *Revista de Política Agrícola* 19 (2010): 93–106.

9. Elisio Contini, Marcos A. G. Pena Júnior, Carlos Augusto M. Santana, and Geraldo Martha Júnior, "Exportações Motor Do Agronegócio Brasileiro," *Revista de Política Agrícola* 21, no. 2 (2012): 88–102.

10. Centro de Gestão e Estudos Estratégicos, *Sustentabilidade e Sustentação Da Produção de Alimentos No Brasil: O Papel Do País No Cenário Global*, Vol. 1 (Brasília: CGEE, 2014).

11. Center for Advanced Studies in Applied Economics, "PIB Do Agronegócio e PIB Total—Brasil," 2015, https://www.cepea.esalq.usp.br/br/.

12. Food and Agriculture Organization of the United Nations, "Food and Agriculture Data," 2015, http://www.fao.org/faostat/.

13. United States Department of Agriculture, "Agricultural Projections," February 1, 2014, http://www.ers.usda.gov/publications/oce081.

14. For a detailed summary on the CMS method and a numerical example, see F. M. A. Carvalho,"Metodo Constant Market Share," in *Métodos Quantitativos em Economia*, ed. M. L. Santos and W. C. Vieira, (Viçosa, Brazil: 2004).

15. David J. Richardson, "Constant-Market-Shares Analysis of Export Growth," *Journal of International Economics* 1, no. 2 (1971): 227–39.

16. Data was collected from the Food and Agriculture Organization of the United Nations. It refers to the dollar value of Brazilian and world exports of the following agricultural products: soybeans, corn, orange, sugar, wheat, cotton, roasted coffee, coffee beans, pork, beef, and chicken meat from 1992 to 2013. For the purposes of this analysis, the markets of South America, North America, Central America, Europe, Africa, Asia, and Oceania are considered.

7. AGRICULTURAL EXPANSION AND LOW-CARBON EMISSIONS

1. This chapter is based on a study for the World Bank with the objective of evaluating the expansion of livestock production in Brazil and its impacts on climate change. The volume was subsequently published as World Bank, *Agricultural Productivity Growth in Brazil: Recent Trends and Future Prospects* (Washington, D.C: World Bank, 2017).

2. For a bibliographical review of the determinants of deforestation, see Jonah Busch and Kalifi Ferretti-Gallon, "What Drives Deforestation and What Stops It? A Meta-Analysis," *Review of Environmental Economics and Policy* 11, no. 1 (March 2017): 3–23. These authors conclude that economic returns from deforestation decrease as transportation costs increase. Economic activities with higher logistical costs tend to be located close to cities and urban environments, whereas those with lower costs are established in more remote areas, which is typical of livestock production.

3. Paulo Barreto and Elis Araújo, *O Brasil Atingirá Sua Meta de Redução Do Desmatamento* (Belém, Brasil: Imazon, 2012).

4. Armindo Neivo Kichel, Davi José Bungenstab, Ademir Hugo Zimmer, Cleber Oliveira Soares, and Roberto Giolo de Almeida, "Sistemas de Integração Lavoura-Pecuária-Floresta e o Progresso Do Setor Agropecuário Brasileiro," in *Sistemas de Integração a Produção Sustentável*, ed. Davi José Bungenstab (Brasília: Embrapa, 2014), 1–10.

5. Roberto Giolo de Almeida and Sérgio Raposo de Medeiros, "Emissão de Gases de Efeito Estufa Em Sistemas de Integração Lavoura-Pecuária-Floresta," in *Sistemas Agroflorestais: A Agropecuária Sustentável*, ed. Fabiana Villa Alves, Valdemir Antônio Laura, and Roberto Giolo de Almeida (Brasília: Embrapa, 2015), 97–116.

6. For a detailed calculation of the land-saving effect, see Appendix C.

7. Agricultural productivity is understood as yield; that is, production per land unit.

8. Almeida and Medeiros, "Emissão de Gases de Efeito Estufa Em Sistemas de Integração Lavoura-Pecuária-Floresta."

9. The slaughter rate is the number of animals slaughtered divided by the total herd. In Brazil this rate was around 14 percent in recent years. Ivan Wedekin, *Economia Da Pecuária de Corte: Fundamentos e o Ciclo de Preços* (São Paulo: Wedekin Consultores, 2017).

10. CO_2 equivalent is a measure used to compare the emissions from various GHG based on their global warming potential (IPCC, *Guidelines for National Governmental Greenhouse Gas Inventories*, 2006). Greenhouse gases are divided into four groups: carbon dioxide (CO_2), methane (CH_4), nitrous oxide (N_2O), and fluorinated gases (or F-gases). The latter is a family of artificial gases used in a variety of industrial applications. Because they do not harm the ozone layer, they are used as substitutes for substances responsible for ozone depletion, but F-gases have a strong greenhouse effect, with a global warming potential up to 23,900 times higher than CO_2.

11. With the change in the U.S. political landscape in 2017, President Donald Trump announced that the country will no longer honor U.S. commitments under the Paris agreement.

12. Angelo Costa Gurgel and Roberto Domenico Laurenzana, "Desafios e Oportunidades Da Agricultura de Baixo Carbono," in *Agricultura, Transformação Produtiva e Sustentabilidade*, ed. José Eustáquio Ribeiro Vieira Filho and José Garcia Gasques (Brasília: Ipea, 2016), 343–66.

13. Roberto Guimarães Júnior, Robélio Leandro Marchão, Karina Pulrolnik, Lourival Vilela, Giovana Alcantara Maciel, Kleberson Worslley de Souza, and Luiz Gustavo Ribeiro Pereira, "Neutralization of Enteric Methane Emissions by Carbon Sequestration Under Integrated Crop-Livestock and Crop-Livestock-Forest Systems in Cerrado Region," in *Anais* (Brasília: Embrapa, 2016), 282–85.

8. THE STRUCTURAL HETEROGENEITY OF FAMILY FARMING IN BRAZIL

1. This chapter utilizes an earlier study, José Eustáquio Ribeiro Vieira Filho, "Structural Heterogeneity of Family Agriculture in Brazil," *CEPAL Review* 111, LC/G.2597-P (Santiago de Chile: Economic Commission for Latin America and the Caribbean [ECLAC], December 2013). Refer to that article for full bibliographic references.

2. For a discussion on family agriculture and the barriers to technological innovation, see Antonio Buainain, ed., *Agricultura familiar e inovação tecnológica no Brasil*, (Campinas: Unicamp, 2007).

3. Eliseu Alves and Geraldo da Silva e Souza, "Pequenos Estabelecimentos Também Enriquecem? Pedras e Tropeços," *Revista de Política Agrícola* 24, no. 3 (2015): 7–21.

4. A technical cooperation agreement was established between IPEA and ECLAC to study the structural heterogeneity of the Brazilian economy.

5. Analyzing wealth creation by considering only land endowment is a mistake. The results reported here testify to the high level of productive heterogeneity in Brazilian agriculture. Technology is a key issue for discussing this problem.

9. IS THE OIL OURS?

1. Eva Dantas and Martin Bell, "Latecomer Firms and the Emergence and Development of Knowledge Networks: The Case of Petrobrás in Brazil," *Research Policy* 38, no. 5 (2009): 829–44.

2. The history of oil production in Brazil can be divided into five time periods: (i) 1864–1918, pioneer explorations; (ii) 1919–1939, beginning of state explorations; (iii) 1940–1973, search for reducing oil imports; (iv) 1974–2006, trajectory for self-sufficiency production; and (v) (2006 to the present, pre-salt exploration. José Mauro de Morais, *Petróleo Em Águas Profundas: Uma História Tecnológica Da Petrobrás Na Exploração e Produção Offshore* (Brasília: Ipea, 2013). This work focuses on the period after the creation of Petrobrás, and we have utilized this source extensively.

3. The Offshore Technology Conference (OTC) was founded in 1969 to improve existing technologies in the oil industry. The first conference was held in Houston. To focus on local issues, regional conferences were held in Brazil (2011) and Asia (2012). For more information, see Offshore Technology Conference, "OTC Distinguished Achievement Awards for Companies, Organizations, and Institutions," September 23, 2015, http://www.otcnet.org/.

4. Offshore Technology Conference, "OTC Distinguished Achievement Awards."

5. João Maria de Oliveira and Calebe De Oliveira Figueiredo, "Caracterização Dos Investimentos Em P&D Da Petrobrás," In *Impactos Tecnológicos Das Parcerias Da Petrobrás Com Universidades, Centros de Pesquisa e Firmas Brasileiras*, ed. Lenita Maria Turchi, Fernanda De Negri, and João Alberto De Negri (Brasília: Ipea, 2013), 139–62.

6. There are several types of offshore drilling and production records, including the measurement of depth in floating facilities, subsea Christmas trees, and drilling activities. Petrobrás has a central role in the worldwide progression of deep water oil exploration, especially in the installation of floating platforms.

7. Also known as "hydraulic fracturing," this technique drills into the ground to extract gas or oil. The advantage of this technology is the ability to access areas that are unreachable by traditional methods. However, the environmental impacts caused in the subsoil are controversial. For this reason, fracking is prohibited in some European countries. Regardless of environmental issues, the technique has been expanding and changing supply and demand curves.

8. The Bank of the State of Paraná (Banestado) was a public bank that was privatized in 2000. In 2003, an investigation was initiated into the corruption and drug trafficking scheme that transferred financial resources to tax havens through fake accounts, and to the so-called CC5 accounts (created to allow legal international transfers). Between 1996 and 2002, billions of reais were diverted to these accounts, with Banestado being the main mediator of fraudulent remittances.

9. With a law degree from the State University of Maringá, Sérgio Moro completed a master's and doctorate degree at the Federal University of Paraná (UFPR), with a focus on constitutional law. Because of the nature of his work, when he became a federal judge in 1996, he switched to the criminal law area, specializing in financial crimes and money laundering. He became Minister of Justice in the Bolsonaro government.

10. THE TECHNOLOGICAL EVOLUTION OF EMBRAER

1. The regional market was of interest to several manufacturers, including Embraer, Bombardier, ATR (Franco-Italian company), DeHavilland, Saab, Fokker, Dornier, and British Aerospace. Most of these companies ceased operations, shifted to a different market, or merged with other companies. In fact, Boeing and Airbus (the latter created in the late 1970s for the A300 project) were not focused on the so-called regional market.

2. The C47, the military version of the DC3, was widely used in World War II and helped the Allies in that conflict.

3. The first commercial airplane powered by jet engines was the DeHavilland Comet; it was launched in 1949 and began operating in 1952 on the London-Johannesburg route of the British Overseas Airways Corporation (BOAC).

4. The higher fuel consumption of larger aircraft does not determine the company's cost of operation. The rise in fuel prices has negatively affected purchase of less economical aircraft.

5. See Airbus, *The Success Story of Airbus* (2015), www.airbus.com/company /history.

6. For a historical overview of the nascent aeronautics industry in Brazil, see Embraer, *Centro Histórico Embraer*, 2015, https://historicalcenter.embraer.com /global/en.

7. The Convertiplane was a revolutionary airplane project that would take off vertically and fly horizontally, acting as a helicopter at take-off but flying like an airplane. The helicopter-airplane hybrid was designed by a German engineer and professor, Heinrich Focke, who was hired by ITA because of his expertise and experience in aeronautical construction.

8. Paulistinha was a high-wing single-engine airplane, considered to be one of the best pilot flight-training aircraft at the time.

9. Given the challenge of designing an aircraft, Embraer hired the experienced aeronautical engineer Max Holste. Invited by Ozires Silva, the then IPD director, the French engineer worked with two other renowned designers: the Brazilian José Carlos de Barros Neiva, founder of Construtora Aeronáutica Neiva, and Joseph Kovacs, a naturalized Hungarian-Brazilian who had been working in Brazil since the late 1940s. Collaboration with foreign engineers, renowned for designing aircraft, was central to sharing and transferring knowledge to Brazilian engineers.

10. Claudio R. Frischtak, "Learning and Technical Progress in the Commuter Aircraft Industry: An Analysis of Embraer's Experience," *Research Policy* 23, no. 5 (1994): 601–12.

11. Giovanni Dosi, "Technological Paradigms and Technological Trajectories: A Suggested Interpretation of the Determinants and Directions of Technical Change," *Research Policy* 11, no. 3 (1982): 147–62. He later produced a book in 1984, *Technical Change and Industrial Transformation*, and a review article in 1988 in the *Journal of Economic Literature* that are helpful.

APPENDIX B

1. If $F(y)$ is differentiable, then there is a unique solution to the following initial value problem (IVP): $y'(t) = F[y(t)]$, with $y(t_0) = y_0$. That is, if $z(t)$ and $w(t)$ are solutions to the same ordinary differential equation, such that if $z(t_0) = w(t_0)$, both functions $z(t)$ and $w(t)$ are identical. This result, known as the theorem of existence and uniqueness of IVP, implies that, $z(t)$ and $w(t)$ are two different solutions from the same ordinary differential equation, $z(t) \neq w(t), \forall t$. This argument can be applied to the logistic equation, since, in this case, $F(y)$ is a differentiable function with respect to y. Finally, as the constant functions $z(t) = 0$ and $w(t) = N$ are solutions from the logistic equation, any solution $y(t)$ of the ordinary differential equation with $y(0)$ different from 0 and N must be such as $y(t)$ is different from 0 and $\forall t$. According to this, the separation procedure may be used without problem in these cases. The general solution of the logistic equation is then given by the constant solutions $z(t) = 0$ and $w(t) = N$, as well as the solutions obtained by the separation process adopted in this study.

INDEX

Page numbers in *italics* indicate figures or tables.